For the Good of the Nation

Jews of Poland

Series Editor: Antony Polonsky (Brandeis University)

For the Good of the Nation

Institutions for Jewish
Children in Interwar Poland

A Documentary History

Edited and Translated
by SEAN MARTIN

Boston
2017

Library of Congress Cataloging-in-Publication Data

Names: Martin, Sean, 1968- author.

Title: For the good of the nation: institutions for Jewish children in interwar Poland / Sean Martin.

Description: Brighton, MA: Academic Studies Press, [2017]

Series: Jews of Poland

Identifiers: LCCN 2016052709 (print) | LCCN 2016053281 (ebook) |

ISBN 9781618115676 (hardback) | ISBN 9781618115683 (e-book)

Subjects: LCSH: CENTOS (Organization)—History.
| Jewish children—Institutional care—Poland—History—20th century. | Jewish orphans—Poland—History—20th century. | Jewish orphanages—Poland—History—20th century. | Poland—Ethnic relations—History—20th century. | BISAC: HISTORY / Jewish. | RELIGION / Judaism / General.

Classification: LCC HV1215.7 .M37 2017 (print) | LCC HV1215.7 (ebook) | DDC 362.73/2--dc23 LC record available at https://lccn.loc.gov/2016052709

©**Academic Studies Press, 2017**
ISBN 978-1-61811-981-0
ISBN 978-1-61811-568-3 (e-book)

Book design by Kryon Publishing Services (P) Ltd.
www.kryonpublishing.com

Published by Academic Studies Press in 2017
28 Montfern Avenue
Brighton, MA 02135, USA
P: (617)782-6290
F: (857)241-3149
press@academicstudiespress.com
www.academicstudiespress.com

Contents

Introduction	vii
I A History of Centos	1
II Descriptions of Homes for Children	60
The "Orphanage in Pinsk" *Ben-Levi*	60
The Publication of the Home for Orphans in Lwów, Zborowska 8 *Maks Schaff*	64
Childish Stubbornness: Notes of a Teacher *Tsvi Tarlovski*	72
Pen Strokes (From My Inspections in the Provinces) *A. Goldin*	75
Images of Youth in School Publications *Leon Gutman*	88
The Strike: An Image of Dormitory Life *Yakov Sarner*	91
III Home for Jewish Children and Farm in Helenówek	94
Education or Crime? From the Diary of an Educator *Yekhiel Ben-Tsiyon Kats*	94

IV CENTOS in Otwock   142

The Therapeutic and Educational Institution in Otwock
(Three Months of Activity)   142
Zofia Rosenblum

Awakening in an Institution (Images of an Institution
for Defective Children in Otwock)   149
Kalman Lis

Two Visits in CENTOS   154
Helena Boguszewska

Five Years of CENTOS Activity in Otwock   166
Zofia Rosenblum

A Report on Five Years of CENTOS Activity in Otwock   172
Zofia Rosenblum

Working with Abnormal Children: On
Eight Years of CENTOS in Otwock   198
Abraham Berger

Afterword   206
Acknowledgments   213
Index   216

Introduction

CENTOS is the name of a Jewish child welfare organization in Poland that existed for less than twenty years, from 1924 until 1940, when the Nazis delegalized Poland's prewar Jewish organizations. Its name is well known to scholars, and the organization provided significant support to Jewish children, especially orphans. The group's leaders continued its activities throughout the war, and the work of CENTOS comes up often in the history of the Warsaw ghetto. Yet the story of this group has not been told. Nor have scholars focused on how, after 1918, Jewish social workers helped to transform their community by improving the lives of children.

I first became interested in the history of Jewish child welfare when I realized many of the sources from the 1920s and 1930s that related to charity and philanthropy among Jews focused on support for children. CENTOS, an awkward Polish acronym for the Centralny Związek Towarzystw Opieki nad Żydowskimi Sierotami, or Central Union of Associations for Jewish Orphan Care, served as an umbrella organization for hundreds of smaller associations and institutions scattered throughout Poland, primarily in the *kresy*, or the eastern borderlands.[1] I became further

---

1 CENTOS is usually mentioned only in secondary sources on general relief work after 1918. For example, see Yehuda Bauer, *My Brother's Keeper: A History of the American Jewish Joint Distribution Committee, 1929–1939* (Philadelphia: Jewish Publication Society of America, 1974). For a brief entry on CENTOS in English by Moshe Landau, see *Encyclopedia Judaica*, s.v. "CENTOS," accessed May 21, 2016. http://go.galegroup.com/ps/i.do?id=GALE%7CCX-2587504106&v=2.1&u=cuyahoga_main&it=r&p=GVRL&sw=w&asid=257eea69361e79fd-5995c638bbc6e218. See also the entry by Rafał Żebrowski, *Polski Słownik Judaistyczny*, s.v. "CENTOS," accessed May 27, 2016, http://www.jhi.pl/psj/CENTOS. CENTOS is written in some sources without capital letters (as Centos). Additional Yiddish and Polish versions of the name include Farband fun Tsentrales far yesoymim farzorgung in Poyln; Farband far

intrigued as I read through the pages of one of its journals, the Polish language *Przegląd Społeczny* (Social review). A frequent tagline that appeared whenever necessary to fill blank space (for example, at the end of an article) was "The Child! The Future of the Nation." There was never any mention of which nation this child belonged to, but CENTOS was a private Jewish institution. Its support came primarily from private donors and the American Jewish Joint Distribution Committee (hereafter, JDC), but CENTOS groups also received subventions from municipalities and the Polish government. CENTOS published journals in both Polish and Yiddish, but the articles on child psychology and proper hygiene do not betray any strong ideological tendency. I wanted to learn more about CENTOS and its work in order to understand how Jewish community leaders tried to overcome the daunting practical challenges of life in Poland between the wars and how they wished to shape the future of the nation.

As I learned more from the CENTOS journals and archival sources, I began to understand the importance of the contribution the leaders of CENTOS made to Jewish life. These leaders participated in the transformation of Jewish life. The successful work of these secular leaders—teachers, doctors, lawyers, and others—increasingly removed authority from the *kehilot*, the official governing bodies of Poland's Jewish communities (*kehilah*, singular). They then began to forge relationships with governmental institutions, including public schools. I decided I wanted to present the words of these social work professionals to readers directly, because much of what I was reading described precisely how community leaders could rebuild after the tragedy of war and what they actually did to shape their community into a modern nation. Their writings reveal the actions of these leaders, what they thought about their work, and how they affected the lives of the children they recognized as the future of the nation. *For the Good of the Nation: Institutions for Jewish Children in Interwar Poland* thus presents both a history of Jewish child welfare and a

---

kinder shuts un yesoymim farzorgung; Centrala Towarzystw Opieki nad Sierotami; Centrala Związku Towarzystw Opieki nad Sierotami i Dziećmi Opuszczonymi. See also Bajla Lewin, "Związek Towarzystw Opieki na Żydowskimi Sierotami i Dziećmi Opuszczonymi Rzeczypospolitej Polskiej (CENTOS)," Prace magisterskie napisane przed 1939 rokiem (sygn. 117), 1931–39, Żydowski Instytut Historyczny im. Emanuela Ringelbluma.

INTRODUCTION

Leib Neustadt, Director, Joint Distribution Committee in Poland and member of Executive Board of CENTOS, Warsaw (American Jewish Joint Distribution Committee Archives)

selection of readings that describe the work of Jewish community leaders and the lives of the children in their care. It is my hope that this book can serve as an introduction to the topic and encourage further research into both the field of social work and the lives of Jewish children. The overview of Jewish child welfare included here addresses the indispensable role of the JDC in providing funds, guidance, and leadership; the development of CENTOS; and the debate between providing foster care or building orphanages. A review of the accompanying primary sources shows that more topics deserve further exploration, including the backgrounds of many of the workers and leaders of CENTOS and, perhaps most importantly, the development of vocational education.

The foremost leaders in Jewish child welfare during this period were Janusz Korczak (born Henryk Goldszmit, 1878/79–1942) and Stefania Wilczyńska (1886–1942). They were involved in CENTOS in different ways, but, because their work has received comparatively greater attention, this study addresses less well-known organizations in order to examine a wider range of experiences of both social workers

Children at play, summer day camp organized by the Association for Jewish Orphan Care, Kraków, 1930 (Narodowe Archiwum Cyfrowe, Warsaw)

and children.[2] The works translated here have been chosen to reflect the activities of Poland's Jewish social work professionals and to illustrate the diversity of experiences of Jewish children in need. They were published in CENTOS journals or in cooperation with CENTOS, and thus they reveal the values and concerns of Poland's most prominent organization for Jewish children. The writings selected exemplify the

---

2 The most complete volume on Korczak and his work is Aleksander Lewin's *Korczak znany i nieznany* (Warsaw: Wyższa Szkoła Pedagogiczna, 1999). See also Joanna Olczak-Ronikier, *Korczak: Próba biografii* (Warsaw: Wydawnictwo W.A.B., 2011) and Magdalena Kicińska, *Pani Stefa* (Wołowiec: Wydawnictwo Czarne, 2015). Also outside of the scope of this study are children's health-care institutions, such as the Medem Sanatorium in Miedzeszyn, run by the Bund. See Magdalena Kozłowska, "'In Sunshine and Joy'? The Story of Medem Sanatorium in Miedzeszyn," *East European Politics and Societies and Cultures* 28 (February 2014): 49–62, and Ryszard Zabłotniak, "Sanitorium Dziecka im. Włodzimierza Medema w Międzeszynie," *Archiwum Historii i Filozofii Medycyny* 55, no. 3/4 (1992): 317–22. For a history of Towarzystwo Ochrony Zdrowia Ludności Żydowskiej (Society for the Protection of the Health of the Jewish People), see Ignacy Einhorn, *Towarzystwo Ochrony Zdrowia Ludności Żydowskiej w Polsce w latach 1921–1950* (Toruń: Wydawn. Adam Marszałek, 2008).

INTRODUCTION

range of issues confronted by social work professionals in the 1920s and 1930s, including the ongoing search for funds, the need to train children to live independently, and how to provide care for children with special needs.

The readings have been divided into three sections. The first highlights descriptions of homes for Jewish children. A report from Pinsk describes care for orphans in a smaller city. A review of publications written by children reveals life at an orphanage in Lwów. Reports of teachers portray children in the classroom, and brief inspection reports of children's homes summarize care for orphans in both small towns and larger cities. The second section highlights the Home for Jewish Children and Farm in Helenówek, near Łódź. Helenówek is of special interest because its founder was Khayim Mordkhe Rumkowski (1877–1944), who later became the leader of the Łódź ghetto. More importantly, though, Yekhiel Ben-Tsiyon Kats offers an extended look at life inside Helenówek in his publication *Dertisiung oder farbrekhn? Funm togbukh fun a dertsier* (Education or crime? From the diary of an educator), translated here in its entirety. The third section features a group of articles describing the work of the CENTOS Therapeutic and Educational Institution in Otwock. This institution (often simply referred to, confusingly, as CENTOS in Otwock) served children with special needs and exemplifies how child welfare leaders aimed to help children with mental and physical challenges. Taken together, the articles by Zofia Rosenblum, Kalman Lis, Helena Boguszewska, and Abraham Berger offer a surprisingly complete picture of the work of the doctors and teachers and the lives of many of the children.

Most of the authors of the articles included here worked directly with children. They were social work professionals engaging in vital work in the aftermath of war. Some of the authors have not left behind any trace of biography beyond their published work. This is especially true of the authors in the first section. There is no information about Ben-Levi, the author of the short sketch of the orphanage in Pinsk, or about Yakov Sarner, who describes a strike of the children in an unidentified home. Similarly, details of the career of Tsvi Tarlovski, who recounts an instance of childish stubbornness, have been lost. Two of the authors, A. (Aron)

Goldin and Leon Gutman, worked as representatives of the JDC. Maks Schaff, a lawyer and Jewish community leader in Lwów, is among the more prominent of these authors.

The selection of readings describing homes for children begins with Ben-Levi's description of the orphanage in Pinsk. This is a typical description of how a local committee provided for war orphans. Significantly, Ben-Levi shows awareness of the role of the JDC and the significance of the JDC's support. Both gratitude for the support of the JDC and tension with the community's "foreign brothers" are apparent in his remarks. Maks Schaff's reviews of the Special Issues published by the orphanage in Lwów reveal much about the lives of the children. The institution was a stable one, with the resources that allowed children to put out sixty-page issues of a publication including children's writings. Schaff shows the range of the children's interests, their love of the outdoors and animals, and their knowledge of both Polish and Yiddish literature. Leon Gutman's account of images of youth in school publications, published in the Polish language *Przegląd Społeczny*, quotes the children in Yiddish, illustrating the interaction between Polish-speaking leaders and Yiddish-speaking children. The classroom and schoolyard scenes portrayed by Tsvi Tarlovski and Yakov Sarner depict some of the normality of childhood. The children were stubborn; they often did not want to go to school and teachers often confronted them. Though institutionalized, some children went to other private and public schools and, in addition to whatever traumas led to their being orphaned, experienced the same trials and tribulations of any child. They were playful, stubborn, cheerful, disobedient, vulnerable, and strong-willed. The inspection reports of A. Goldin yield fascinating insights into the histories of the committees and associations of CENTOS. Goldin makes short, summary judgments about the organization of a committee or about the level of the community's financial support for an institution. His judgments are those of a bureaucrat, concerned with doing his job and improving the general effectiveness of his agency's work. His reports reveal the range of activities of those involved in Jewish child welfare, in both small towns and large cities.

Yekhiel Ben-Tsiyon Kats describes his experiences teaching at the Home for Jewish Children and Farm in Helenówek. He worked as a

INTRODUCTION

teacher there before publishing his text with the support of the CENTOS journal *Dos kind*.³ His text, *Dertisiung oder farbrekhn?*, is a slim volume—less than sixty-five pages—excerpts of which were previously published in *Dos kind*. The text is an exposé of life in Helenówek and so demands, more than the other writings, additional explanation. Khayim Rumkowski ran Helenówek from its founding through the 1930s. An insurance salesman and manufacturer of velvet, Rumkowski was active as a member of the *kehilah* in Łódź and a Zionist. He is best known for his role among the community during World War II, when he was appointed *Judenälteste* (Eldest of the Jews). In this leadership role, Rumkowski adopted a policy of productivization, hoping that the Germans would not kill those who were able to work. This led him to concur with the deportation of Jewish children. As he explained in a public speech in September 1942, "The ghetto has been hit with a painful blow. They are demanding from us our most precious fortune—children and the elderly. I was not privileged to have a child of my own, so I gave the best years of my life to children ... In my old age I must stretch out my hands and beg: 'Brothers and sisters, turn them over to me! Fathers and mothers, give me your children ...'"⁴

It is difficult to overestimate Rumkowski as a tragic figure. Rumkowski has been condemned for what many have described as an act of collaboration. Yet it remains true that nearly seventy thousand Jews remained alive in the Łódź ghetto in 1944. Moreover, he was the founder of an orphanage; he had spent a significant part of his life working on behalf of Jewish children. In addition, rumors of sexual abuse cloud any evaluation of Rumkowski, before or after the war. As Robert Moses Shapiro writes in his biographical sketch of Rumkowski in the *YIVO Encyclopedia*, "Unsubstantiated prewar rumors alleged that Rumkowski sexually abused a number of orphans and staff members at Helenówek; similar unconfirmed allegations about his wartime behavior

---

3 There is no information about his career later in the 1930s.
4 An English language version of the original Yiddish speech appears in a work by Isaiah Trunk, *Łódź Ghetto: A History*, trans. and ed. Robert Moses Shapiro (Bloomington: Indiana University Press, 2006), 272–74.

were made by some survivors of the Łódź ghetto."⁵ Kats's book is at least one source of these prewar rumors, which account for only a small portion of the entire text.⁶

Shapiro's statement about unsubstantiated prewar rumors and unconfirmed wartime allegations is perhaps the most just and evenhanded judgment that can be made about the situation. While Kats's text does offer details, some of which could yet be confirmed through the additional work of researchers and genealogists, the rumors are unsubstantiated, even if often repeated in fictional treatments of the Łódź ghetto. The Polish scholar Monika Polit offers an interpretation of Rumkowski based on an especially thorough and analytical review of the sources describing Rumkowski's life and experiences in Helenówek in both Yiddish and Polish. She concludes that the incidents Kats describes are most likely exaggerated, and, indeed, the tone of Kats's work is far from objective. She also points out that, whatever the truth of the allegations against Rumkowski, he was not a pedophile. The rumors concern older teenagers. Polit asks the difficult question, "Can the sincere engagement of Rumkowski redeem him for his guilt toward several, even more than

---

5   Robert Moses Shapiro, *YIVO Encyclopedia of Jews in Eastern Europe*, s.v. "Rumkowski, Khayim Mordkhe," accessed August 30, 2015, http://yivoencyclopedia.org/article.aspx/Rumkowski_Khayim_Mordkhe.

6   Philip Friedman referred to this book in an essay on Rumkowski, "Pseudo-Saviors in the Polish Ghettos: Mordechai Chaim Rumkowski of Lodz," in *Roads to Extinction: Essays on the Holocaust*, ed. Ada June Friedman (New York: Jewish Publication Society of America, 1980). Referring to Rumkowski, Friedman wrote, "His enemies accused him of being excessively familiar with female students and teachers." He provided additional information in an accompanying note: "He was publicly accused of that in a book written by a physician, which I read in the late 1930s. It was published in Yiddish in Lodz or Warsaw. The author was, to the best of my recollection, a Dr. Pecker, or Preger. I do not recall if Rumkowski took legal action against the author." Ibid. 335, 349n. Dr. M. Peker wrote the introduction to Kats's book, and so I think that *Dertsiung oder ferbrekhn* must be the book to which Friedman refers. Friedman's essay first appeared in Hebrew as "Goalei sheker ba-gitaot polin," *Metsuda* 7 (1954): 602–618. Referring to Friedman's imprecise recollection of Kats's text, Isaiah Trunk cites this "brochure" by "a certain Doctor Preger, or Peker" in *Łódź Ghetto*, 456n85. In this same note, Trunk also cites the work of Lucille Eichengreen as "a first-hand, eyewitness testimony that Rumkowski was, in fact, a sexual predator." See Lucille Eichengreen, *From Ashes to Life: My Memories of the Holocaust*, with Harriet Hyman Chamberlain (San Francisco: Mercury House, 1994), and *Rumkowski and the Orphans of Lodz*, with Rebecca Camhi Fromer (San Francisco: Mercury House, 2000).

INTRODUCTION

several, teenage girls?"⁷ Similarly, the Israeli scholar Michal Unger points to "the gray zone" described by Primo Levi, suggesting that any assessment of Rumkowski and his behavior must avoid definitive judgments.⁸

Kats's allegations against Rumkowski clearly served as the primary motivation for his writing. He presents his work with prefatory and concluding remarks from Jewish leaders who attest to the truth of his descriptions, juxtaposing them with testimonials from former teachers and residents of Helenówek. But the image Kats leaves of Helenówek is not entirely negative. Helenówek was a substantial institution, an effort to improve the lives of Jewish children and, not least, a reflection of the Zionist goals of Rumkowski and others.⁹ The home was established in what was then the country surrounding the city. The establishment of a farm was meant to offer the children the facility they would need to prepare for one of their possible futures, a life in Palestine. Kats's "diary" includes what we might think of as several set pieces, descriptions of incidents that must have occurred in other locations as well. These incidents show us something of what must have happened countless times in both the *shtetlakh* (small towns) of the *kresy* and the larger cities. For example, he describes a widower with a daughter already in Helenówek, bringing in two more of his children, one tugging his hand and the other in his arms clinging to him. He recounts the roughhousing of a boy and girl in their early teens, acting out their sexual impulses. He tells of young women and girls turning to the dormitory of the Froyen-shuts fereyn (Women's Defense Association) for assistance. His descriptions reveal how teachers and children interacted and how children interacted with each other. Kats also raises the important question of just how far courts of children could go in their prosecution of teachers for what children deemed offenses. The notion that children can rule themselves, while important pedagogically, was never entertained without the concomitant notion of adult authority.

---

7 Monika Polit, "Mordechaj Chaim Rumkowski: Prawda i zmyślenie" (Warsaw: Stowarzyszenie Centrum Badań nad Zagładą Żydów, 2012), 39 (translation mine).
8 Michal Unger, *Reassessment of the Image of Mordechai Chaim Rumkowski* (Jerusalem: Yad Vashem, 2004), 13.
9 For the institution's own approach to child-care issues, see *Der yosem: tsaytshrift gevidmet di inyonim: fun yesoymin-farzorgung, kinder-dertsiung, un froyen-shuts* (Lodz: Internat far yidishe kinder un ferme in Helenuvek: Yidish froyen-shuts-feryn in Lodz, 1926).

Kats depicted Helenówek as an institution that catered to the whims of adults and neglected the well-being of those it was meant to serve. It stands in contrast to the CENTOS Therapeutic and Educational Institution for Children in Otwock. This home for children with special needs, founded in 1928, was the subject of much interest in its day and remains of interest to historians.[10] The authors describing CENTOS in Otwock were better known than the other authors whose works appear here. Zofia Rosenblum (later Szymańska, 1888–1978) was a leading figure in Warsaw's medical community. She was from a linguistically and culturally assimilated Jewish family, well educated, and, until her involvement in social welfare, generally unaware of the living conditions of her Yiddish-speaking neighbors. She lived a long life, surviving the Holocaust in hiding and establishing herself as one of Poland's most respected health professionals after World War II. Her memoir, *Byłam tylko lekarzem ...* (I was just a doctor), details her career before and after the war and includes much information about her years at CENTOS in Otwock.[11]

Kalman Lis (1903–42) was prominent in a different field. He was a well-known Yiddish poet, first published in the late 1920s. Born in Kowel in Wołyń and educated in both the *kheyder* and in a Polish high school, and later at the University of Warsaw and Vilna University, Lis was a writer, teacher, and administrator. Lis specialized in working with developmentally delayed children. He became director of CENTOS in Otwock in 1937. Lis published several books of poetry and became known as an anti-Fascist proletarian poet.[12] His poems, criticism, and reportage

---

10 The most thorough overview of this institution is Marzena Pękowska, "Organizacja Zakładu Leczniczo-Wychowawczego 'CENTOS' dla żydowskich dzieci niepełnosprawnych intelektualnie w Otwocku (1928–1939)," *Przegląd historyczno-oświatowy* 57, no. 1/2 (2014): 141–56. In Polish this institution is most often referred to as Zakład Leczniczo-wychowawczy "CENTOS" and in Yiddish as the Hayl-pedagogisher anshtalt "TSENTOS." CENTOS appears as an entry in the Glossary of Terms and Concepts in the comprehensive work on the Warsaw ghetto by Barbara Engelking and Jacek Leociak, *Getto warszawskie: Przewodnik po nieistniejącym mieście* (Warsaw: Wydawnictwo IFiS PAN, 2001), 787. Translated by Emma Harris in *The Warsaw Ghetto: A Guide to the Perished City* (New Haven, CT: Yale University Press, 2009), 835. Engelking and Leociak refer to this institution in Polish as Klinika Medyczno-Pedagogiczna w Otwocku, translated as the Medical and Pedagogical Clinic in Otwock.

11 Zofia Szymańska, *Byłam tylko lekarzem...* (Warsaw: Instytut Wydawniczy Pax, 1979).

12 Salomon Łastik and Arnold Słucki, *Antologia poezji żydowskiej* (Warsaw: Państwowy Instytut Wydawniczy, 1983), 14.

appeared in Yiddish publications throughout Poland, including in *Literarishe bleter*. In spite of his significant work in both literature and social work before the war, he is perhaps best known for his verses written during the Holocaust. He was seriously wounded in the German bombardment of Poland on September 1, 1939, but he was able to return to his work in Otwock. During the liquidation of the Jewish population of Otwock in August 1942, the children under his care were shot, and he attempted, briefly, to hide with the help of a peasant before being shot and killed by the Germans near Otwock.[13]

Helena Boguszewska (1886–1978), author of a sketch describing her visit to the institution in Otwock, was known as a writer with leftist sympathies. She also published with Zofia Rosenblum.[14] In the mid-1930s Boguszewska was one of the leaders of *Przedmieście* (City Outskirts), a writers' group project that aimed to tell the stories of everyday people who were otherwise neglected in the period's contemporary fiction.[15] Boguszewska often wrote and collaborated on this "literature of fact" with Jerzy Kornacki (1908–81).

These accounts of the institution—by a doctor and teacher who worked there and two outside observers—reveal a much different kind of institution than Kats's Helenówek. Rosenblum, a medical doctor with an interest in children's health, outlined the work of the institution in essays in *Dos kind* and *Przegląd Społeczny*. Her view of the institution is perhaps best described as clinical. She is most interested in how and why the organization operates. She describes the process for the selection of the children, the need for an isolation ward, and the staff's therapeutic and educational methods. Lis, in contrast, offers a colorful picture of the boys in his care, describing how he woke them up every morning. Boguszewska, a Polish writer with a deep interest in child welfare, describes her two

---

13 Zofia Borzymińska, *Polski Słownik Judaistyczny*, s.v. "Lis Kalman (Kałmen)," accessed May 29, 2016, http://www.jhi.pl/psj/Lis_Kalman_(Kalmen). A more complete entry for Kalman Lis written by Khayim-Leyb Fuks can be found in the *Leksikon fun der nayer yidisher literatur*, ed. Shmuel Niger and Yankev Shatski (New York: Alveltlekhn Yidishn Kultur-Kongres, 1956–81).
14 Helena Boguszewska and Zofia Rosenblum, *Co się należy wszystkim dzieciom*, from *Życie dziecka* (Life of the Child) (Warsaw: Polski Komitet Opieki nad Dzieckiem, 1928).
15 See Czesław Miłosz, *The History of Polish Literature* (London: Macmillan, 1969), 427.

visits to the institution in Otwock and offers another set of images of children's lives. Abraham Berger, a representative of the JDC, wrote an account of eight years of CENTOS activity in Otwock that suggests both what was achieved and how much more was yet to be done.

The sources describing CENTOS in Otwock outline the types of children accepted and the process for admission. The language of the day identified the children as, quite literally, stupid, feeble-minded, idiotic, or psychopathic. Other terms used were less directly derogatory, such as developmentally delayed or mentally underdeveloped. In each instance I have chosen English phrases that reflect the Yiddish or Polish as closely as possible. The writings about Otwock reveal an institution that made a sincere effort to improve the lives of children who faced greater challenges than others. Included is a teacher's description of "days of independence," when the children assumed the roles of the staff in order to show they could handle the tasks of day-to-day living. The authors show that those who led Otwock were aware of changes in both pedagogy and medical practice. But their work had limits. The statistics offered by Rosenblum reveal that many children left CENTOS in Otwock because CENTOS no longer had the money to care for them. I have included the texts on Otwock to draw attention to a unique institution and to the history of special education.[16]

The leaders of CENTOS prepared children to live productive lives, whether in Poland or Palestine. The question of the nation to which these children belonged has perplexed more than one writer. Stanisław Vincenz (1888–1971) was a close friend of Maks Schaff, the Jewish community leader from Lwów. In one of his many essays on Jewish themes, Vincenz recalled a visit, at Schaff's invitation, to a home for Jewish boys in Lwów during Passover.[17] Vincenz recalled how the children sang songs for the

---

16 Polish scholars have covered the topic. See Marian Balcerek, *Rozwój wychowania i kształcenia dzieci upośledzonych umysłowych* (Warsaw: Wydawnictwa Szkolne i Pedagogiczne, 1981) and *Dzieje szkolnictwa i pedagogiki specjalnej*, ed. Stanisław Mauersberg (Warsaw: Państwowe Wydawnictwo Naukowe, 1990). For additional context from another country, see Michael Grossberg, "From Feeble-Minded to Mentally Retarded: Child Protection and the Changing Place of Disabled Children in the Mid-Twentieth Century United States," *Paedogigica Historica* 47, no. 6 (2011): 729–47.

17 Stanisław Vincenz, *Tematy żydowskie* (Gdańsk: ATEXT, 1993), 47. The visit is also mentioned by Teresa Schaff in her memoir of her life with her husband Adam Schaff, the

holiday in Hebrew and how he, not for the first time, made a mistake. Vincenz took his hat off during a moment he deemed celebratory enough to command respect. Others left their heads covered. The children sang in Hebrew and conversed among themselves in Polish. One child even read a verse in Polish dreaming about the land of Israel. The child, "a typical Polish type," provoked Vincenz to ask Schaff, "Where are we? With people from which nationality?"[18]

Schaff proudly explained that the goal of those working with the children was to connect Israel and Poland, for now and for the future, even if—or especially if—some of these children might eventually emigrate to Palestine. Vincenz approved of this goal. Schaff, a leader of the Jewish community who had assimilated linguistically and—at least to some extent—culturally, was one of the foremost leaders of Jewish child welfare in Poland after 1918. He wrote often for *Przegląd Społeczny*. Vincenz's observation highlights the fact that children in institutions led by Schaff grew up belonging to two nations. The work of Schaff and others like him benefited Poland's Jewish children, who spoke in Polish, sang Hebrew songs, and prepared for a possible life in Palestine.

Vincenz was simply not sure to which nation these Jewish children belonged. The cultural flexibility of the Jewish children shocked the educated and cosmopolitan Vincenz, more familiar than most with the cultural diversity of his native Galicia. Many professionals like Schaff devoted their careers and their philanthropy to Jewish children. They worked tirelessly on behalf of the most needy and vulnerable, those who had been orphaned as a result of violence and pogroms during and after World War I. The organizations of which they were a part were most certainly Jewish institutions, established by Jews, run by Jews, for the benefit of Jewish children. They provided aid and imparted ideals of national belonging but, most importantly, they aimed to prepare children to live independently, wherever that might be.

Beset by challenges from the conclusion of the war in 1918 and obviously constrained financial circumstances, the associations of CENTOS

---

son of Max Schaff. *Mój Adam* (Warsaw: "Kto jest Kim," 2012), 103–4. Vincenz was a Polish writer known for his love and knowledge of the Hutsul region of Galicia.

18 Vincenz, *Tematy żydowskie*, 47.

were quite literally still in the middle of figuring out the parameters of their work in the 1930s. CENTOS leaders wrestled with questions such as which children should be institutionalized and which children *could* be institutionalized, given money and resources. At the outbreak of war in 1939, CENTOS itself was still a teenager, just sixteen years old. The leaders of CENTOS had yet to define the precise roles of private and institutional care. They were still setting up organizations and programs to train child welfare workers. Jewish community leaders, abroad and in Poland, had done much to improve the community's material circumstances and to transform how children grew into Jewish adults. Their pioneering social work serves not only as a reminder of the vibrancy of the interwar Polish-Jewish community but also as a call to examine the relationships among nations living together in one state. Their legacy is an urgent appeal to protect the rights of children.

A Note on Translations and Names

All translations and errors are mine. I have made an effort to follow the rules of YIVO for transliteration, but, when they exist, I have used common English spellings for place names and some terms. In other cases, I have rendered place names in Polish, whether published in Yiddish or Polish. I have also indicated the Yiddish name if given in the original text. In the few instances when Polish language authors employed Yiddish phrases, I have retained the Polish transliteration of words in Yiddish. I have adopted the modernized spelling Zofia Rosenblum for Zofja Rosenblum. Rosenblum (also occasionally spelled Rozenblum) adopted the name Szymańska during the war and used the name Zofia Szymańska professionally in the postwar period.

I

A History of CENTOS

The system of social care that emerged among Jews in Poland after 1918 was radically new. It brought together laws and institutions from the period of the Partitions and a national Jewish child welfare movement whose leaders were perhaps the clearest example of the community leadership's transformation from religious to secular authority. Some of them, like Maks Schaff and Zofia Rosenblum, came from Polonized Jewish families. Others, such as Kalman Lis, came from more traditional, Yiddish-speaking backgrounds. They came together because of the crisis that resulted from years of war. Collectively, their work reflects the values of the Jewish community in Poland.

Poland in the 1920s was a place of turmoil and growth. Its diverse populations sought many different ways to improve living conditions, outside of and within the already established communal and governmental structures. Poland's Jewish community leaders responded to the formation of the Polish state by founding organizations to reach their goals and by working with the new Polish government. There were some continuities in philanthropy from the prewar period throughout the 1930s, but the newly independent Polish state and the position of Poland's Jews as members of a community with ties abroad conditioned the development of social welfare.

Jews made up about ten percent of the population of the newly formed Polish state.[1] Four-fifths of Jews were urban, and in most large

---

1 Joseph Rothschild, *East Central Europe between the Two World Wars* (Seattle: University of Washington Press, 1974), 36; Ezra Mendelsohn, *The Jews of East Central Europe between the World Wars* (Bloomington: Indiana University Press, 1983), 23; Ezra Mendelsohn, "Interwar

cities Jews accounted for a quarter of the population or more.² Jews also lived in the smaller towns and villages of Galicia and the *kresy*, the eastern borderlands. While there were some who attained high positions in commerce or the professions, the Jewish community is perhaps best described as generally lower middle-class or proletarian, with the same economic challenges as their neighbors but the additional burden of exclusion from certain types of work and general economic, political, and social discrimination.³ The increased pauperization of the Jewish community became a pressing issue during this period.⁴ In addition, the war was not truly over in 1918. Violence continued as the new state consolidated its borders and was exacerbated by accompanying pogroms.⁵ The challenges of war and the ethnic violence that followed often devastated smaller communities.

Seeking solutions to the political, social, and economic conditions under which they lived, many Jews turned to the ideologies of nationalism and socialism.⁶ Many strove to develop national identities grounded in different conceptions of Zionism. Still others held fast to conceptions of Jewish identity grounded in the practice of religion, but even the Orthodox were increasingly involved in political life. Through the brief period of Polish independence, the Zionists, Bundists, Orthodox, and Folkists (advocates of Jewish cultural autonomy) would compete for the attention of Poland's Jewish population. The question of language exacerbated the political and religious differences. Interwar Polish Jewry was a tri-lingual culture.⁷ Most Jews in Poland spoke Yiddish in the home, but the use of

---

Poland: Good for the Jews or Bad for the Jews?" in *The Jews in Poland*, ed. Chimen Abramsky, Maciej Jachimczyk, and Antony Polonsky (Oxford: Basil Blackwell, 1986), 130–39.

2 Rothschild, *East Central Europe*, 35.
3 Mendelsohn, *The Jews of East Central Europe*, 27.
4 Rothschild, *East Central Europe*, 40; Antony Polonsky, *The Jews in Poland and Russia*, vol. 3, *1914–2008* (Oxford: Littman Library of Jewish Civilization, 2012), 62.
5 For an overview of the pogroms and continued violence, see Polonsky, *The Jews in Poland and Russia*, vol. 3, 45–50.
6 See Ezra Mendelsohn, *On Modern Jewish Politics* (Oxford: Oxford University Press, 1993) and Polonsky, *The Jews in Poland and Russia*, vol. 3, 59–66.
7 Chone Shmeruk, "Hebrew-Yiddish-Polish: A Trilingual Jewish Culture," in *The Jews of Poland Between Two World Wars*, ed. Israel Gutman et al. (Hanover, NH: Brandeis University Press, 1989), 285–311.

Polish—as well as Hebrew—increased during this period as it was often strongly advocated by Zionist leaders. The multiplicity of political parties and variations in national ideology and national feeling are indeed staggering. What these parties shared, however, was the goal of improving the living conditions of the community, often both materially and, in some way, spiritually.

The Jewish community in Poland was a significant presence in the country, concentrated in urban neighborhoods and, in spite of a stratum that was relatively wealthy, largely poor and in economic distress. The community was both national and traditional; that is, the appeal of Jewish nationalism led to the popularity of the many different Zionist parties, but many in the community came from and were still rooted in a traditional religious environment. Impoverished Jews lived next to impoverished Poles. (As historians have noted, Polish Jews were poor because they lived in a poor country.)[8] At the same time, they were living during a time of rapid political and economic change, not always for the better. The first years of independence concluded with the Constitution of 1921 and were followed by a period of unstable democracy that collapsed with the coup of Marshal Józef Piłsudski in 1926.[9] Piłsudski's authoritarian regime was not dictatorial.[10] Moreover, he was not an anti-Semite and was viewed favorably by the Jewish community.[11] After his death in 1935, the Polish government became increasingly autocratic and conflicts among government leaders could not be contained. Anti-Semitism increased and came to play a greater role in Poland's politics, and the anti-Semitic stance of the Roman Catholic Church contributed to the hostile atmosphere. A wave of anti-Jewish violence occurred from 1935 to 1937. The government supported an economic boycott of Jewish businesses, and a law passed in 1936 forbade ritual slaughter (though the law was later amended to allow

---

8 Polonsky, *The Jews in Poland and Russia*, vol. 3, 57; Joseph Marcus, *Social and Political History of the Jews in Poland, 1919–1939* (Berlin: Mouton, 1983).
9 This periodization follows that outlined by Polonsky, *The Jews in Poland and Russia*, vol. 3, 58–59.
10 Polonsky, *The Jews in Poland and Russia*, vol. 3, 73.
11 Natalia Aleksiun, "'Regards from My Shtetl': Polish Jews Write to Piłsudski," *The Polish Review* 56, no. 1/2 (2011): 57–71.

ritual slaughter in areas where Jews made up more than three percent of the population).[12]

These twenty-one years of independence were turbulent, presenting significant challenges for Polish Jews, both those taking leadership positions in social movements and political parties and those just trying to make a living. Adaptation was a feature of Jewish life in Poland at this time, in response to a new government and to the cultural norms of a new Poland. This is perhaps most clearly seen in the community's increasing linguistic assimilation and in the high numbers of Jewish children participating in public education in spite of a vibrant network of private Jewish schools.[13] As the Jewish community was becoming increasingly active in both Zionism and Bundism, Jews were also speaking Polish, reading Polish newspapers and literature, and participating in the culture of Poland much more extensively than before 1918. The signal achievement of the Jews in Poland between 1918 and 1939 was the creation of nationally conscious, nearly autonomous organizations of civil society intended to train a generation of Jewish leaders to realize Jewish goals in Poland.[14] Those organizations include CENTOS and its institutional members, all of which were supported to a great extent by private donors. These donors included both wealthy patrons and those who could only make modest donations for a worthy cause. That cause was making the most basic improvements in the lives of the neediest children. Reviewing the demographics of the Jewish community in Poland, the historian Joseph Marcus concluded that "for most, a childhood spent in the midst of a Jewish family in eastern Europe was a chilly, sombre experience."[15] The associations of CENTOS served full orphans (those who had lost both parents), half orphans (those who had lost one parent and needed outside assistance), and the families of the poor or those with special needs. Orphans found

---

12   Mendelsohn, *The Jews of East Central Europe*, 73.
13   Mendelsohn, *The Jews of East Central Europe*, 67. For an examination of private Jewish educational alternatives in interwar Poland, see Shimon Frost, *Schooling as a Socio-political Expression* (Jerusalem: Magnes, 1998).
14   For an overview of organizations that focused on children and youth, see Sean Martin, "Polish Jewry between the World Wars," in *The Wiley-Blackwell History of Jews and Judaism*, ed. Alan T. Levenson (Malden, MA: Wiley-Blackwell, 2012), 393–408.
15   Marcus, *Social and Political History*, 182.

themselves at the mercy of community leaders struggling to design a safety net that had not existed previously.

The chaos of war exposed the weaknesses of the organized Jewish communities (the *kehilot*) and opened the opportunity for civic leaders and activists to make significant changes. The CENTOS associations were grassroots efforts based on the work of volunteers, some of them wealthy and some of them skilled in working with children.[16] These associations grew organically during the war, consolidating into CENTOS in 1924. This was the beginning of the institutionalization of Jewish child welfare in Poland and part of the well-developed Jewish civil society that emerged in Poland after 1918. They sought support from locals, from foreign relief agencies, and from municipal authorities. CENTOS operated as a professional association, distributing funding, publishing journals for its members, offering training, and inspecting sites of member associations.

The transformation of philanthropy and social work was an evolution, brought about by the development of imperial laws in the nineteenth century, the physical violence of war, the improved education received by so many Jewish women and men throughout Europe, and, not least, the aid provided by Jews from abroad. The leaders of the associations of CENTOS worked outside the traditional *kehilot* and aimed to change local conditions in ways not previously imagined by Jewish leaders in Poland. The transformation imagined—and to a great extent realized—by these associations placed responsibility in the hands of leaders distinguished by their educational achievements and their involvement in philanthropy or political activism, not their knowledge or practice of religion. The transformation sharpened the secular identity of the Jewish community while at the same time enhancing its ties to the larger Jewish community abroad.

While CENTOS was a strong organization that brought together the work of hundreds of professionals, it was always in need of funds. Throughout the 1920s, CENTOS received support from the JDC, but the JDC withdrew that support at times. But by the early 1930s the worldwide economic depression eventually made a sense of financial crisis permanent. Thus, the

---

16 The best overview of the sites of CENTOS and the types of facilities sponsored can be found in a fold-out map in Moshe Shalit, ed., *Fun yor tsu yor: ilustrirter gezelshaftlekher yorbukh* (Varshe: Farband fun tsentrales far yesoymim-farzorgung in poyln, 1929).

generous and well-organized philanthropy of American Jews was central to the development of Jewish child welfare on the local level in Poland. The aid from the JDC began during the war, establishing a dynamic that continued for the next two decades. The JDC aimed to provide relief and eventually to withdraw their support when Polish Jewish institutions were able to take over. While the establishment of CENTOS in 1924 may represent the readiness of Poland's Jews to care for themselves on their own, economic stability in Poland remained elusive and so the need for additional funds never abated. The story of the transformation in leadership of local Jewish communities—from a focus on specifically religious concerns to an awareness of the need for organizations with a practical effect on the Jewish community—cannot be told without an explanation of the American role and the reaction of local Jewish leaders. This cooperation between American and Polish Jewish leaders exemplifies the cooperative nature of the Jewish community. Unable to draw on their own resources, Polish Jews reached out to their relatives abroad. Their relatives rose to the challenge. Though only a part of the complex Jewish civil society that was then developing, children's welfare organizations are worthy of study because they represent the Jewish community's investment not just in Jewish children but in Poland as well. Institutions of social work, much like institutions of elementary and secondary education, can teach us much about how specific groups experience social and political change. In this case, they demonstrate the transformation from religious to secular authority and illustrate the implications of that change for both Jews and Poles. The sources reveal the enormity of the catastrophe after 1918, the concerns of community leaders, and, not least, how the most vulnerable children grew up during this period.

While there is relatively little source material about the Jewish community in Poland before World War II, many different kinds of sources help us to determine the outline of the history of Jewish child welfare. Recently there has been significantly greater interest in the history of Jews in Poland and, among Polish scholars, in the history of child welfare.[17] Local studies of Jewish communities in specific locations have

---

17 See especially Izabela Szczepaniak-Wiecha, "Traditions of the Social Work Profession in Interwar Poland (1918–1939)," in *Amid Social Contradictions: Towards a History of Social Work in Europe*, ed. Gisela Hauss and Dagmar Schulte (Opladen: Barbara Budrich

helped to fill gaps in our knowledge, and scholars have begun to address a broader range of topics, including histories of specific institutions, biographies of influential individuals, and the histories of philanthropy and child welfare.[18]

Scholars in Poland have made significant efforts to evaluate the history of child welfare in this period. The older work of Marian Balcerek and Czesław Kępski is especially helpful for putting together a picture of the kinds of institutions developed and the aid provided by both state and private groups.[19] In addition, newer scholarship by Stefania Walasek and Izabela Szczepaniak-Wiecha has done much to broaden our perspectives of the history of children and to highlight the contributions of Polish

---

Publishers, 2009), 79–87; Izabela Szczepaniak-Wiecha, Agnieszka Małek, and Krystyna Ślany, "The System of Care for Abandoned Children in Poland, 1900–1960: The Development of Family-Forms of Care," in *Need and Care: Glimpses into the Beginnings of Eastern Europe's Professional Welfare*, ed. Kurt Schilde (Bloomfield Hills, MI: Barbara Budrich Publishers, 2005); Agnieszka Małek and Izabela Szczepaniak-Wiecha, "Female Organisers of Social Care in Poland: From Charity to Professional Social Assistance," in Schilde, *Need and Care*; Aleksandra Bilewicz and Stefania Walasek, eds., *Rola mniejszości narodowych w kulturze i oświacie polskiej w latach 1700–1939* (Wrocław: Wydawnictwo Uniwersytetu Wrocławskiego, 1998); Stefania Walasek, *Wśród "swoich" i "obcych": Rola edukacji w społeczeństwach wielokulturowych Europy Środkowej (XVIII–XX wiek)* (Kraków: Impuls, 2006); Stefania Walasek, ed., *Opieka nad dziećmi i młodzieżą* (Kraków: Impuls, 2008).

18 See Rebecca Kobrin, *Jewish Bialystok and Its Diaspora* (Bloomington: Indiana University Press, 2010); Cecile Kuznitz, *YIVO and the Making of Modern Jewish Culture: Scholarship for the Yiddish Nation* (New York: Cambridge University Press, 2014); Natan Meir, "From Communal Charity to National Welfare: Jewish Orphanages in Eastern Europe before and after World War I," *East European Jewish Affairs* 39, no. 1 (April 2009): 19–34; and Kalman Weiser, *Jewish People, Yiddish Nation: Noah Prylucki and the Folkists in Poland* (Buffalo, NY: University of Toronto Press, 2011). Significant gaps in the field remain. For example, there are no comprehensive studies of Jews and their experiences in both public and private education. One wishes, too, for studies that would compare more probingly the experiences of Poland's national minorities at different times and in different places.

19 See Marian Balcerek, *Rozwój opieki nad dzieckiem w Polsce w latach 1918–1939* (Warsaw: Państwowe Wydawnictwo Naukowe, 1978) and *Dzieje opieki nad dzieckiem w Polsce: Ze szczególnym uwzględnieniem rozwoju kształcenia dzieci upośledzonych umysłowo* (Warsaw: Wyższa Szkoła Pedagogiki Specjalnej im. Marii Grzegorzewskiej, 1977); Czesław Kępski, *Dziecko sieroce i opieka nad nim w Polsce w okresie międzywojennym* (Lublin: Wydawnictwo Uniwersytetu Marii Curie-Skłodowskiej, 1991). See also Lidia Jurczyk, "Dziecko jako szczególna kategoria w opiece społecznej okresu międzywojennego," *Zeszyty naukowe WSPS*, ed. Ludwik Malinowski and Małgorzata Orłowska (Warsaw: Wyższa Szkoła Pedagogiki Specjalnej, 1998), 23–37 and Rafał Pląsek, "System opieki społecznej w II Rzeczpospolitej: Kontrolne aspekty funkcjonowania instytucji," *Praca Socjalna* 29, no. 4, (2014): 118–231.

scholars working in the field. Impressively, this newer work also features a commendable focus on multiculturalism. Zdzisław Cutter and Edyta Sadowska have written an important introductory article on the history of social work in the interwar period with special attention to the Jewish community.[20] But much work remains if we wish to understand more about the care provided for children and about how children experienced that care. For example, no scholar has yet considered Jewish institutions alongside Polish institutions, comparing the way these two different nations—living as neighbors among other nations—aided their children. *For the Good of the Nation* is offered as an introduction for others interested in exploring the topic further and as an effort to understand this social work from the perspective of those providing the care.

Scholars recognize social work as "the starting point for the emergence of a civil society that takes care of each member of the community."[21] The construction of the state after 1918 provided a framework for centralization that demanded compliance from the private religious and national groups of this civil society.[22] Unfortunately, governmental records are of limited use in the study of child welfare and related topics. Only about 5% of the records of the Ministry of Labor and Social Care have survived. The records of the Ministry of Religious Confessions and Public Enlightenment—which would have included material related to the Jewish community—fared a little better: an estimated 26% of those records have survived.[23] In the absence of this significant source of information, the archives of the JDC provide one of the most important sources of information for the study of Jewish social work in Poland. The bureaucrats of the JDC filed reports, usually in English, from inspections in the field to the JDC's various offices in Warsaw, Vienna, and New York. The reports of visits to orphanages and aid committees offer basic information such as a home's address or the number of children under care,

---

20 See Zdzisław Cutter and Edyta Sadowska, "Opieka nad ludnością II Rzeczypospolitej ze szczególnym uwzględnieniem mniejszości żydowskiej" in Walasek, *Opieka nad dziećmi i młodzieżą*, 59–118.
21 Dagmar Schulte, "Dual Mandates, Many Faces: Histories of Social Work," in Hauss and Schulte, *Amid Social Contradictions*, 254.
22 Walasek, *Opieka nad dziećmi i młodzieżą*, 9.
23 Kępski, *Dziecko sieroce i opieka nad nim*, 7.

information that is difficult to find elsewhere. The view of an outsider here is obviously problematic, but in many cases these reports may be the only descriptions of an aid committee's work. These sources reveal both the role of the American Jewish community and the situation on the ground in Poland.

Material from the perspective of local Jewish leaders is fragmentary in the JDC archives, consisting of miscellaneous documents and correspondence related to the formation of aid committees and orphanages but in no way reflecting the comprehensive nature of relief efforts after 1918.[24] Fortunately, the CENTOS publications themselves provide us with significant detail of the achievements of the various associations, albeit from an institutional point of view. These publications include the journals of professional Jewish social work, *Dos elendste kind* (The neediest child), *Przegląd Społeczny* (Social review), *Dos shutsloze kind* (The defenseless child), *Dos kind* (The child), and *Unzer kind* (Our child), the annual reports many associations published, and the few publications edited and written by the children themselves, perhaps the most important sources for the study of this topic. The journals offered Jewish child welfare leaders a way to exchange information about the work of local committees and a platform for discussion of their views on institutionalization and private care. These journals, designed to serve the needs of an increasingly numerous group of social workers, teachers, and other child-care professionals, included brief, opinionated discussions of important issues, reviews of current and past research, and regular reports of the activities in each of the CENTOS branches.[25] They reveal specific information about the groups and tell us more about the lives the children lived and sometimes include names and places. Publications for Jewish children may also

---

24 This material can be found in the archives of the YIVO Institute for Jewish Research in New York and in local and state libraries and archives in Poland, Ukraine, and Lithuania.
25 While so many records from these institutions and those who worked in them have been lost, important traces remain in the Jewish and Polish press. The press, a fundamental source admittedly neglected here, could reveal much about how these institutions were viewed by the general public and, by the highlighting of different incidents that led to conflict, about issues of special concern to the public and Jewish community leaders. In addition, materials from archives of smaller towns in Poland, accounts in the popular press of the efforts of relief workers and community activists, and information from the *yizker-bikher* (memorial books) published after World War II may yield further insights.

help us to understand how Jewish community leaders and parents understood childhood. More significantly, these publications also include the writings of many children. The best example of this is Janusz Korczak's *Mały Przegląd* (Little review), a supplement of the independent Polish-language Jewish daily, *Nasz Przegląd* (Our review).[26] There were several important Yiddish-language publications for children,[27] but I have yet to find one written by children and published by a Jewish children's institution.

This review of Jewish child welfare in Poland offers an overview of the Jewish community's response to the war starting in 1918, an evaluation of the role of the JDC, and an outline of the history of CENTOS, with special attention paid to the essential question of institutionalization versus foster care. This seemingly narrow topic—the study of efforts to aid Jewish children across all of Poland during this period—is actually quite broad and part of many different fields of study within history, including the histories of family life, childhood, and gender. The leaders of these institutions and the children they helped generally adapted well to the conditions of life in the fledgling Polish state and learned to cooperate with authorities to meet their own needs. This study helps to answer questions about how Polish authorities both encumbered and aided Jewish community leaders in their efforts to improve the living conditions of their community. Scholars focusing on family relations or on the role of women in the development of modern social work would also do well to consider how these groups provided care and how they prepared children to live independently. In addition, this topic is at the nexus of the history of national groups and the history of the professional discipline of social work. The efforts of social workers were at least as important to the development of the national communities of Jews and Poles as those of politicians. In addition, an examination of child welfare offers us a rich view of individual and family experiences during the period between the wars.

---

26 For excerpts of children's writings, see *Dom na Krochmalnej na łamach "Małego Przeglądu"* (Warsaw: Agencja Edytorska, EZOP, 1997).

27 Adina Bar-El, *Itonut yeladim beyidish ube-ivrit be-polin, 1918–1939* (Nir-Israel: Ha-mehaberet, 2002).

A Response to War

When considering the role of Jewish children's organizations in rebuilding Poland after the 1914–18 war, Jewish community leader Maks Schaff stated that the historian looking back on the postwar period would have "to solve the puzzle of how people so poor could do so much to survive the war."[28] The answer may lie simply in the combined efforts of individuals and local institutions that aimed to protect Jewish children. The work of Jewish leaders in large cities such as Kraków and Lwów and small towns such as Stryj and Zwiahel suggests that Jewish community leaders were able to meet the challenge presented by the devastation of war and the difficult economic circumstances that followed. In doing so, they not only improved the lives of individual children, but they also began to redefine the relationship of the Jewish community to the *kehilot* and to the state. Scholars have long recognized the breakdown of the *kehilot* during World War I and its implications for the development of the Jewish community. As Steven Zipperstein has written, "the war created an institutional vacuum that was filled by a technically skilled cadre of relief workers."[29]

How did local Jewish communities respond to the crisis of the war? Writing in 1929 in *Przegląd Społeczny*, Maks Schaff stated, "Anyone who reads the annual report of any regional committee knows already what will be in the report. Everywhere it's the same history, everywhere it's the same work, the same difficulties, . . . the same lack of understanding for the importance of our actions and our needs."[30] Schaff made these remarks in a column of the journal devoted to a review of the annual reports of Jewish children's organizations. His comments suggest that, in spite of

---

28   Maks Schaff, "Wśród sprawozdań," *Przegląd Społeczny* III, no. IV (April 1929): 145.
29   Steven Zipperstein, "The Politics of Relief: The Transformation of Russian Jewish Communal Life During the First World War," in *Studies in Contemporary Jewry* (1988): 33. Rebecca Kobrin has shown that, with the development of modern voluntary associations in late nineteenth-century Russia, more independently minded lay leaders began to replace the weak *kehilot* well before 1914. "The Politics of Philanthropy: Migration, Emigration, and the Transformation of Jewish Communal Governance in Bialystok, 1885–1939," in *The Jews of Eastern Europe*, ed. Leonard J. Greenspoon, Ronald Simkins, and Brian Horowitz (Omaha: Creighton University Press, 2005), 237.
30   Schaff, "Wśród sprawozdań," 146.

varying local conditions, these Jewish children's organizations shared something of a common history.

In the period before the rebirth of the Polish state, social care differed significantly in each of the three different areas governed by the partitioning powers of Russia, Austria, and Prussia. Religious organizations predominated in the field of social care in the Polish lands under Prussian rule, while philanthropic organizations of different kinds were active in the Austrian Empire. Charitable work faced significant restrictions in the Russian Empire, curtailing private initiatives.[31] The *kehilot* were officially charged with the care of the Jewish community, but the rise of private philanthropy in the mid-nineteenth century was also a significant development.[32] In addition, the early twentieth century was a period of growth in the area of education, when a new cadre of Jewish professionals was being trained in universities throughout Europe and when the work of pedagogues such as John Dewey (1859–1952) and Maria Montessori (1870–1952) was receiving wide acclaim. Working with children was one field in which new professionals could find an outlet for their skills and talents.

Perhaps the most important institution to emerge from the period before the war was Pomoc (Help), the association that established the orphanage where writer and physician Janusz Korczak began his work with Stefania Wilczyńska. Korczak and Wilczyńska represent a specific stratum of the Jewish community in Poland: comparatively wealthy, well-educated professionals, linguistically and culturally assimilated yet still active within the Jewish community. The two worked together from the 1912 opening of Warsaw's Jewish Orphans' Home on Krochmalna Street until their deaths in August 1942. They had met a few years earlier in 1909. A fellow doctor, Izaak Eliasberg, asked his friend Henryk Goldzmit to work in the Berson and Bauman Jewish Children's Hospital. Through his involvement with Eliasberg, Korczak became a member of Towarzystwo "Pomoc dla Sierot" (Help for Orphans Association), the group that

---

31 For a review of social care in the period before World War I, see Cutter and Sadowska, "Opieka nad ludnością II Rzeczpospolitej," 70.

32 For example, see Józef Bąk, "Dwa zapomniane zakłady wychowawcze dla opuszczonej i zaniedbanej młodzieży w Krakowie," *Studia historyczne* 37, no. 1 (1994): 91–102.

eventually built the Jewish Orphans' Home. One of the most active leaders in the association was Eliasberg's wife, Stella Eliasbergowa. She hired Wilczyńska, the daughter of friends, to help with the children in the orphanage in 1909. Korczak and Wilczyńska became a remarkable team. The success of Korczak's pedagogical ideas is due in significant measure to their implementation by Wilczyńska. Wilczyńska managed the Jewish Orphans' Home. She cared for the children on a daily basis, nursed the children's wounds and illnesses, established procedures for the home's operation, determined the budget, and ordered supplies, among other tasks. She and Korczak were, arguably, the two most successful administrators of homes for children in Poland. Korczak admitted that he simply could not manage without her.[33] Just as Korczak has been described as the father of the children in his care, so Wilczyńska has been described as their "no-nonsense mother."[34]

Soon after fighting began in 1914, Jewish community leaders established and further developed a range of associations and institutions for Jewish children. These groups initially focused on relief and on efforts to aid war orphans. The Jewish community in the United States, especially the newly formed JDC provided significant aid to the Jews in Eastern Europe. Jewish community officials, local philanthropists, and volunteers established day-care facilities, orphanages, and summer colonies. Often with help from the JDC, they arranged for foster care, sponsored after-school programs, and developed vocational opportunities, among other tasks. Some of these associations and institutions were quite specialized, focusing on providing care or resources for specific groups of children, such as infants or those with special needs.

The violence of World War I orphaned nearly a million and a half children in Poland, approximately fifteen percent of the total number of children in the country.[35] According to the census of 1921, seven percent of this total (or 115,200) were full orphans; the vast majority (1,447,100 children) were

---

33 Betty Jean Lifton, *The King of Children: A Biography of Janusz Korczak* (New York: Schocken Books, 1988), 155.
34 Ibid.
35 Kępski, *Dziecko sieroce i opieka nad nim*, 13–14.

half-orphans.³⁶ All of them were considered war orphans, though it was recognized that not all were orphaned due to the circumstances of war. As expected, the number of war orphans declined as the years passed and orphans grew up. There were still some war orphans in the late 1930s, primarily older teenagers still in school and receiving some kind of assistance.

Only a small number of these war orphans (around sixty thousand) were Jewish, yet the destruction of the war took a disproportionate toll on Jewish communities in eastern Galicia, which had been subjected to the harsh Russian occupation.³⁷ American Jewish leader Henrietta Szold believed the situation of the Jews in Eastern Europe would eventually be "described as the third *Hurban*, or catastrophe, following the destruction of the first Temple by the Babylonians in 586 BCE and the second by the Romans in 70CE."³⁸ The three million Jews of Poland's Second Republic made up the largest Jewish population in Europe, but the community was devastated.

While the JDC was providing much needed assistance during the war, Jewish community leaders formed local committees in hundreds of towns throughout eastern Galicia.³⁹ The formation of the JDC set in place the dynamic of international aid, the dependence of Polish Jews on such aid, and the efforts of Polish Jews to stand on their own. The JDC continued

---

36 Ibid.
37 The best overview of Jewish child care in interwar Poland is the article by Nina Bar-Yishay and Marek Web, "Yesoymim-farzorgung un kindershuts in poyln (1919–1939)" [Care of orphans and child welfare in Poland (1919–1939)], in *Studies on Polish Jewry, 1919–1939*, ed. Joshua Fishman (New York: YIVO Institute for Jewish Research, 1974), 99–136. Also see Jessie Bogen, "The Problem of Jewish War Orphans," American Jewish Joint Distribution Committee Archives, New York City (JDC Archives), 1919/1921, File 88. For a description of the effect of occupation on the Jewish community in Eastern Europe, see S. Ansky, *The Enemy at His Pleasure*, trans. Joachim Neugroschel (New York: Henry Holt, 2002). Originally published as *Khurbn Galitsiye* [The destruction of Galicia] in S. Ansky, *Gezamlte shriftn* [Collected works], (Warsaw: S. Shreberk, 1925). Yehuda Bauer gives a number of seventy-five thousand orphans in his history of the JDC, *My Brother's Keeper*, 9.
38 Mary McCune, *The Whole Wide World, Without Limits: International Relief, Gender Politics, and American Jewish Women, 1893–1930* (Detroit: Wayne State University Press, 2005), 52, 216n19. For responses to the destruction of the war, and an example of the language Jews used to describe this destruction, see David Roskies, *Against the Apocalypse: Responses to Catastrophe in Modern Jewish Culture* (Cambridge, MA: Harvard University Press, 1984).
39 American Jewish aid continued throughout the end of the 1930s and—to the extent possible—during and after World War II. Reviewing international aid to Jews in Poland over the course of the twentieth century, one can see clearly the importance of this aid, always present in formal and informal contacts from the beginning of the twentieth century.

its role aiding Jews in Eastern Europe after the war, though the non-Jewish context in which they worked had radically changed. With the help of the JDC, the associations for children united into CENTOS in 1924. CENTOS grew into the most important institution of modern Jewish social work in Poland, sponsoring hundreds of sites throughout the country dedicated to improving the lives of Jewish children and publishing professional journals.[40] Its initial effort was focused on care for orphans but in later years its mission broadened to include care for all children in need.

The crisis in child care was brought on by the extreme circumstances of war and, within the Jewish community, by the ensuing postwar violence of pogroms. The crisis reveals how differently child care was viewed in the early twentieth century. The often economically strained circumstances of single parents were recognized immediately as a legitimate reason for giving a child into institutional care. In lands where empires had fallen and state authorities were still learning how to govern, there was no system yet in place to address the needs of parents and children. Emerging from war as an independent—if embattled—democratic state, Poland faced several immediate challenges, including immediate relief and integration of the country's numerous national groups (Ukrainians, Jews, Belorussians, and Germans foremost among them).

The Minorities Treaty of 1919 obliged Poland to treat all of the country's citizens equally, a task the Polish nation never fulfilled.[41] The Constitution of March 1921 declared the theoretical equality of all citizens, but the legislation and government institutions later put into place determined the reality of this theoretical equality. The independent Polish state thus faced a difficult challenge: how to ensure adequate care for all needy children, regardless of religious, ethnic, or national difference.[42] The need for

---

40 For the most thorough overview of the work of these and related associations, see Shalit, *Fun yor tsu yor*, and Moshe Shalit, ed., *Oyf di khurves fun di milkhomes un mehumes: Pinkes fun Gegnt-komitet "Yekopo" in Vilne: 1919-1931* (Vilne: Gegnt-komitet "Yekopo," 1931).

41 Polonsky, *The Jews in Poland and Russia*; Marcus, *Social and Political History*; Celia Stopnicka-Heller, *On the Edge of Destruction: The Jews of Poland Between the Two World Wars* (Detroit: Wayne State University Press, 1994); Jerzy Tomaszewski, *Mniejszości narodowe w Polsce w XX wieku* (Warsaw: Editions Spotkania, 1991).

42 Illustrating that this was not an easy principle to put in practice, Yehuda Bauer recounts a 1919 incident in which food from the United States was distributed separately to Jewish and Polish recipients. *My Brother's Keeper*, 10.

separate social service agencies stemmed from the pre-war separation of the Jewish and Catholic communities and the natural inclination of both communities to preserve their religious traditions. The Jewish community shared the Catholics' concern that orphaned children might be raised by parents of another faith. The desire to take care of Jewish children within Jewish institutions came from a fear of baptism. Jewish nationalism likely played a role as well.

As a result, the child welfare associations that Jewish community leaders established during World War I remained private institutions run by Jews for Jewish children. Mentions of this issue can be found throughout the sources. A child's faith mattered. For example, a court case in Lwów in 1925 suggests the reasons why the religious identity of the child (determined by the mother in Polish law) was an issue of such concern: the desire of the Jewish community not to "lose" any of its children to Christianity and the practical need of individuals and community associations to pay for the care of the child.[43] In another incident, a 1930 report on the work of the CENTOS committee in Gorlice mentions the group's efforts to find as many places for Jewish children in institutions as possible, because of the fear of baptism.[44] In her study of education for the deaf and blind in Lwów, Marzena Pękowska points out that non-Catholics could attend Catholic institutions, but they had to agree to teach their children Catholicism.[45] This practice of segregation persisted through the late 1930s. In the summer of 1939, new laws on the adoption of underage children stated that a Roman Catholic child could only be adopted by a person belonging to that faith or by a married couple, one of whom had to be Roman Catholic.[46] However, such restrictions appear to have been in place informally much earlier.

---

43 For example, the headline of a newspaper article asked, "Who should be the caretaker of a Jewish child?" See "Kto ma być opiekunem żydowskiego dziecka," *Chwila*, 4 August 1925, 3.
44 "Z Centrali krakowskiej," *Przegląd Społeczny* IV, no. VI (June 1930): 235–37.
45 Marzena Pękowska, "Wielokulturowa społeczność uczniów lwowskich szkól dla głuchoniemych i niewidomych (1830–1939)," in Walasek, *Wśród "swoich" i "obcych,"* 177–86.
46 Kępski, *Dziecko sieroce i opieka nad nim*, 29. For a discussion of this issue of segregation, see Susan L. Tananbaum, "Childcare Dilemmas: Religious Discourse and Services among Jewish and Christian 'Orphanages,'" *Jewish Culture and History* 12, no. 1/2 (2010): 159–74.

Evidence from the Jewish children's homes suggests that the relationship between the Polish state and the Jewish associations developed slowly throughout the interwar period. A 1923 law on child welfare (and related future legislation) legally obliged the private Jewish associations to conduct their work within specific legal guidelines. The adoption of legislation protecting children and their mothers ultimately strengthened the position of the Jewish social worker struggling to raise funds and awareness about the plight of Jewish children.

One leader in the field identified 1928 as the date for the transition from philanthropy to social work. Claiming that social work was under threat because so many had come to see it as a part of everyday life, Ada Reichensteinowa pointed out the difference between the poetic phrases "philanthropy," "charitable works," and "mercy," juxtaposing them with the harsh sounding "social work."[47] While the word "orphan" previously evoked shudders, she claimed it was now seen as quite normal. Social work had evolved into a system of organized services in need of collective support. Writing about the Week of the Orphan, Reichensteinowa recognized that there was always only one goal: collecting the greatest amount of money with the least amount of effort. She had seen those collecting money on the street for various causes give fresh flowers to passersby if a donation was given. This turned into passing out artificial flowers and then into simply giving donors a piece of paper with an official stamp. The importance of the Week of the Orphan lay in collective effort and in its character as an "official" event with the support of state authorities. The Week of the Orphan represents the change from charity to social work, a change that community leaders of the early 1920s participated in and led.

The publications designed and written by children include several short sections on subjects relevant to their lives and illustrate how the transformation in social work affected them. For example, a section of brief autobiographies in *Nasze Życie* (Our life), a publication of the Institution for Jewish Orphans in Stryj, allows us to see where the children came from and to understand their position as orphaned children.[48]

---

47 Ada Reichensteinowa, "Tydzień sierocy," *Przegląd Społeczny* II, no. IV (April 1928): 1–3.
48 "Życiorysy," *Nasze Życie*, January 1930, 3–4. Other articles describe the children's reactions to an exhibit in Poznań and detail Stanisław Staszic's contributions to Poland.

Lea Wurm was born in Stryj and her family lived well enough until the war. But after her father was disabled and her mother became mentally ill, she wrote, "we do not have an apartment, and we live almost on the street." As a result, Wurm was taken to the home for orphans. She reported that she was doing well in school but that she still suffered because she knew her parents would never be able to get themselves out of poverty. Lipe Eichen, born in Stryj in 1914, was in the fourth class at gymnasium. His mother died when he was a year old. He then contracted rickets and he was unable to walk for five years. He could walk only on all fours. To get out of the house in the summer, he sat on the steps, where he often fell asleep. Once, the sound of a broken glass startled him and he fell off the steps and lost consciousness, so he never sat on the steps again. Eichen took the entrance exam for the gymnasium in the fourth grade, but he did not pass the first time because of difficulties with Polish grammar. When he took the exam again, he passed, and he finished the first class of gymnasium well. His father died suddenly one summer, leaving Eichen again in a perilous position but for the support of the orphanage. The stories of Wurm and Eichen are not unusual. As their lives changed, so did the Jewish community that formed new institutions to help them. The devastation of war and subsequent political changes transformed the East European Jewish community. As the history of Jewish child welfare in Poland shows, the 1920s and 1930s were a period of renewal and growth.

The JDC in Poland

The JDC was formed in 1914 to aid the Jews of Palestine during World War I.[49] Its role quickly expanded to include aid to Jews in Europe. The JDC was formed to distribute the funds raised by the Central Committee for the Relief of Jews Suffering through the War, founded by Orthodox Jews from Eastern Europe, and the American Jewish Relief Committee, made up primarily of Jews from Germany. The group's formation illustrates the generosity of the predominantly German-Jewish philanthropists and the connections between Jews from very different backgrounds. As Yehuda

---

49 Bauer, *My Brother's Keeper*, 6–7.

Bauer points out, the German-Jewish leaders of the JDC described the Jews of Poland as their coreligionists, emphasizing the group's religious identity. The Jews of Poland, though, had much different notions of Jewish communal identity, most of which were explicitly ethnic and national. The formation of the JDC is an example of stronger ties among Jewish communities in the United States, Europe, and the Middle East.

From the beginning, the JDC intended to be a temporary presence in Poland, though economic circumstances meant it never entirely withdrew its support. For financial reasons, support from the JDC was withdrawn at various points from different regions, but it was often restored later in a different form (such as clothing donation or educational assistance). At the most basic level, this financial support paid for food, clothing, and shelter, but it also made possible extensive training courses, regional conferences for Jewish social workers, and a level of organization that aimed to implement the highest standards of care for all Jewish children in Poland. The crucial, and arguably equally important, contributions of the JDC were money and organization. The generous financial support of American Jews allowed many of these small associations to sustain themselves and to grow throughout the early 1920s.[50] The JDC fostered the centralism of Jewish community leadership in Poland at the same time as it made a real difference for the individuals and associations it supported.

The specific circumstances of how children were cared for reveal the dynamics at work among these individuals and institutions. The JDC's work in child welfare began in Galicia because the Jewish communities there were better organized and orphaned children were already identified through a registration process initiated by local leaders, according to Simon Peiser, the first director of the JDC's Child Care Department in

---

50 The support of the JDC and its role in relief have been well examined. See especially the works of Zosa Szajkowski, "Disunity in the Distribution of American Jewish Overseas Relief, 1919–1939," *American Jewish Historical Quarterly* 3 (March 1969): 376–407; "Disunity in the Distribution of American Jewish Overseas Relief, 1919–1939 [Conclusion]," *American Jewish Historical Quarterly* 4 (June 1969): 484–506; "Budgeting American Jewish Overseas Relief (1919–1939)," *American Jewish Historical Quarterly* 1 (September 1969): 83–113; "'Reconstruction' vs. 'Palliative Relief' in American Jewish Overseas Work (1919–1939)," *Jewish Social Studies* 32, no. 1 (1970): 14–41; Chiara Tessaris, "The War Relief Work of the American Jewish Joint Distribution Committee in Poland and Lithuania, 1915–1918," *East European Jewish Affairs* 40, no. 2 (August 2010): 127–44.

Warsaw.[51] In 1920, the JDC undertook to provide relief to twenty thousand war orphans registered in Galicia, only 2,448 of whom were full orphans.[52] The JDC established a territorial office in Lwów with district offices throughout the region, including one in Kraków. The central office in Warsaw was meant to coordinate the work of the vast number of smaller associations with the assistance of the provincial offices in cities like Kraków; this organizational insight, combined with continued persistence in managing this complex system, was the real triumph of the JDC—and later CENTOS—in child welfare. Peiser offers a succinct explanation for the operations of the JDC in its early years in Poland, showing us just how the JDC worked with the associations that eventually became CENTOS:

> we . . . either availed ourselves of existing children's committees in the towns of which the districts consisted or appointed new ones. The duty of the members of these town committees consisted of taking complete charge and exercising supervision of the orphans in their respective communities. They were expected to turn in a financial account of expenses incurred in the maintenance of the child, and to report upon this progress to the district office. From this office visitors were sent out from time to time to confer with our representatives in the smaller towns and to inspect the homes in which the children had been placed.[53]

The majority of local aid associations founded during and after the war were affiliated with the JDC. Money was certainly the most

---

51   Simon Peiser to War Orphans' Committee, 15 November 1921, JDC Archives, 1921/1932, File 339. Peiser was a Prussian-born rabbi, trained at Hebrew Union College, who had been supervisor of the Jewish Orphan Asylum in Cleveland from 1914 to 1919.
52   Jewish War Orphans in Galicia (Statistical Report), JDC Archives, 1921/1932, File 339. Note that this is nowhere near the total number of war orphans, only those registered according to JDC guidelines. The report mentions that 344 children in Kraków were provided with direct financial support in 1920; this support went toward food, schooling, medical aid, and clothing, amounting to JDC expenditures totaling 410,686 marks for the month of December 1920.
53   Simon Peiser to War Orphans' Committee, 15 November 1921, JDC Archives, 1921/1932, File 339.

important motivating factor. While the JDC coordinated the work of the local committees, they subventioned only a fraction of those in need of care, at least in part because of the JDC's insistence that aid be strictly limited to aid for war orphans (which included aid to children who were the victims of disease outbreaks during the war and aid to children whose parents were killed in anti-Jewish violence). Still, a substantial number of Jewish children did not receive direct aid from the JDC, though they may have been affected by the JDC's actions (such as the JDC's encouragement to improve standards at an orphanage or, indirectly, through the JDC's seminars to train Jewish social workers). The JDC aimed to improve standards gradually. By providing for some children, they meant to encourage the local communities to support the others.

The relationship between the JDC and local committees was complex. The source material indicates that at times it was quite positive; other evidence suggests the tensions inherent in relief work and the resentment felt by East European Jews. Not surprisingly, the relationship seems to have been considerably smoother when local committees contributed substantially to their own financial operations. The JDC did fund some committees entirely from JDC resources, though most local groups received support to varying extents from membership dues, the local magistrate, and the *kehilah*, an arrangement of finances that suggests the complexity of this kind of work and also indicates the role of the child welfare association in the larger community. Some smaller committees were able to fund their needs entirely from membership dues, indicating the generous nature of the community's donors and, in general, greater community support to meet the local need. The JDC insisted on local support for the committees. Because they saw the orphan crisis as temporary, they did not want to remain in Poland indefinitely and they hoped to hand over responsibility to local committees who would have to be prepared to raise the funds and administer care on an ongoing basis.

The presence of a JDC official was not all that uncommon in towns throughout Poland in the 1920s and 1930s. In a 1921 letter to the American chairman of the JDC Felix M. Warburg, James N. Rosenberg, the European director of the JDC, described a visit to a relief kitchen in Sochaczew, a town just west of Warsaw:

> We hunted up Simche Grundwag, who was the remittance-paying agent for this town for the Joint Distribution Committee. Grundwag is one of the solid and substantial citizens, a man of my own age, who looks at least twenty years older. He is a member of the Council of the town and of the Board of Magistrates. Grundwag first took us to the Polish-American Relief Administration kitchen. We walked in and there was a portrait of Mr. Hoover, with an American flag. The children were eating, and I do not mind if you send a copy of this letter to Mr. Hoover and let him get a picture of those hungry youngsters getting their food in that kitchen. We each had a little of the food to see what it was like. It was a sort of gruel or rice or hominy, not sweet enough to eat but hot and nourishing and it tasted pretty good after those two hours of riding in an open car in zero weather.... The sad thing about it was there were separate rooms for the Jewish and Christian children. When we try to develop our work in Poland we must realize the depth of this separation. One great room for the Christian children, a smaller room for the Jewish children.[54]

Rosenberg's letter, a version of which also appeared in the *New York Times*, captures the efforts of both Polish and Jewish Americans to provide relief after World War I and suggests the level of involvement of local activists like Simcha Grundwag who responded to the crisis of the war. His observation that Jewish and Christian children were cared for separately strikes the reader

---

54 James N. Rosenberg to Felix M. Warburg, 15 December 1921, JDC Archives, 1921/1932, File 324. An edited version was published under the headline "Main Street East," in *The New York Times* on February 19, 1922. Herbert Hoover was head of the American Relief Administration in the years after World War I. In his memoir of his time in Poland after the war, Rosenberg's JDC colleague Boris Bogen commented on Herbert Hoover's attitude toward this segregation: "To Mr. Hoover all hungry stomachs looked alike, and the hunger of a Pole was precisely the same sort of affliction as the hunger of a Polish Jew." *Born a Jew* (New York: Macmillan, 1930), 126.

as remarkable, both because it seems natural not to make such distinctions during such a time of great need and because the remark is somewhat naive. Social services in interwar Poland made distinctions between Christians and Jews because both communities sought to provide for the children within community guidelines, including kosher food and religious instruction.

Inspection reports done by JDC officials offer a significant amount of detail regarding local committees and their cooperation with the JDC. A few examples from small towns will illustrate what can be learned about these institutions from the JDC archives. The details are fragmentary, but similar reports from other towns offer concrete details from which tentative conclusions can be drawn about the nature of JDC involvement in child welfare in Poland and about the efforts of local leaders. Unfortunately, these reports were not filed as systematically as the modern researcher would like; while there are reports from different periods, there is no comprehensive set of reports from each town for an entire period. Still, JDC inspectors traveled widely throughout Poland and visited a variety of institutions. The JDC's system of administering funds and policies included local oversight of finances and care and held local committees accountable to JDC officials and their communities. In this way, they were able to unite the communities working toward the goal of insuring better futures for Jewish children.

Conditions in the town of Zwiahel, near Równo, reveal the difficult environment in which these Jewish child welfare leaders began their work after the war and the consequences of the postwar conflict between the Poles and Soviets. In the absence of institutions for children, JDC officials established three homes for orphaned children in the town in 1920. In a report of the JDC's Orphans' Relief Section for July 1920 to July 1921, officials wrote,

> How little the Jewish public of Volhynia know about the protection and the care of children may be seen from the following instances. After the second occupation of Zwiahel by Bolshevist troops, when the JDC was taking over the children that had been evacuated from Zwiahel to Rowno, all children from Zwiahel, 70 in number, were found on one pile of dirty and rotten straw, on the floor of the home for the aged, in a wet building, in incredible sanitary condition; children of both sexes and of all ages

were crowded together; healthy children were in immediate touch with the sick ones. Most of these children were roving about in various ends of the city, often suffering hunger, and many among them affected with favus or other skin diseases, as well as with typhus. The mortality among the children due to those diseases attained up to five a day.[55]

Such was the crisis to which both individuals and institutions responded. As the report indicates, local communities' poverty and their lack of knowledge of proper hygiene and medical care made this response more difficult.

Additional fragmentary evidence from JDC reports on committees aiding children throughout Poland's eastern borderlands suggests the complexity of providing care to children. The town of Słonim offers a fairly positive, simple example.[56] A JDC inspector reported in 1921 that the Jewish orphans in Słonim (about sixty from the town itself and forty from the district) received very good care and the orphanage made a positive impression. Those children between ages thirteen and fifteen were taught a trade. For the JDC inspector, all was in order. The situation in Pinsk, however, was much different. A 1921 report does not even mention the briefest of details describing the town's three orphanages.[57] Instead, the report is simply an account of a meeting of a central committee that united the three autonomous orphanages. JDC representatives were not able to learn much about any of the orphanages at this meeting, as committee members simply argued among each other. Somewhat unusually in these accounts, the JDC representatives note ideological differences among those involved in child-care work; some were described as Zeire Zionists and others as Bundists. The representatives left a meeting where committee

---

55 Work of the Orphans' Relief Section, Report from July 1, 1920 to July 1, 1921, JDC Archives, 1921/1932, File 207.
56 Letter No. 1354/236, From War Orphans Bureau, Warsaw, To Mr. M.D. Waldman, European Director, Child Care Department, Vienna, 30 November 1921, JDC Archives, 1921/1932, File 339.
57 Letter No. 1353/234, From War Orphans Bureau, Warsaw, To Mr. M. D. Waldman, European Director, Child Care Department, Vienna, from M. Raskin, 20 November 1921, JDC Archives, 1921/1932, File 339.

members "were thrashing out local misunderstandings," but over the next few days they succeeded in setting up a JDC Child Care Committee in Pinsk. The committee included representatives from each of the three committees and from each of the town's different political factions.[58]

Partisan committee members were not the only local particularity encountered by JDC representatives. Two hundred orphans in private homes were supported by the Orphans' Council in Stanisławów. JDC inspectors in this town found that the council kept two separate ledgers, each of which showed a different balance. The local representative finally admitted that the council had received money from a district committee to liquidate its work; that money, however, had not been spent. When the JDC renewed activity, the local council did not report that they still had this money in reserve. The need for JDC officials to oversee their work at the local level was real. The response to the plight of these children involved the local agencies of a non-territorial national minority group (the smaller associations founded by Jewish leaders), international aid (from the JDC and other groups), and local governmental leaders. Nearest the situation, the newly formed associations took the lead in providing care, but they always looked to outside sources such as the JDC for funds and tried, with some success, to gain the support of municipal leaders. Local circumstances varied significantly.

An early report from the town of Dubno in 1921 indicates that of the nine hundred war orphans registered in this town and the surrounding area, two hundred to three hundred of them were already being supported on an individual basis.[59] Dubno had suffered comparatively greater losses than other towns in the Wołyń region and the recovery there was slow. Army troops were still housed there in April of 1921 (the time of the report) and so life had not yet returned to normal. The town had a hospital, three schools, a home for the aged, and an orphan asylum with twenty-three children. The JDC provided the majority of the funds for the orphan asylum. The JDC inspector was impressed that local leaders were raising their own funds but noted that there were few wealthy individuals left in

---

58 See also Ben-Levi, "The 'Orphanage in Pinsk,'" translated below.
59 Report from JDC Rowno to JDC Warsaw, from A. Shohan, Director, Rowno branch, 24 April 1921, JDC Archives, 1921/1932, File 324.

the area; those who had acquired fortunes during the war were apparently "not the type to help." There is no explicit mention of the education the children in the orphanage received, but there is a note regarding the schools in the town. The Yiddishists of the Kultur-Lige had received money from another relief group, the People's Relief Committee, and taken over a school previously run by the Zionists. In addition, the town was home to a large Talmud Torah, meant to be non-political but influenced by religious Zionists. Dubno offers a good example of the way the JDC worked; there is a mention of the registration of orphans, insisted upon by the JDC before any aid could be offered. A majority of children were in private care (foster homes), but the JDC also supported an orphanage. Significantly, the report included mention of the town's own means for contributing to the cause of child welfare. In addition, the report noted that the Dubno *landsmanshaft* (association of immigrants usually from the same region) should be compelled to ensure the existence of the orphanage.

In comparison to Dubno, the larger town of Brześć nad Bugiem was home to a comparatively well-established orphanage and children's aid committee. According to a 1926 report, 260 children were in foster care and 94 children lived in the town's orphanage.[60] In both groups, there was a nearly equal division between half and full orphans. The children attended a range of schools, including the traditional Talmud Torah, the Tarbut schools with an emphasis on Hebrew culture, Mizrakhi (religious Zionist) schools, and public schools. The majority were in the Talmud Torah or the Mizrakhi school. One hundred seventeen attended schools in which they received some kind of vocational training, and many were apprenticed to locksmiths, shoemakers, tailors, dressmakers, and others. I. Fridman, the 1926 inspector, noted that the orphanage contributed only twenty-five percent of its "own means" to its financial operations, indicating that the children were heavily subsidized by the central committee of CENTOS, supported by the JDC. Fridman noted that this twenty-five percent consisted of governmental and communal support, and that the town itself, meaning individual donors through membership dues,

---

60 Report No. 16, From I. Fridman, Brest, To Financial Section of the J.D.C., Warsaw, 26 December 1926, JDC Archives, 1921/1932, File 337.

Portrait of the managing committee of CENTOS, Zaromb, 1938 (YIVO)

contributed little to the orphanage. The implications of governmental support were clear upon another inspector's visit two years later. D. Towbin arrived just an hour after a visit of the *wojewoda* (provincial governor) to the orphanage.[61] The official's visit was unexpected, but nonetheless Towbin reports that all the rooms were "arranged nicely, clean and airy," and that, though some of the rooms needed repairs, the home presented a "rich appearance." The mayor, however, reacted negatively to seeing only Jewish inscriptions on several of the doors, tearing one of them down in protest. (Towbin did not note whether they were in Yiddish or Hebrew.) Although there is no indication of the orphanage's response, the home clearly operated in conditions that called for sensitivity to the majority Polish environment, to expressions of Jewish culture, and—not least—to its financial supporters.

One of the most important questions asked about the development of these local committees concerns the ideological nature of the various groups' activities. The views of the leaders of these institutions reflected the communities in which they lived. Some were Zionists, some were

---

61 Control Report No. 40/61 "Orphan House in Brest – by D. Towbin," 5 June 1928, JDC Archives, 1921/1932, File 330a.

Bundists, and some were from more traditional backgrounds.[62] While there is some evidence that local committees aimed to expose Jewish children to only one aspect of Jewish national life, whether religious or secular, there is also evidence that Jewish children's aid associations made efforts to abide by the wishes of the child's relatives concerning education. In many cases, it is difficult to discern if an aid association had any specific kind of ideological orientation. The fragmentary nature of the records from the children's aid associations in the early 1920s offers very little evidence about this important question. Fortunately, the JDC archives help to illuminate this issue.

While Yehuda Bauer has written that most of the leaders of the JDC were left-wing Zionists,[63] support from the JDC was predicated on the fact that such ideological distinctions could not be made on behalf of children and were out of place in the environment of the orphanage. Because of its position as an outsider, the JDC simply had to remove itself from these conflicts internal to the Jewish community in Poland. As one JDC official remarked as late as 1926, "A soup kitchen in Poland is not only a means by which to feed the hungry, but immediately becomes, as well, a political instrument."[64] Complicating the issue was the fact that each group wanted support from the JDC; the Americans' non-partisan stance thus seems less like an insistence on political neutrality and more like a practical response to the demand for charity. The JDC simply could not support thousands of small institutions in Poland. The JDC was better able to serve more individuals and communities by taking refuge in an organizational bureaucracy that set up regulations such as the registering of orphans and the agreement to provide for all children regardless of the parents' ideological views.

While the descriptions of children's homes collected here do not reflect the ideological differences among Polish Jews, the various

---

62 For a good description of the effect of ideology in child welfare, see Azriel Shohet, *The Jews of Pinsk, 1881 to 1941*, ed. Mark Jay Mirsky and Moshe Rosman (Stanford, CA: Stanford University Press, 2012), 619.
63 Yehuda Bauer, *American Jewry and the Holocaust: The American Jewish Joint Distribution Committee, 1939–1945* (Detroit: Wayne State University Press, 1981), 32.
64 Letter from B. Kahn to Felix M. Warburg, 21 February 1926, JDC Archives, 1921/1932, File 324.

inspection reports from JDC officials indicate that ideology played a role in several areas. JDC inspectors carefully reported the number of children cared for in specific orphanages and noted the educational institutions which children attended, perhaps the best indication of the strength of a given group in an area. There was a definite range, from public schools to private Jewish schools of all types, including the Talmud Torah, Yiddishist schools, and Tarbut schools. The diversity of institutions attended by children affiliated with the same aid association suggests that the aid associations did not insist on any kind of uniform, ideologically based education. The inspection reports show that the JDC subventioned children who attended all kinds of institutions and that individual orphan homes cared for children whose parents preferred religious education and others who were more secular and ideological in their approach. If JDC officials had a bias, the bias favored secular education that was expected to prepare children for a career in the future. Religious education was at times disparagingly described as old fashioned, even if it was being provided for the students in an adequate way.[65]

An example involving the most vulnerable children, those orphans who were developmentally delayed, suggests that there were issues more important than ideology for social workers to consider. The plight of officially stateless Jewish children after the war illustrates the importance of citizenship, the need for both state intervention and private associations, and the challenges of defining national communities. As organizations aimed to help orphaned children whose citizenship status was unclear after the war, they arranged for financial adoptions and foster care in a variety of ways. From 1914 to 1923—that is, from the period of the war until five years after the reestablishment of the Polish state—the state did not regulate orphanages and other organizations caring for children, regardless of their nationality. During this period, child welfare organizations did not register with any central state body. After 1918, however, they increasingly turned to the state for financial assistance.[66] Even after the

---

65 See for example D. Towbin's report on Kalisz, Report No. 30, From: D. Towbin, To: Financial Section of the Child Care Committee for Boys, Kalisz, 28 February 1927, JDC Archives, 1921/1932, File 337 and Dr. Bogen's Diary, 16 July to 20 July 1921, JDC Archives, 1921/1932, File 324.

66 Kępski, *Dziecko sieroce i opieka nad nim*, 39.

newly formed Ministry of Labor and Social Welfare assumed responsibility for statewide regulation of children's welfare agencies, the government limited its role in child welfare to caring for war orphans, leaving the care of other orphaned children to the specific locality of the child's residence.

Thus, a child's legal place of residence or citizenship mattered greatly, especially to children like Miriam Sherman. Sherman was one of seven "feeble-minded" children whose story is told in the files of the JDC and who was deported to Europe immediately upon arrival in the United States.[67] It certainly seems likely that there were more than seven Jewish children diagnosed as "feeble-minded" upon their arrival in the United States, but I have not yet found a way to determine the number or fate of these children. Leaders in the JDC, active in caring for children in Eastern Europe and in cooperation with the many Jewish social service agencies in the United States, seem only to have documented these seven cases. Their story deserves some attention since it reveals the range of challenges faced by parents, the JDC, local leaders, and educators.

Young Miriam Sherman came to the United States from Poland with her parents in 1921.[68] Judged to be "feeble-minded," she was deported. While her parents remained in the United States, impoverished and unable to provide for their daughter, the JDC, with the cooperation of the Council of Jewish Women, arranged for Miriam to be cared for in a private Jewish institution in Poland for "feeble-minded" children under the age of six. The JDC could not assume care for the child, or for other children in the same position, indefinitely. By virtue of her parents' birthplace, Miriam was a Russian subject and not a Polish citizen eligible for aid from the Polish state. Wanted neither in the United States nor in Poland, Miriam found a temporary home in a private Jewish institution.

The challenge of caring for these stateless children involved no less than four private social service organizations: the JDC; the Council for

---

67 The vocabulary of the time meant these children were variously described as "feeble-minded" or "defective." Since their specific conditions are never adequately explained, I will describe them here simply as developmentally delayed.

68 For the story of Miriam Sherman and other children in her situation, see JDC Archives, 1921/1932, File 114.

Jewish Women; Ezra (a group in Antwerp that cared for the children temporarily on their return from New York to Eastern Europe); and the Committee for the Care of Orphans in Warsaw (a Jewish association that sponsored a home for Jewish children with disabilities in Warsaw, where the children ultimately received adequate care). Not surprisingly, the most significant challenge in providing care concerned money. The Warsaw home where the children received care was far from their parents' home in the United States. Only the preserved correspondence between the social service organizations concerning payment for care and the infrequent reports on the children's condition allow us a look into the children's lives and the effects of immigration restrictions and states' discriminatory definitions of citizenship.

The story of these seven children begins in the summer of 1922, when the JDC was called upon to find a solution to their dilemma. A letter from Bernhard Kahn, the acting chairman of the JDC's European Executive Council, described the situation in stark terms: the only possibility for such children deported from America was that an individual or institution guaranteed continued payment for their care; otherwise, the children would have to return to their communities of origin, east of the Polish border in the territory of the Soviet Union.[69] The latter meant that these children would certainly not receive the care they needed, as their closest family members were already in the United States and they did not have other close relatives able to provide for them in the Soviet Union. Realistically, returning the children would simply mean leaving them on the street. At the same time, the JDC, whose resources were already near exhaustion as a result of their extensive relief activities throughout Eastern Europe and Palestine, could not accept indefinite responsibility for the children's needs.

To respond to the needs of the children, who stayed temporarily in Antwerp while a solution could be found, the JDC searched for an institution in a state that would accept children from another state. The only state that might have accepted the children was Germany, but only if an individual or outside agency guaranteed the cost of maintaining the child.

---

69 Letter from Bernhard Kahn to the Department of Immigration Aid, Council of Jewish Women, New York, 1 September 1922, JDC Archives, 1921/1932, File 114.

Even if an institution in Germany had been willing to accept the children without such a financial guarantee, the state would not have permitted the institution to do so. The New York office of the JDC's War Orphans Bureau asked its counterpart in Warsaw to arrange temporary care in Kraków or Vienna, where there were institutions that might have taken the children, or to arrange care with a family until these institutions had vacancies. In the meantime, care was arranged at an institution in Warsaw, where the children remained indefinitely. The Committee for the Care of Orphans, run by D. Rundstein (referred to as Mrs. Rundstein throughout the correspondence), had a solid reputation as a provider of care for the children of middle-class Jewish families. However, like other institutions of its kind, it could not provide care for free. The JDC negotiated with Rundstein that the families would sign contracts for their children's care and advance a $150 deposit, a sum that at first would be remitted through the JDC to the Warsaw institution and then directly to Warsaw.[70]

Thus began the correspondence that details the requests for payments, the parents' financial condition, and the health of the children. The institutions involved did their best to provide adequate care, even when the parents did not meet their presumed financial obligation. The files tell the story of the children from 1922 to 1924. The fate of the children after that time is not indicated in the files, and I have not been able to determine what happened to them after that date. Several times Rundstein extended care for the children, even after she had repeatedly threatened to return them to the Soviet Union.

Some of the conflict over money owed by the parents in the United States may have been due to the kind of care the children received at the Warsaw institution. The institution is described as one that cared for comfortable middle-class Jewish children,[71] and it is likely that these parents would not have been able to afford such care had they been living in the Soviet Union or Poland. Reports from Rundstein and another social worker

---

70 Memorandum from War Orphans Bureau, Warsaw to War Orphans Bureau, New York, Subject: Care of deported mentally defective children, 6 June 1922, JDC Archives, 1921/1932, File 114.

71 Letter from A. Shohan, War Orphans' Bureau, Warsaw, to War Orphans' Bureau, New York, 4 October 1922, JDC Archives, 1921/1932, File 114.

with the Committee for the Care of Orphans (identified as Mrs. Welfle) repeatedly stressed the need for special education classes for the children, classes that could only be provided if the parents remitted additional payments.[72] While it is at least likely that this was simply an attempt to get as much money as possible from the parents in America, the orphanage did pay for the children's maintenance—above and beyond the normal level of care other children in similar circumstances received—even after it must have been clear that the parents in the United States would never entirely meet their financial obligation. Moreover, the JDC never accused the institution of caring for the children simply for financial gain.

The JDC was in the awkward position of acting as intermediary between the children's parents and the institution in Warsaw. When neither Rundstein nor the JDC received money or communication from Max Sherman (Miriam's father) the JDC sent Mr. Sherman a letter, saying, "Your unconcerned attitude is more than overbearing." Sherman's replied, "I'm sorry you think I take so little interest; my wife is worried to death; what to do? Can you send the child to Canada where I have a brother-in-law to take care of her?" In subsequent correspondence, the JDC pointed out that sending the child to Canada was simply not an option, writing, "Canada no more desires to have feeble minded children admitted into their country than the United States. . . ."[73] In any case, Max Sherman would have had to bear the cost of transport as well, and he already owed money for the care Miriam had already received. An announcement by the Polish government in 1923 that all Russian subjects would have to leave Poland by the fifteenth of April of that year occasioned a flurry of correspondence about what to do with Miriam. The JDC could not guarantee that Rundstein would not deport the child once the deadline had passed. Sherman did send small sums of money from time to time upon learning that deportation was an imminent probability. As of December 1923, Rundstein agreed to continue caring for the children (roughly a year past the threat to return them to

---

72 Letter from Mrs. D. Rundstein to Mr. Sherman, 20 March 1943, JDC Archives, 1921/1932, File 114.
73 Letter from M. B. Sherman to Miss A. Kottler, 27 December 1922, and Letter to Mr. Max Sherman from War Orphans Bureau, 29 December 1922, JDC Archives, 1921/32, File 114.

their countries of origin), but she continued to stress that she needed financial support from the parents to be able to do so.

The exact physical condition of the children is unknown, but descriptions of the children's progress indicate that the children were, at the very least, developmentally delayed both physically and mentally. A few of the children required electrical treatments for paralysis. For example, in a report from the JDC's Child Care Department in Warsaw to the War Orphans Bureau in New York, we learn about the progress of Chaim Flaxman:

> The boy's leg and arm have been treated with electricity since 2 months.... The doctor advises to continue the treatment as he believes that the boy will partly recover the use of his arm and leg, which are now inert. The boy lost his awkwardness. He moves quite easily and dresses himself. His guardians at the Home pay special attention that he should make use of both of his hands when writing or eating. The boy gets the treatment and massage at a reduced price, but the treatment is quite expensive.[74]

The care provided by the Warsaw Committee for the Care of Orphans made a real difference in the lives of these children. Private associations intervened successfully to improve the living conditions of at least some of Poland's most vulnerable Jewish children.

As the plight of these children suggests, citizenship mattered, and the leaders of the JDC recognized its importance. American Jewish leaders considered the growth and development of the Jewish community in Poland to be one of their goals, but they also realized that this meant that local Jewish leaders would have to operate within the bounds of Polish government and society. A conversation in 1921 between two JDC leaders involved in child welfare, Boris D. Bogen and J. B. Rosenberg, reveals some of the goals of the American Jewish leaders relevant to cultural education.[75] Speaking of the Polish Jews, Bogen admitted, "I am very proud to say that

---

74 The letter is dated January 31, 1923. JDC Archives, 1921/32, File 114. Child Care, Feebleminded Children, p. 1054.

75 Memorandum of Conversation between Dr. Boris D. Bogen and J. B. Rosenberg, Esquire, Far Rockaway, New York, 16 August 1921, JDC Archives, 1921/1932, File 324.

they are now divided into territorial instead of political groups. They are developing an extreme patriotism for their particular territories." In response, Rosenberg asked, "Do you mean you feel it might add to the importance of the status of the Jews in Poland that they should get some territorial sense of loyalty and thereby become an important part of the citizenship of the country?" Bogen responded, "That is my purpose. It is rather a purpose of construction than destruction." Making the point that he wanted Polish Jews to be "interested in one specific social effort, like child care, and organize along functional lines"—and himself aware of the difficulties caused by the presence of so many active political movements—Bogen stated, "My purpose is to break up the political perplexities. Now we have another problem. I want them to be interested in the entire country, rather than in the locality." American Jewish aid aimed to provide concrete assistance but also had larger goals in mind, including the breaking down of political divisions and the increasing of awareness of a Jewish commitment to life in Poland. As Rebecca Kobrin writes in her study of philanthropy in Białystok, "Émigré philanthropists should not be viewed as mere altruistic welfare workers who wrote checks from afar hoping to ease the suffering of their compatriots abroad. Interwar émigré philanthropists acted as revolutionary forces, using their funds to restructure Jewish communal life in the manner they saw fitting and supporting institutions that challenge the authority of the Polish state."[76] The goals of these philanthropists included altering the ways in which Jews in Poland defined their relationship to the country. Leaving aside the very real question of the JDC's chances for success in reaching their goals, we are left with a picture of a Jewish community active across international lines, taking care of its own, and reestablishing itself as a national community concerned with questions of social welfare, education, and long-term survival in Poland.

The Development of CENTOS

Boris Bogen served with the JDC in Europe from 1917 to 1924. In his role overseeing relief operations, Bogen visited many different facilities

---

76 Kobrin, "The Politics of Philanthropy," 253.

throughout Poland. He related in his memoir an incident from 1921 that demonstrated that Polish Jews were ready to shed any dependence on the American JDC. The JDC announced that they were withdrawing funds from an orphanage and school run by the Mizrachi organization (Orthodox Zionists). Pretending that he was going to show Bogen the awful conditions in which orphans lived, the Mizrachi political leader Yehoshua Heshel Farbstein took Bogen on a tour of a "new orphans' home recently built and full of well-nourished and most cleanly children."[77] This example illustrates the dynamic between American and Polish Jewish leaders and the need of Polish Jews to care for themselves. By 1924 the private associations for Jewish children united to form CENTOS, a result of the combined efforts of local leaders and American Jewish relief workers.[78] CENTOS, an institution that had grown organically from the efforts of Jews in hundreds of locations, exemplifies the independence of Poland's Jewish leaders. CENTOS brought together hundreds of smaller associations formed throughout Polish lands during the war, and, with the support of the JDC distributed funds to the associations, established communications between the groups, and promoted the cause of Jewish child welfare to the larger Jewish and Polish communities. It quickly became the leading organization in Jewish child welfare in Poland.

The Polish scholar Izabela Szczepaniak-Wiecha has explained that the cooperation between the authorities and private groups is a legacy of the Partitions, when voluntary associations began to play a significant role in providing care. After 1918, private groups and the new authorities continued the relationships begun during the period of the Partitions. The August 1923 law on social work legally obliged Polish communities to provide for the country's poor, including abandoned and orphaned children, without regard to religious faith, race, or nationality, thus marking the turn from philanthropy to state action.[79] The law set the conditions for

---

77 Bogen, *Born a Jew*, 248–49.
78 Szczepaniak-Wiecha, "Traditions," 85.
79 Tadeusz Jałmużna and Nella Stolińska, "Formy opieki nad dzieckiem w łódzkich mniejszościach narodowych (1918–1939)," in *Rola mniejszości narodowych w kulturze i oświecie polskiej w latach 1700–1939*, ed. Aleksandra Bilewicz and Stefania Walasek (Wrocław: Wydawn. Uniwersytetu Wrocławskiego, 1998): 237–44; and Szczepaniak-Wiecha, "Traditions."

further development in the field, codifying methods for providing care and establishing that economic need entitled children to services such as foster care.[80] By 1937, CENTOS encompassed 250 associations with forty-five thousand members paying fees to support the associations' work.[81]

With the help of the JDC, child welfare work was centralized and divided among regional and local committees. The seven central offices of CENTOS were in Warsaw, Białystok, Wilno, Pińsk, Równo, Lwów, and Kraków. In 1926, 349 local committees operated in 335 towns. In 1937, 276 committees operated in 201 towns.[82] Each of these committees enjoyed the financial support of members, perhaps better described as annual donors. The total number of members of CENTOS associations throughout the interwar period never went lower than forty thousand and reached nearly fifty-four thousand in 1931. These members enabled CENTOS to support a record high number of children (29,648) in 1937. Support ranged from an educational subsidy to a place in an institution and over the years included direct relief (food and clothing), participation in after-care organizations and activities, and attendance in summer colonies.

The extant annual reports of CENTOS associations, many of which are in the collection of the National Library in Warsaw, provide some of the best information for a history of Jewish social work.[83] They often include lists of board members for a given year, a brief introduction outlining the financial situation and activities of the past year, a budget, a few pictures, and lists of contributors. They range from ten to thirty pages in length, and they can be quite detailed, providing the number of shoes, coats, shirts, dresses, and gloves distributed in a given year. Fortunately, some of the reports provide information of a more general nature, which is especially helpful. For example, a report might comment on the educational background of the organization's children or the reason for financial

---

80 Ludwik Malinowski, "Geneza opieki socjalnej w Drugiej Rzeczypospolitej," 18.
81 Marcus, *Social and Political History*, 143.
82 These numbers are taken from Bar-Yishay and Web, "Yesoymim-farzorgung," 112, table 2. Bar-Yishay and Web took their numbers from *Przegląd Społeczny* and reports in the JDC archives.
83 See Barbara Łętocha, Alina Cała, and Zofia Głowicka, eds., *Dokumenty życia społecznego Żydów polskich (1918–1939) w zbiorach Biblioteki Narodowej* (Warsaw: Biblioteka Narodowa, 1999).

difficulties. Many reports stem from one association in a particular location; others are regional reports written and distributed by the regional committees of CENTOS. Still others are reports commemorating the fifth, tenth, or even thirtieth anniversary of an association.

Two areas addressed in most annual reports, the budget and the education of the orphans, help us to understand how these associations propelled and reflected change within the Jewish community. An examination of the budgets published in several of the reports suggests the associations shared an important similarity. With few exceptions, Jewish children's associations received their greatest income from dues-paying members. This reflects the grassroots nature of their development. While some Jewish children's associations and orphanages (such as Korczak's) had been founded before World War I, the crisis of the war spurred the development of many more. Those behind the organization of Jewish children's groups, whether in Poland's largest cities or smallest *shtetls*, were individuals—usually doctors, lawyers, or teachers—who recognized the need and responded accordingly. A report published on the fifteenth anniversary of the Association for the Care of Jewish Orphans in Lwów reveals that dues-paying members sustained the group.[84] Each Jewish children's association was supported by members who paid dues, not to receive any benefits but to pay for the care of the most impoverished Jewish children. An association had anywhere from one hundred to five hundred members, whose names were often listed in the annual report. In addition to raising money from dues, associations sponsored parties and events to raise money, often raising more funds in a year than an association received from either the *kehilah* or local and state governments. Those private individuals who had founded the Jewish children's associations continued their support throughout the interwar years and attracted the support of others. As private Jewish leaders, they acted outside the authority of the legal Polish state and the official Jewish community, though they longed for—and desperately needed—the support of both.

Committees were often hampered by a severe lack of funds. Typically, the children's aid committee of a small town such as Dąbrowiec or Stryj

---

[84] *Sprawozdanie Towarzystwa dla Opieki nad Żyd. Sierotami we Lwowie za 15-lecie 1916–1930* (Lwów: Towarzystwo dla Opieki nad Sierotami Żyd. we Lwowie, 1931), table 1.

consisted of a small group of leaders, perhaps five to ten individuals, who sought to use existing resources to respond to the needs of their communities.[85] In some cases, the committee saw the need to expand or revive the activities of an already existing orphanage or children's aid group. Other groups were completely new organizations. The local committee typically provided subsidies to single parents, arranged for the placement of children in foster homes, and supervised a small orphanage with perhaps as few as ten or as many as fifty children. Local efforts depended primarily on the resources and skills of the local community organizers. Those with more money were able to build and maintain institutions; those with less advocated placing children in the homes of relatives or strangers and providing a regular subsidy to the foster parents.

A 1928 report in *Przegląd Społeczny* offers a statistical snapshot of the work provided by the associations of CENTOS.[86] In total, 344 committees operated in 316 locations. This work was supported by 52,652 members, 2,498 of whom served on the boards of their committees. Lwów hosted the greatest number of institutions, at thirty-nine. Warsaw was home to thirty-five institutions, while Równo and Pińsk had eleven each. There were eight institutions in Białystok, five in Wilno, and six in Kraków. The committees cared for 13,614 orphans, of which 3,750 were full orphans (1,762 were boys and 1,988 were girls) and 9,864 were half-orphans (4,778 boys and 5,086 girls). From October to December 1927, 692 orphans had left care and 386 had been taken into care. In the same period, 136 children had become independent (working in a trade) and 239 had been removed from care because their relatives were living in improved material circumstances. Fifty-nine children had emigrated. Two had died, nine passed the upper age limit for care, and 247 had been removed from care for lack of funds.

---

85 Report No. 10, From: I. Fridman, Dąbrowiec, To: Financial Section of the J.D.C., Warsaw, Subject: Control-report of the cash and bookkeeping of Orphans' Maintenance Committee, Dąbrowiec, 22 December 1926, JDC Archives, 1921/1932, File 337 and Letter from A. Shohan, Warsaw, to JDC Warsaw, Report of trip to Lwów and Rowno, 14 August 1921, JDC Archives, 1921/1932, File 324. Dąbrowiec had a smaller orphan home, with twelve children, compared to the one in Stryj, with eighty-seven children.

86 "Stan akcji opiekuńczej nad sierotami żyd. w Polsce a dniem 1. stycznia 1928," *Przegląd Społeczny* II, no. IV (April 1928): 37–38.

Striking among these numbers is the high figure of 247 for those removed from care because of lack of funds. The need was real. The numbers show the fluidity of the situation confronting community leaders. Children came and went, sometimes for good reasons, because their families' fortunes had improved, and sometimes for bad, because of lack of funds. Eight and a half percent of the 692 who left care had emigrated, suggesting that emigration was a real possibility. Unfortunately, the place of emigration is not indicated in this statistical profile.

Institutional care was an important alternative for impoverished parents, as indicated by the fact that 2,683 of 4,657 orphans in institutions were half-orphans. In addition, 7,472 children were living with relatives and 1,495 were in foster families not their own. The total number of children attending schools of various types was 9,743; the number attending more than one school was 877. Some did not attend school because of development issues, illness, or because of the lack of an appropriate school. The total number of children learning a trade was 4,450; the vast majority, 3,439, studied with private masters while 1,011 children attended trade schools. For various reasons, including lack of funds, failure to complete elementary school, unemployment, a lack of masters, or because of physical or mental disabilities, 539 of the 4,981 children past school age were not learning a trade. Most of those working were in the needle trades, as dressmakers, tailors, seamstresses, or embroiders. Others were carpenters, locksmiths, shoemakers, barbers, or furriers. To make vocational education possible, 987 orphans had been transferred from a committee in a small town to one in a larger city.

By 1938, the institutions within CENTOS included, among other associations: twenty-six orphanages, seventy-five day-care facilities, three clinics for mothers and children, and summer colonies in over thirty locations. Together, the institutions of CENTOS served nearly thirty thousand children in 1938.[87] In his history of the JDC in the 1930s, Yehuda Bauer notes the increase in the number of children CENTOS cared for in the

---

87 "Wykaz instytucji," *Sprawozdanie Centralnego Stowarzyszenia Opieki nad dziećmi i sierotami żydowskimi "CENTOS" za czas okres od 1/4 1937 do 31/3 1938* (Warsaw: Zakł. Graf. "Feniks," 1938).

1930s, from 15,102 in 1932 to 32,066 in 1937.[88] The work of CENTOS was simply vital to the strength of both the Jewish community and of Poland, and it was largely the result of private initiative. Almost thirteen percent of the CENTOS budget came from the JDC. The government provided an additional seventeen percent. The remaining seventy percent came entirely from dues-paying members.[89] Thus, while the support of both the JDC and the government was quite significant, the associations of CENTOS were clearly Polish Jewish organizations. The work of CENTOS was most decidedly a collective effort, even, one might say, a national undertaking.

The community leaders who sought to aid Jewish children, whether in the United States or Poland, were subject to the limitations of legal systems beyond their control. The limited historical record of the few associations for which information is available suggests that the relationship with the Polish authorities was not entirely a negative one. Local governing bodies did provide subsidies to Jewish institutions, which at times equaled or exceeded those of the official Jewish communities (though, as noted above, they were far less than the funds provided by private Jewish donors). Though this was not an explicit goal, the leaders of the government and Jewish civil society in Poland both forged unique institutions, private yet partially funded by the public and meeting both private and public needs. More than one government had abandoned children like Miriam Sherman. The institutional ties between local Polish government and Jewish child welfare associations suggest that Jews and Poles had begun to fundamentally reorganize the way their communities worked. Maintaining the distinction between private need and public responsibility, the leaders of Jewish civil society in pre-World War II Poland demonstrated the admittedly tenuous possibilities of growth for a religiously and ethnically distinct nation within a multinational state. They also began to show that, with the help of the Jewish diaspora, they could take care of themselves.

Assistance from the Polish state for Jewish children's associations was minimal. For example, over the fifteen-year period of its report, the Lwów

---

88 Bauer, *My Brother's Keeper*, 204.
89 Ibid.

association received only small subsidies from the Polish government for five of the fifteen years. Only in three of the years did the Lwów association receive any funds from the Lwów municipal authorities. A report of the regional CENTOS association in western Małopolska, based in Kraków, describes the relationship of the children's associations to the Polish government throughout the 1920s and 1930s and corroborates the situation in Lwów.[90] CENTOS officials in Kraków had worked diligently to establish positive working relationships with city and state authorities, and, through their tremendous progress aiding Jewish children, they won the sympathy and respect of Polish officials. When small subventions from municipalities were diminished further because of economic crisis, regional CENTOS leaders intervened and in some cases were able to restore the subvention, which saved more than one children's association. Unfortunately, though, the respect of the authorities never translated into adequate material support for the children's groups.[91]

Worsening the situation, Jewish children's associations received only nominal support from the *kehilot*. The Lwów association received funds from the Lwów *kehilah* for only six of its fifteen years. Annual reports of Jewish orphanages in Warsaw, Wołyń, and Kołomyja reveal a similar distribution of funds in each location.[92] The lack of support from the *kehilot* is striking and raises several questions, not the least of which concerns which group in society should be responsible for assisting children of a specific group. The Jewish community leaders who founded the associations after World War I acted outside the *kehilot* and formed new organizations. Their very existence challenged the prevailing model of

---

[90] *Sprawozdanie jubileuszowe, Zachodnio-Małopolskiego Związku Towarzystw Opieki nad Sierotami Żydowskimi, z okazji 15-lecia działalności 1923-1938* (Krakow: Zachodnio-Małopolski Związek Towarzystw Opieki nad Sierotami żydowskimi "CENTOS-KRAKÓW," 1938), 17–18.

[91] A. Goldin addresses such issues in "Pen-Strokes (From my Inspections in the Provinces)," translated below. Goldin notes that in Pinsk Jewish children received what the law said they should receive.

[92] See *Tetigkayts-barikht fun Ts. K. far der tsayt fun ershtn yanuar 1927 bizn ershtn april 1928* (Równo: Gezelshaft far yesoymim farzorgung af volin, 1928); *Tsu der draytsiker yeriker ekszistents funem „Beys yesoymim" in Kolomey: Draytsik yor yudishe yesoymim farzorgung: 1918–1938* (Kołomyja: Druk. M. Dalfen i M. Ohringer, 1938); and *Sprawozdanie Domu Sierot "Eszel" w Warszawie* (Warsaw: Druk. "Bristol," 1939).

Jewish community life with *kehilah* leaders as local authorities acting as intermediaries with Polish officials. The annual reports of the children's associations complained frequently that they did not receive adequate support from the *kehilot*. CENTOS officials in Kraków stated simply that *kehilah* leaders were not interested in modern social work.[93] Some *kehilot* were still beneficiaries of government support. These funds from local and state authorities were then distributed to individuals who had petitioned the *kehilah* for support, not to modern institutions such as those that belonged to CENTOS. From the point of view of CENTOS officials in western Małopolska, such charity undermined their efforts to practice social work professionally and was simply ineffective. The *kehilot* did distribute some funds to children's associations, but as they too experienced deficits during the interwar period, this support was, like that from the city and state, inadequate. Stubbornly defending their mission to protect children, the CENTOS officials in Kraków refused to accept the argument that the *kehilot* could not support them because of financial considerations and encouraged the *kehilot* leadership to organize their finances so that greater support of children could become a reality.

Cooperation between Jewish groups and municipal authorities could take various forms. The innovative programs designed by Jewish leaders had real results during the interwar period. For example, from 1921 to 1925, the Board of Education in Lwów sponsored a course for illiterate Jewish children organized by the Association for the Care of Jewish Orphans in that city.[94] After taking the course, the children could take the exam for the fourth class of elementary school. If they passed, they were entitled to work as apprentices, which would in turn provide them with the skills to make a living. The course enabled nearly two hundred Jewish children to enter a trade. In another instance, a kitchen for an after-school facility in Kraków was developed with the support of school authorities.[95]

---

93 *Sprawozdanie jubileuszowe*, CENTOS-Kraków, May 1938, 18.
94 *Sprawozdanie Towarzystwa dla Opieki nad Żyd. Sierotami we Lwowie za 15-lecie 1916–1930*, 19–20.
95 Henryk Leser, "Obecny stan opieki społecznej w Zach. Małopolsce, List z Krakowa," *Przegląd Społeczny* II, no. I (January 1928): 31–34.

Court cases from the eastern Galician town of Złoczów in 1935 suggest the difficulties that could arise in the relationship between Polish authorities and private institutions.[96] In 1935, the board of the orphanage for Jewish children in Złoczów lodged a complaint in regional court because the town had failed to provide any funds for the orphanage in its annual budget. The town had provided an annual subsidy for many years. The Polish court decided in favor of the town, ruling that the l923 law on social work legally obligated Polish communities to provide care for children in private institutions only when a prior agreement had been established. The Jewish community argued that such an agreement existed because the town had already provided for the orphanage for many years, long enough that community leaders had a reasonable expectation that the funding would be continued. The board of the orphanage appealed the ruling, but lost again. The leaders of the orphanage in Złoczów argued that they acted for the state in providing care to the poor and that the 1923 law legally established the local government's responsibility in providing for a community's poorest citizens, regardless of faith or nationality. Turning to the Central Committee of Associations Caring for Jewish Orphans in Lwów, the leaders of the orphanage asked for support in their efforts to hold the town of Złoczów legally accountable.

The issues here are important ones, for which, unfortunately, there is little source material. Was the failure of Złoczów to provide funds for the orphanage simply due to budgetary considerations during one of the most difficult years of the Great Depression? To what extent did similar conflicts occur in other communities? At issue was the role of the private institution within local government and the local government's (and hence the state's) responsibility to care for all of its citizens. The case of Złoczów suggests the unique task faced by both Polish authorities and Jewish community leaders: not simply to provide care for the country's poor, but to do so fairly and equitably. That this did not happen is not surprising; that Polish authorities and private Jewish institutions had such contacts and relationships suggests that the reality of Polish-Jewish relations was more complex than we usually assume.

---

96 Maks Schaff, "O należytą interpretację ustawy," *Przegląd Społeczny* IV, no. XII (1935): 257–63.

The interactions between the organized Jewish community (both in Poland and abroad) and local and state authorities reveal how the ceremonial side of bureaucracy formalized the changing relationships between two national communities in one state. In 1930, when the Polish state conferred upon Cecylja Klaftenowa (1888–194?) the order of Polonia Restituta, one of the highest awards conferred by the state on civilians, the citation noted her "state-creating" work and declared that "the Jews on whose behalf Dr. Klaftenowa works are citizens of the Polish state, and whoever works to economically benefit Polish Jewry also renders the state meritorious service."[97] Klaftenowa, a doctor of biology, played a significant role in the history of Jewish social welfare and, as a member of the city council, in the history of Lwów.[98] As the founder of vocational schools for girls and the driving force behind the founding of vocational schools for boys, Klaftenowa dedicated her life to improving educational opportunities for Jewish children. Her practice of social work, her Jewish activism, and her journalism advanced her cause: to educate Jewish youth and provide them the means to live independently. As the state's award suggests, this was a cause that found favor with the Polish government. While it is clear that the political state served by Klaftenowa's work was Poland, it is less clear that her efforts benefited two nations, a nation of Poles who formed the majority population in a political state and a nation of Jews who, though a minority in Poland, nonetheless had developed a strong national identity.

In another example, a ribbon-cutting ceremony for a day-care facility in Białystok included a performance of the Polish national anthem and a special blessing for Józef Piłsudski. In the guest book for the occasion, the provincial governor wrote on the first page, "Whoever cares for the good of the Nation cannot be indifferent to the fate of the child. I look forward to your institution raising competent citizens, sensitive to the fate and needs

---

97 "Cecylja Klaftenowa—Polonia Restituta," *Przegląd Społeczny* IV, no. XI (November 1930): 404–7.
98 For a brief biographic sketch by Rafał Żebrowski, see *Polski Słownik Judaistyczny*, s.v. "Klaften (Klaftenowa, z domu Beigel) Cecylia," accessed May 28, 2016, http://www.jhi.pl/psj/Klaften_(Klaftenowa_z_domu_Beigel)_Cecylia. Klaftenowa was killed in Lwów during the war, but the exact circumstances of her death are unknown.

of humanity."⁹⁹ The children who were to benefit from the facility prepared a special program for the opening, with songs in both Polish and Yiddish, and the assembled guests enjoyed a small reception. Such occasions were common in Poland when Jewish leaders opened a new facility. The visit by Polish officials was simply a ceremonial function of state authorities, an obligatory visit to a new local institution. Nonetheless, the governor's remarks in the guest book suggest both the cooperation between local Jewish leaders and, as mentioned earlier, the tension between the Polish and Jewish nations. While the Jewish leaders who established such institutions worked in close cooperation with the newly formed Polish state, they also acted from a motivation to benefit a separate group, the Jewish nation. The governor's remarks are very carefully and imprecisely phrased; none could take offense. Yet the efforts to establish private day-care facilities, orphanages, and other such institutions were fraught with obstacles, and the relationship between the Jewish associations that founded these groups and the Polish state was equally tense. Polish officials viewed the support from American Jews as threatening, seeing the Minorities Protection Treaty as imposed by foreign interests. This resentment betrayed a lack of understanding of the national identity of Jews and an understandable confusion regarding the support and development of national minority communities. Yet the minimal support the state did provide suggests a recognition of the vital work of Jewish community leaders.

The institutions of CENTOS reflected other changes the Jewish community experienced at this time, including a marked growth in the participation of Jewish children in public education and the development of opportunities for young Jews to develop practical, technical skills in specific trades. In a 1927 annual report on efforts to help orphans in Eastern Małopolska, Józef Kohn wrote, "Is it generally understood that this is not the plaything of community leaders, but the difficult, heroic struggle for the existence of the entire nation, for the future of each of us? If we want to live, we must create institutions that will teach us how to work!"¹⁰⁰ He described the need for dormitories and orphanages, for

---

99 "Wiadomości z central sierocych," *Przegląd Społeczny* III, no. II (February 1929): 84–85.
100 Józef Kohn, "Rok 1927 w akcji sierocej Małopolski Wschodniej," *Przegląd Społeczny* II, no. II (February 1928): 41.

medical care, and, especially, for vocational education. Jewish youth needed such programs in workshops and schools in order to learn how to make a living. In Kohn's view, these programs and this kind of social work were essential for the community's very existence. The educational possibilities for Jewish orphans were both more underdeveloped and more numerous than we might expect.

Most of the annual reports include at least a brief mention of the educational level of the children under the group's care. Jewish leaders were primarily concerned with the ability of the children to make a living once they reached adulthood. For that reason, Jewish child welfare associations encouraged all forms of education, especially vocational training. Each association met a different need in a different location, yet the struggles were similar. The leaders of these associations recognized the need to make some kind of provision for education, whether this meant placement in a public school, placement with a master craftsman, or the establishment of a school at the association's own orphanage. Most institutions sent their children to public schools and then supplemented that education with courses in Jewish language, history, and culture during after-school hours. Jewish children often had the opportunity to attend lectures, plays, and performances and, in some cases, even participate in their own productions. In addition, they often had access to a small lending library in the orphanage, with books and newspapers in Polish, Yiddish, Hebrew, and German.

To take one example, the author of a regional report of the Association for the Care of Jewish Orphans in Wołyń assessed the situation fairly positively, stating that most children in their care were receiving an education.[101] The writer of the Wołyń report admitted that, while Jewish leaders had succeeded in providing their children with an education, the rhetoric of Jewish community leaders at conferences on child welfare encouraged the promotion of a secular, nationalist Jewish education. In this area, the writer claimed, there had been no real success.[102]

The author of the Wołyń report noted a couple of reasons why more Jewish children attended public schools than Jewish schools. The report

---
101 *Tetigkayts-barikht fun Ts. K. far der tsayt fun ershtn yanuar 1927 bizn ershtn april 1928*, 8.
102 Ibid.

indicated that branches of CENTOS throughout the Wołyń region continually argued with representatives from Jewish schools over the issue of tuition. According to the report, representatives of Jewish schools, often impoverished themselves, treated the branches of CENTOS just like they did the "richest of the parents" because they knew that the CENTOS branches received support from the American JDC. Jewish leaders simply could not always afford to send the children in their institutions to private Jewish schools. Moreover, the government offered plenty of free public schools where Polish was the language of instruction. Comparatively, there were fewer private Jewish schools, whether oriented toward Yiddish or Hebrew culture. There was some good news for proponents of Jewish education, however. In spite of the cost of private education, the number of Jewish children in Jewish schools in Wołyń was slowly increasing, as tables in the report show. Still, it appears that children in private Jewish orphanages most often attended public Polish schools, an indication that the orphanages prepared children for participation in the larger Polish society and that these private Jewish associations did not serve to separate Jewish children from their surroundings but rather imparted the skills necessary for survival and success.

Vocational education was always a priority for Jewish community leaders. Jewish children in the handworkers' dormitory in Kraków were in a unique situation that illustrates the pragmatic goals of Jewish community leaders.[103] Children in this dormitory had already left an orphanage, having attained the age (usually around fourteen or fifteen) when children could be thought independent, but they still needed practical skills in order to make a living. The dormitory offered them a home and the opportunity to be trained as a locksmith, tinsmith, carpenter, pastry cook, or hairdresser, among many other occupations. The dormitory in Kraków was an especially well-developed institution in a larger Polish city, which meant that its children had access to more resources than those in smaller

---

103 Piotr Trojański, "Stowarzyszenie Rękodzielników Żydowskich Szomer Umonim w Krakowie," *Kraków: Studia z dziejów miasta*, ed. Jerzy Rajman (Kraków: Wydawnictwo Naukowe Akademii Pedagogicznej, 2007), 229–30; and Sean Martin, "Future Generations: Associations for Jewish Children in Kraków, 1918–1945," *Polin: Studies in Polish Jewry* 23 (2011): 291–320.

towns. In some locations, craftsmen were reluctant to take on apprentices because they did not have enough work themselves. The majority of children in the dormitory were from Kraków, but nearly a third came from elsewhere in Poland. The children worked from seven in the morning until four in the afternoon, with evening hours free for other activities. The dormitory offered midday meals around the work schedules of the children and offered a range of activities, including journal publication, sports, lectures, and access to a library. Education in both vocational fields and in other subjects meant the residents of the Kraków dormitory were especially well prepared for the tasks of adulthood.

The work of the leaders of CENTOS changed the Jewish community. A comment on the development of summer colonies in Western Małopolska points to some interesting trends, at least as viewed by the anonymous author of the report.[104] Summer colonies had originally been organized for the poor, as charitable, philanthropic initiatives to aid the poorest and least healthy children. The author notes that colonies were now encouraged for all children, even healthy ones. Parents' committees of different types of schools, youth organizations, and sports clubs had all established summer colonies. The author was intrigued that Orthodox institutions and organizations had also established colonies. The author wrote, "Would someone have even thought of this just a few years ago? This is an unprecedented revolution in worldview, in thinking about health, hygiene, and the culture of the body. This action is a turning point, the best sign for the future of the summer colonies. It gives to us a new, healthy Jewish generation."[105] The author's comments suggest the distance of the Orthodox from the kinds of activities initiated by the CENTOS committees and supported by the JDC. But they also suggest real progress and reveal a noteworthy optimism in the achievements of CENTOS. In a relatively short time, the associations and institutions of CENTOS had brought about significant change within the Jewish community in Poland.

---

104 "Z Centrali Krakowskiej, Żydowska akcja kolonijna w zachodniej Małopolsce," *Przegląd Społeczny* VI, no. XI (November 1932): 324–27.
105 Ibid., 325.

Foster Care and Orphanages

Should orphaned children remain with family members or be placed in institutions? This was the most pressing question facing child welfare leaders worldwide in the early decades of the twentieth century. While the devastation of World War I and the creation of the new Polish state meant Jewish child welfare leaders were working under remarkably changed conditions, they could draw on their knowledge of prewar institutions and of trends in child welfare work in other countries and in Poland. The trend toward foster care in the United States occurred long before 1914. The White House Conference of 1909 made clear that professional child-care workers preferred foster care to institutions.[106] By 1917, Jewish leaders in the United States, many of whom would be involved in the relief efforts in Poland, also saw foster care, or "placing-out," as a better option than institutions.[107] Thus, the question of which method of care was more effective had already concerned leaders in child welfare well before the crisis faced by Poland's Jewish leaders in the 1920s. In addition, Polish social work leaders also advocated different systems of care within family settings, settings that disrupted the traditional notion of children sleeping in bunk beds crowded along a wall. Kazimierz Jeżewski pioneered the idea of "nests" where children could learn and grow, and Czesław Babicki developed a "family system" that rejected the more usual conception of a home for children. Scholars see foster care as one of the achievements of social work in interwar Poland.[108]

The CENTOS journal *Dos kind* published a heartfelt appeal to support the establishment of a home for young Jewish workers in 1924. The orphan

---

106 For an overview of the shift away from institutionalized care in the early twentieth century, see Duncan Lindsey and Paul H. Stuart, "Orphanages in History and the Modern Child Welfare Setting: An Overview," in *Home Away from Home: The Forgotten History of Orphanages*, ed. Richard B. McKenzie (New York: Encounter Books, 2009).

107 See the comments of Boris D. Bogen in his book *Jewish Philanthropy* (New York: MacMillan, 1917), 160. Bogen served as Director General of the JDC from 1917 to 1924.

108 Izabela Szczepaniak-Wiecha, Agnieszka Małek, and Krystyna Ślany, "The System of Care for Abandoned Children in Poland 1900–1960," in *Need and Care: Glimpses into the Beginnings of Eastern Europe's Professional Welfare* (Opladen & Bloomfield Hills, MI: Barbara Budrich Publishers, 2005), 179–96; Sean Martin, "How to House a Child: Providing Homes for Jewish Children in Interwar Poland," *East European Jewish Affairs* 45, no. 1 (2015): 26–41.

Tereza Rozenboym told of her life circumstances: she was the child of an honest Jewish worker who was killed during a pogrom. Her mother died in the hospital. A poor woman took her in and sent her out to beg. Later, she lived in an institution for several years. At the age of fifteen, she was ready to leave the children's home, as she had to give up her place to another "miserable" child, in her description. "Where should I go now?" she asked. "Back to the old woman, who sells onions in the market? Back to her, sleeping in the cellar on a straw sack? Often the question comes to me, why was I, a desolate stranger, made to feel like I was cared for, that I was just like other children?"[109] Her appeal and her circumstances, not unknown to those concerned about child welfare, forced readers to assess the long-term impact of the care Jewish children received in private children's homes in Poland. There is no simple answer to Rozenboym's question: why did you help me, knowing you would have to throw me out? Community leaders like Schaff and Korczak attempted to address the needs of children by establishing homes where orphaned or neglected children could live twenty-four hours a day with appropriate educational support and medical care, but they could only do so much once the children had matured. Such institutions were just one of the ways Jewish community leaders supported children, but these institutions fell short when it came to helping young teenagers make the transition to independent living.

Throughout the interwar period, Jewish child welfare leaders struggled with Rozenboym's question, periodically evaluating the institutions and the systems of care they had established. The discussion regarding institutions and private care reflected the desire to provide effective and efficient services, but it was also a sign of the institutional immaturity of the organizations that had emerged to address the needs of children. The care of children in private homes (called at times private care, home care, or foster care) was seen as the most practical solution to the crisis faced after World War I and a real alternative to the establishment of brick-and-mortar institutions. Proponents of institutions and private care advocated greater supervision of these services and more organization of both child welfare workers and the children themselves. Believing that such

---

109 Tereza Rozenboym, "Tsu aykh, foters un muters! (a brif fun a yesoyma)," *Dos kind* 4, no. 4 (April 1924): 33–34. *Dos kind* was published in Warsaw by CENTOS.

supervision would make the children under their care into more productive, responsible adults, the leaders of Jewish children's aid associations in Poland approved of the increasing involvement of non-governmental organizations and the state in the intimate lives of families.

The pages of the CENTOS journals included discussion on the most effective methods of child care. Several writers, including Stefania Wilczyńska, addressed the advantages and disadvantages of foster care and institutionalization and made recommendations for reform. A few clearly favored institutions, but most advocated care for children in private homes, perhaps not least because of the burden on the increasing number of institutions.

The advantages of care in a private home, whether the child was placed in the home of an extended family member or a stranger, were clear: the home provided a family environment where the child could grow naturally with adult supervision and the companionship of other children. The child could attend school and, as necessary, learn the discipline of work outside the home. Growing up with other children, the orphan would learn to live in the world and be able to cope with the challenges of adulthood. In a home, the child had familial support, a network on which to rely in the present and in the future. This was a significant advantage for all of those writing on this issue, even those who favored the development of separate institutions to house Jewish children. The only advantage of care in a private home that was consistently considered more important than growing up within a family was financial.

The disadvantages of private care were also clear: often, the families taking care of these children were poor themselves. As one author stated, the "bourgeoisie," able to care for their own children, did not see the need to care for others' and did not need the subsidy provided the family for assuming the care of another child. Those taking on the role of raising the child of a relative or fostering a child were often impoverished themselves and saw the subsidy from CENTOS as a payment to cover the needs of the family rather than the needs of a specific child; indeed, they were seen as "professional shnorrers."[110] Thus, in effect, associations supported by Jews

---

110 Rokhl Shtayn, "Private adoptatsie oder kolektive," *Dos kind* 1, no. 1 (January 1924): 11.

with the necessary means to make charitable contributions outsourced the care of poor children to other poor families. From the viewpoint of the bureaucrats of CENTOS and the JDC, the monies given to families could not be controlled easily. In an article in the first volume of *Dos kind*, Rokhl Shtayn describes some examples of the lives of children in foster care. She describes one woman, A., with four "adopted" girls, three aged fourteen to sixteen, and one aged ten. A. lives in a room with a kitchen. Living in the kitchen are her son, his wife, and four children. In the main room the four girls sleep two to a bed. Shtayn describes the relationship of the foster mother to the children. At the beginning of the month, when she has received the subsidy from the JDC, the foster mother is cheerful and friendly. But her mood changes as the days go by and the money becomes tight. She begins to use insults like "pig" and "lazy bum."[111] Shtayn's example shows the negative side of private care, the use of a child simply to obtain a subsidy from a social service agency. Those favoring private care recognized the child might be subject to these kinds of conditions in addition to facing cold and hunger, but the role of the family was still privileged. Poor living conditions were not seen entirely as negative aspects of a child's life. L. Neustadt, head of the JDC's Child Care Department in Warsaw, admitted that the child in private care might grow up cold and hungry. This hunger and cold would, in Neustadt's words, "build character."[112]

Reports of inspections by JDC officials reveal the challenges community leaders faced. A 1921 visit to Równo by Dr. Bogen and Leib Neustadt (author of the article discussed above) revealed a more or less typical situation. A war widow was raising eight children on her own. She lived in what the JDC officials described as "a tumbledown shack with a broken roof and walls."[113] She refused to move from the shack because she owned the land. As Dr. Bogen wrote, "This is one of the cases of persistent stubbornness on the part of an ignorant mother, so that the conditions were not due to neglect or inability on the part of the

---

111 Ibid., 11–12.
112 L. Neustadt, "Private farzorgung oder antshtaltn (sic)," *Dos shutsloze kind* 1, no. 1 (January 1928): 21.
113 Dr. Bogen's Diary, 16 July to 20 July 1921, JDC Archives, 1921/1932, File 324.

management." While the report does not tell us how the mother made a living, we know she was not able to provide sufficiently for her large family, nor did her circumstances allow her to accept improved living facilities the JDC would have provided. While there is no indication in the report that the JDC wished to remove the children from the care of their mother, the JDC did wish to move the family from their home, an action which certainly would have had unintended consequences. While we have no further evidence about this specific situation, half-orphans were sometimes removed from families and did receive care in institutions throughout Poland. This mother's stubbornness shows us just one interaction between social workers and individuals, between the organized community and a client in need of help. Private care had its limitations; the JDC could only do so much to improve this woman's plight. The intent of the leaders of the JDC and others involved in child welfare was certainly noble, but the consequences of their actions may not always have been entirely positive.

Certain trends in the work of CENTOS had become clear by the late 1930s. In 1926, 11,108 children were in private care.[114] This number declined to a low of 3,470 in 1932 but then grew to 6,592 in 1938. Most significantly, the number of children in institutions climbed steadily from 1926 to 1938, from 4,671 in 115 institutions to 9,799 in 205 institutions. The steady increase of institutionalized children is of special interest, and difficult to explain, not least because it contradicts the conclusion of such a seasoned professional as Wilczyńska. By the 1930s, child welfare leaders had not arrived at a clear policy on how best to aid children in desperate circumstances. In spite of a recognition that foster care was significantly more manageable financially, institutional care continued its influence. In her writings on child welfare, Wilczyńska did not directly address her doubts about the efficacy of the work to which she had devoted her entire life. She did, however, describe the conditions the children faced and outline recommendations for training others working in the field. Wilczyńska was not known for her writing, but she did leave behind a slim record from which we can learn more about her

---

114 Bar-Yishay and Web, "Yesoymim-farzorgung," 112, table 2.

approach to the field. She occasionally wrote articles for *Dos kind* and *Przegląd Społeczny*, journals published by CENTOS. She also described her experiences in Palestine in letters published in Korczak's review for children, *Mały Przegląd*. These writings reveal her concern for the future of the children and her active role in the professional education of social workers and teachers.

In an article published in *Dos kind* in 1937, Wilczyńska asked the same question young Tereza Rozenboym had asked in 1924: what was the point of children's homes when children leaving the homes were not prepared for independence, not prepared to take care of themselves "on the outside"?[115] Wilczyńska's disappointment in the results of the children's home stemmed from the fact that she knew those who left found it difficult to adjust to the outside world. She knew that Rozenboym's despair was real. Korczak's institutions may have been the best examples of homes in which children lived in comfortable circumstances and then faced the harsher circumstances of the real world upon their release. In response to the need, Wilczyńska outlined a system for releasing children from children's homes. She recommended that all fourteen-year-olds be registered officially and that their family's finances be surveyed. She recommended the completion of a questionnaire that would focus on the possibility of the child remaining in the institution and include: a history of the child in the institution; plans for the coming year; and evaluations from the child's school, employer (if the child was working), and the institution itself. These materials were to be started in January and completed in April of the year of the child's release. Wilczyńska also stressed the necessity of sending the children away with proper clothing. She recommended that children spend a month in the summer colony, if necessary, before their final departure from the home. Wilczyńska allowed for the possibility that the child might need to stay in the children's home another year, on the condition that the child find work, finish a course, or improve behavior. Alternatively, the child could become an assistant in the institution or be

---

115 Stefania Wilczyńska, "Próby uporządkowania, albo usuwanie bez bólu," in *Słowo do dzieci i wychowawców*, trans. Ela Frydman, ed. Marta Ciesielska (Warsaw: Muzeum Historyczne m. st. Warszawy, 2004), 74–76. The article was first published in Yiddish in the March 1937 issue of *Dos kind*, but Wilczyńska must have written the article in Polish.

directed to another facility where he or she might receive additional education. The child might return to his or her parents but with the right to receive continued assistance for meals or study. The child might be apprenticed. Finally, the child might be placed in an open institution that would allow for contact with the family and support from the institution (such a facility was called a *półinternat*—literally a halfway house, akin to a day-care center). Wilczyńska allowed for several options based on a child's individual circumstances. Her first thought was for the well-being of the child.

Wilczyńska was ideally suited to the work she carried out for CENTOS as an inspector of children's homes in 1937. She knew what worked, and she could address both the needs of the children and the needs of the staff. However, this work did not seem to satisfy her; in fact, Wilczyńska's work with CENTOS actually solidified her skepticism about the efficacy of boarding homes for children. In an article for *Przegląd Społeczny*, Wilczyńska described the period of her employment with CENTOS inspecting children's homes.[116] Wilczyńska understood the nature of philanthropy in Poland between the wars. She knew that the philanthropists and committees who ran the homes would prepare carefully for inspections from officials who made decisions about funding (whether they represented the Polish state or the JDC). Wilczyńska insisted on sleeping overnight in each of the homes, realizing she would be able to observe much more by spending the night and listening for the behavior of the children. She compared the quality of the mattresses she slept on for comfort and hygiene. She also paid attention to how children ate, not what they ate. For example, if children ate greedily, it was a sign that the food they were eating was not what they received every day. Wilczyńska's most important recommendation was that professionals in the field should share information. She lamented that few seemed to know of the recommendations she had made in her previous article in *Dos kind*. In short, as late as the 1930s CENTOS was still having problems circulating their journals to the staff of CENTOS-affiliated institutions. While an inspection

---

116 Stefania Wilczyńska, "Sprawozdanie z półrocznej działalności Poradni pedagogicznej przy Związku 'Centos,'" in *Słowo do dzieci i wychowawców*, 79–85. The article was first published in *Przegląd Społeczny* XII, no. 3 (March 1938).

system was in place, CENTOS still found it difficult to reach the many different kinds of professionals who worked in CENTOS institutions, both full and part time and with a range of educational backgrounds. Wilczyńska ultimately concluded that a more open environment allowing children greater contact with their relatives should be encouraged, as long as this environment considered the ages, gender, intellectual development, and family circumstances of the children involved. In short, Wilczyńska advised those working with children to consider the best circumstances for the child.

While Wilczyńska herself did not directly address the issue of institutional care versus private care, many involved in child welfare did, expressing their views in brief articles in the CENTOS journals. The advantages of an institution to house needy children were clear. Institutions were able to offer comfortable living standards that individual families simply could not afford, and officials of an institution could control both the finances of the home and, to some extent, the behavior of the children and parents more easily. Korczak, too, questioned the efficacy of the institution. In the 1929 edition of *Jak kochać dziecko* (How to love a child), Korczak wrote,

> Homes for children today are already less like a monastery or barracks; they are almost like hospitals. There is hygiene, but there is no laughter, joy, surprise, free will; the mood is serious, if not raw. Architecture has not helped; there is no 'children's style.' There are only ceilings for adults, adult proportions; such details are chilling. The French say that Napoleon replaced the school bell of the monastery with a drum—good for him; I would add that the factory bell burdens the spirit of education.[117]

This comment does not appear in the original edition of the text; Korczak added this commentary specifically for the 1929 edition, after another ten years of experience and experimenting in homes for children. Tempered with respect for the child, the discipline provided in Korczak's institutions

---

[117] Janusz Korczak, *Dzieła*, t. 7 (Warsaw: Oficyna Wydawnicza Latona, 1993), *Jak kochać dziecko*, 71.

was more positive than negative, an illustration of effective adult care of children. But, as those involved in this debate over methods of care recognized, not all children's homes were run by Korczak and Wilczyńska.[118]

Toward the end of her life Wilczyńska rejected institutional care as a solution for the needs of children. According to Betty Jean Lifton, the biographer of Korczak, Wilczyńska joked with her colleagues about the dishonesty of her career, saying often, "Before I die, I want to write one book, *Abolish the Boarding Home*."[119] Wilczyńska wrote to Fejga Lifszyc in 1937 that she was not a sincere person; she had been against institutions for the past six years yet she stayed out of inertia.[120] While Korczak's children's homes were arguably the best-run institutions in the country, the children leaving his care faced the same challenges as others trying to make it as independent adults. If even the homes for children established by Korczak could not provide adequate care for children, as Wilczyńska suggested, then what conclusions can we make about the solutions Jewish leaders hoped would improve children's lives? Wilczyńska's desire to abolish the boarding home shows that the leaders of CENTOS were far from achieving a consensus about how best to provide for children.

The associations of CENTOS serve as an example of how the Jews of Poland successfully took care of their own needs, albeit with significant help from the American Jewish community and the support of the state of which they were citizens. CENTOS represents an achievement of the developing Jewish civil society that was evident in other areas as well—for example, in the press, the theater, and, indeed, in political life. The leaders of CENTOS managed relationships with private donors, the JDC, and Polish authorities. They sought innovative ways to provide care and

---

118 Shtayn, "Private adoptatsie oder kolektive," 12. In his overview of child welfare in interwar Poland, Marian Balcerek raises the question of how much Korczak's success rested on the leadership skills of just one individual. See *Rozwój opieki*, 325–26.
119 Lifton, *King of Children*, 226. Michał Wroblewski, an apprentice to Korczak and Wilczyńska, told Lifton of Wilczyńska's views. Another apprentice, Roman Bertisch, tells the same story in his recollection of his time at the Jewish Orphans' Home. "Niepowtarzalny pedagog," in *Wspomnienia o Januszu Korczaku*, ed. Ludwika Barszczewska and Bolesław Milewicz (Warsaw: Nasza Księgarnia, 1981), 202.
120 Quoted in Olczak-Ronikier, *Korczak*, 326n24, 454.

education, and in the pages of CENTOS journals they thought critically about how to improve their work. CENTOS grew relatively quickly, harnessing the energies of local leaders and managing their work to improve the quality of care. Significantly, they conducted this work on behalf of the Jewish nation, a nation that was part of a multinational state, even as this work was at least partly—and often explicitly—about the process of integration. While CENTOS leaders often openly supported Jewish nationalist ideals, they also recognized the need to become a part of the larger community in which they lived. The leaders of CENTOS did not work in isolation, separated from the rest of society. Their presence in the public sphere challenged both Jewish and Polish authorities. CENTOS was outside the framework of the *kehilot*, and it took on the work that more properly might have been the task of the official Jewish communities or the state authorities. Yet, in fact, there was little alternative; neither the *kehilot* nor the state was prepared to meet even the most basic needs of the Jewish nation in Poland. The associations of CENTOS thus attempted to meet the need. They worked with Jewish community representatives in Poland and abroad, fostered cooperation with Polish authorities, sent their children to public schools, and taught them the skills to survive in the workforce. Their work was for the good of the nation.

II

Descriptions of Homes for Children

The "Orphanage in Pinsk"*1

Ben-Levi

Ben-Levi's short text describing the history of the orphanage in Pinsk describes the sometimes problematic dynamic between the Jews from Pinsk that were living outside of Poland and their "brethren" back home. This support, often so crucial, led to the resentment expressed here. His description of the crowded conditions and poor financial situation neatly outlines the challenges faced by Jewish community leaders in Poland. The Jewish community of Pinsk is the subject of a comprehensive study, encompassing the entirety of its history.[2] This extensive survey includes an overview of the city's child welfare associations.

"The 'Orphanage in Pinsk'" was published in *Dos kind* 3, no. 8/9 (August–September 1926): 34–35. Nothing is known about the author, Ben-Levi.

From the recent report of the Board of the orphanage in Pinsk, it can be seen from the activity of the past several years that the orphanage, located in the homes provided by the late Reb Yosef Halperin, of blessed

---

1 *Polesier togblat*. The asterisked title is present in the original, indicating that this short article appeared earlier in *Polesier togblat*.
2 See Azriel Shohet, *The Jews of Pinsk, 1506–1880*, ed. Mark Mirsky and Moshe Rosman, trans. Feige Tropper and Moshe Rosman (Stanford, CA: Stanford University Press, 2008), and *The Jews of Pinsk, 1881–1941*, ed. Mark Mirsky and Moshe Rosman, trans. Feige Tropper and Moshe Rosman (Stanford, CA: Stanford University Press, 2012). Originally published as *Toledot ḳehilat Pinsḳ Ḳarlin: 1506–1880* (Jerusalem: Association of the Jews of Pinsk in Israel, 1973) and *Toledot ḳehilat Pinsḳ ḳarlin: 1881–1941* (Jerusalem: Association of the Jews of Pinsk in Israel, 1977).

Descriptions of Homes for Children

Exterior of the building that housed CENTOS until 1931, Pinsk (American Jewish Joint Distribution Committee Archives)

memory, counts in terms of both its economic and hygienic direction and its educational system as the only one that meets the demands of a modern educational establishment. It is a remnant of the three existing orphanages.[3] More than five hundred war orphans have found a home there.

In earlier times the Pinsk relief groups in London and Chicago, in America, would have covered the budget.

Foreign organizations, especially the Pinsk association in London, arranged private adoptions for fifty-two children in London, for forty-four children in Cape Town, Africa (to be supported by the Jewish community), and a group of children in "children's villages" in Palestine.[4]

---

3 For a brief sketch of these three orphanages, see Shohet, *The Jews of Pinsk, 1881–1941*, 618–19.
4 For details of these foreign adoptions and reproductions of original documents written by the children, see *The Pinsker Orphans: The Life and Times of the Children from the Three Pinsk Jewish Orphanages in the 1920s*, compiled by David Solly Sandler (Wanneroo, W.A.: David Solly Sandler, 2013).

Boys and instructors pose in a class for locksmiths in a trade school run by CENTOS, Pinsk, undated (YIVO)

The children in their "new homes" continually send delightful letters about their very good arrangements.

But the funds from overseas have been exhausted. The well-known reductions have begun to have an effect.

The orphanage supports a hundred full orphans today while about 250 are in private care throughout the city.

In hindsight, the education of these orphans was not given enough attention.

Talented children should be developed and given a place for professional development. The orphans should be led to become self-reliant. A shoemakers' workshop and *shoykhet*[5] workshop were added to the orphanage, in addition to the workshops and trade schools in the city.

And new orphanages for children multiply daily. Those who were adopted have become orphaned. Winter is coming. New shoes and new clothes are needed. The Board of the orphanage finds itself in a great dilemma. If they are not able to open the doors of the orphanage more

---

5   Ritual slaughterer.

broadly to victims of the crisis, the war victims will find themselves in no pleasant conditions.

In addition, some of the buildings donated are in complete ruins and desperately need to be renovated.

The kitchen, laundry room, shoemakers' workshop, and *shoykhet* workshop are simply dangerous (they are likely to fall down any minute).

In order to ensure the continued existence of the Pinsk orphanage, the only modern educational establishment in Polesie, on both the inside and the outside, our society must more deeply "love our fellows as ourselves." Love and treat the war and crisis orphans as your own children!

Consider that these poor little souls had their own home once, not long ago.

Do not count on help from overseas, because our brothers in America and London and other places have recently come to a completely different decision. They say:

"If society itself keeps its distance and does not notice or listen to the appeals for relief, it cannot come to us with complaints!"

Let us see, our foreign brothers say, the intensive relief work done there and then we will in double measure support our suffering brothers from the old home . . . only when they come to us again for support.

The Publication of the Home for Orphans in Lwów, Zborowska 8

Maks Schaff[1]

A doctor of law and active Jewish community leader, Maks Schaff wrote often for *Przegląd Społeczny*, usually about important issues of funding and advocacy. He was a member of the Leopolis (Lwów) branch of B'nai B'rith and is a good example of a member of the intelligentsia taking a lead in the field of philanthropy.[2] He had two sons, Adam Schaff (1913–2006), the well-known Marxist scholar and philosopher, and Leon Schaff, a lawyer and legal scholar. Maks Schaff was killed in Lwów during the war.[3]

Schaff reviewed two issues of the special publication put out by the children of the Home for Orphans in Lwów on Zborowska 8. These reviews originally appeared in *Przegląd Społeczny* II, no. V (May 1928): 44–47 and *Przegląd Społeczny* III, no. VIII (August 1929): 321–24.

The association publishes an annual report with activities of the departments and selected agencies. We learn from this report the goals of each department, how many of the plans were realized, what remains to be done, and the reasons something was not achieved. We read in these reports about the eternal battle, between the agency on the one hand and society on the other, to raise the necessary funds. The balance tells us if the battalion achieved a victory or if there will remain a great deficit in the next year, or, if there will be no deficit, that the agency still is not able to

---

[1] The original source gives the author as M. S.
[2] Łukasz Sroka, "Members of the 'Leopolis' Humanitarian Society in Lvov (1899–1938): A Group Portrait," *Scripta Judaica Cracoviensia* 12 (2014): 99–119.
[3] See Filip Friedman, *Zagłada Żydów lwowskich* (Łódź: Centralna Żyd. komisja historyczna w Polsce, 1945).

accomplish anything. But we learn very little about the children. Information about their average state of health, their progress in their studies, their learning a trade, is presented only briefly.

But no one other than the initiated can penetrate the mental development of the child in an institution or understand a child's actual educational direction. It is difficult to ask those in charge of the children's education for an account of their arduous and demanding work throughout the year that considers this question properly.

The children themselves, from some healthy instinct, know how to resolve this difficulty. In different orphanages the children have spontaneously taken the initiative to start their own publications. These are monthlies or single issues edited and compiled solely by the children. They are the best reflection of the mental development of the children and also offer a measurement of the work of the authorities and educators.

Under consideration here is the "Special Issue," published by the Home for Orphans at 8 Zborowska Street. The "Special Issue" is unusually rich in content, as "it is meant to be a mirror . . . of life throughout one year. It includes much of what we thought about through the entire year. We put in it our original work and some studies of general themes on the questions that emerged in the course of our Friday talks. We also offer reports of these talks. These reports illustrate the course of discussions on books or specific topics. We also offer a history of our home, reports of sentences,[4] and farewell letters from those who have left the institution this year."

Such is the summary offered by the Editorial Committee of the "Special Issue" in a foreword.

Part I includes the original works: "Fantasy about the End of the World," "Ratchet," and a survey on friendship by Ignacy Mischel; "Rosa and the Butterfly" by Rela Winkler; "Two Plants" by Süsli Jad; "The Plant and the Person" and a survey titled "Episodes from the Lives or Experiences of Some Animals" by Sala Herbst; "The Adventures of Reks the Horse" by Süsli Jad; "Longing for Freedom" by Rela Winkler; and, finally, "Would I

---

[4] This refers to the punishments the children received for infractions, perhaps imposed by children's courts.

like to be a Human Moon and Why" by Süsli Jad; "What I Feel When I Perform" by Izrael Hass; and "Picture of Life" by Sucher Laszczower.

Each of these works is appropriate for children from eleven to thirteen, exceptional, and worthy of publication. The most original are the works on the themes of "Friendship" and "Episodes from the Lives or Experiences of Some Animals." They show an involvement in the natural world and, in comparing the lives of animals and plants with humans, original and independent thinking. Izrael Hass is the only one to write about what he has personally experienced. The young musician considers what he feels and experiences in his daily life and what he feels and experiences when he performs. If he responds to these feelings and makes progress in his performances, it may turn out the boy has a future as a musician.

While Part I acquaints us with the creative talents of individual children in the institution, the second and third parts offer a picture of the entire school year and an image of the development of the students throughout the year. In this respect Part II, the reports from the Friday talks, is the most interesting. The accounts of these talks come from the pens of different children. It is clear that someone new took the minutes at each meeting. Two children sometimes took the minutes, acting as secretaries for the day. At first the minutes show the incompetence of the children, but they get better from week to week, until they take on the character of real minutes. The minutes reveal the subject of the talk, the course of the discussion, how many children took part, and if the subject was chosen for them or selected by the children. The horizons of the children in the institution are broadened. Their knowledge deepens. There is a certain diversity of themes, but the guidelines remain the same. The children must get to know more deeply the individual and nature and to consider independently the individual and his relationship to daily affairs, the essence of the individual and his relationship to nature, to people, and to the development of character. In addition, the youngest children must make an effort and study "the life of an animal."

The director's plan was realized in its entirety. Her plan to entrust the discussions to the children led naturally to the kinds of talks that correspond to a prepared plan. The children think that they are independently reaching certain results, that they are independently choosing the topics which interest them at any given moment, but at the same time an iron logic applies and, without fail, a carefully arranged plan is carried out. The plan is carried out superbly. The minds of the children are focused, their attention riveted, their imagination excited. Their minds are working and together they build with small building blocks a magnificent building, to the remarkably straightforward intellectual development of the entire "community." Everyone marches forward. Some benefit a great deal, others less, but there is no one who does not benefit from this ongoing, superb work.

Part IV is dedicated to the history of the community. The experiment of the range of schools and institutions is realized here in its entirety. The administration can trust its community and be certain that this eases the dissatisfaction that is usually nurtured in the hearts of students as a result of an imposed program of work. But it is not possible to entrust the system of justice to the community. Incidents multiply, fines come down, and court sessions bring out the most people in the evenings. The most trivial concerns can become the subject of trials. Transgressions, misdeeds, and crimes multiply endlessly. The officials of the court, wanting to prevent a growth in irresponsibility and certain types of depravity, must after a certain time take back authority. This must be done in a delicate way, in order to bring out the appropriate voluntary decision of the community. And to her credit, the director has succeeded here, too. Judging from the excerpts of farewell letters, the work of the entire year did not go to waste. The children bidding their farewell ask about the possibility of staying longer in the institution, which had been their home until this time.

From an outside view the "Special Issue" is tastefully published and rich in content, numbering sixty pages. The publication offers a many-sided picture of the intellectual development of the children of this institution. This is the first "Special Issue," and the children included the work they recognized as the best and what the editorial committee accepted.

The subjects of Parts III and IV include the following: "How Do I Imagine the Souls and Lives of Plants?"; "How does Kończynski Imagine Human Life after the World is Extinct?"[5]; "How does Czyżowski Imagine

---

5 Poet and prose writer Tadeusz Konczyński (1875–1944). His works often focused on psychological themes.

Human Life after the Extinction of the World?"⁶; "The Way of Life and Thinking of the Residents of Polynesia"; "Why Wild People Decorate with Objects of Daily Life"; "My Impressions after Reading Grabiński's Short Story 'Tajemnicza stacja'"⁷; Survey: "Which Ideal Person I Like Best and Why"; "History of our Community"; and extracts from sentences and excerpts from farewell letters.

Our admiration and thanks are due to the director of the institution for so successfully completing her task in this way.

M. S.

Too often we are concerned only with the reports published by branches of our own associations. To the extent that these reports describe fundraising campaigns for orphans, we can say in advance that the reports of all of the different committees will be identical. Nearly everywhere where such associations emerged during the war, all of them had to resolve and manage the same difficulties and concerns. All of these associations, today united into one organization, stand before the same uncertain tomorrow. All of the committees, without exception, are fighting on several fronts with the goal of raising the necessary funds. It is more or less the same story everywhere. Several individuals of good will form a group with the goal of taking on the fate of abandoned and orphaned children. The group begins to search for necessary funds within the community and the circle of those cooperating with the group becomes broader and broader, but there still remains a deficit in the treasury. Personal funds are used to cover the deficit and work continues. The fight goes on everywhere for a final realization of the law on social welfare. The financial outlook is bad everywhere. But a strong faith is placed in the regulations of the law on social welfare and the conclusion of the current fight for money.

Quite naturally, then, little space in these reports is given to the children themselves and it is actually not possible to tell if good will is enough

---

6   Kazimierz Andrzej Czyżowski (1894–1977), a writer for children and youth whose works included elements of science fiction.
7   Stefan Grabiński (1887–1936), Polish fantasy and horror writer.

to carry out the task the group has taken on or if the children are being properly brought up.

The publications of special issues from various orphanages, edited by the children in these orphanages, should then be greeted with enthusiasm. These publications, the work of the children and their answers to surveys, are the best way to see if an institution is ready to meet the demands of the task it has taken on.

With joy and pride we can note that these publications affirm the general conclusion that our institutions are well run pedagogically and that they have reached a high level. The "Special Issue" published by the Home for Orphans in Lwów on Zborowska 8 has now come out. Heartfelt congratulations are due to the leadership of the institution and especially the educator Dr. Vogelówna for the results of the past year of work. Children in the institution from ages six to fourteen are going to elementary school. Starting at the age of nine, older children take part in common readings of books chosen for discussion and in discussions of papers on different topics. Out of these discussions arise many issues brought up both by the children themselves and by the educational staff.

One has the impression from this "Special Issue" that the educators designed a pedagogical-psychological study intended to evoke a strong intellectual reaction from the children to certain questions, as if the educators wanted to see how independent thought arises in children, how it is developed and formed.

From a discussion of Grabiński's book *Maszynista Grot*, a discussion emerged that lasted several evenings.[8] The question: Do I like the character of the machinist Grot, and is liking such a character even possible? The question of the possibility of excluding the machinist from society led to a lively and passionate discussion. We get to know the character and temperament of each of the children from their responses. Responses to the questions about fantasy or the story of a machinist or a pilot leave us with even more colorful impressions.

---

8 This story appears in Stefan Grabiński, *Demon ruchu* (Warsaw: Księgarni J. Czerneckiego, 1919). See also Grabiński, *The Dark Domain,* trans. Miroslaw Lipinski (Sawtry, UK: Dedalus Limited, 3rd edition, 2013).

Another discussion leads to the question: Do I know the feeling of humiliation, and how do I experience this feeling when someone humiliates me? The responses bring on another question: Can a prize be a humiliation?

The children visited the theater and the movies, leading to a discussion on the topic: Which gives me more, the movies or the theater? The visits also stimulated the directorial talents of the children, who took on the task of arranging, after a single reading of the story, a film scenario for Barwiński's "The Last Night of Kreisler."[9]

The children also had the possibility of learning about Jewish literature on Friday evenings. After reading the works of Sholem Asch, the children responded to the question: How does Sholem Asch depict the life and atmosphere of a small Jewish town? Which description in *Miasteczko* (Shtetl) do you like the most?[10]

In the final accounting we can note that 140 works were read in the home, many of them ten, twelve, thirteen, and even sixteen times.[11] It is regrettable that the readers of each book are not mentioned, as this would offer a basis for getting to know the children better.

Knowing the books read, the older children can be asked: Which books did you like best and why?

One can also see in the "Special Issue" how the younger children develop a critical, observational sense, how they think independently, and how they express their views. Young children respond to the questions: How does the bird from our courtyard spend his day? How does the acacia or rose in our courtyard live its life? What they wish for themselves. A description of winter.

Because it was the tenth anniversary of the home, some of the older children sent in their earlier work for the "Special Issue," of which the

---

9 A reference to Henryk Barwiński (1877–1970), a Polish actor and director involved with school theater programs in the 1920s and 1930s.
10 Sholem Asch (1880–1957), Yiddish novelist and playwright. *A shtetl* was a serialized work (in *Der fraynd*) published in 1904. A Polish translation, *Miasteczko*, appeared in 1910 (Warsaw: Biblioteka Dzieł Wyborowych, E. Nicz, 1910).
11 See also Ellen Kellman, "*Dos yidishe bukh alarmirt!* Towards the History of Yiddish Reading in Interwar Poland," *Polin: Studies in Polish Jewry* 16 (2003): 231–43.

most characteristic for the life of the institution was the story titled "Two Friday Evenings."

The "Special Issue" consistently shows that the home functions at a very high level, that it is led by a professional who plans in advance for the entire year and has as her most important, most essential goal the children's intellectual development, teaching them the habits of independent, critical thinking, of freely expressing their thoughts, and of justifying them.

The impression is often given that the children are given issues that are too lofty, that the discussion evenings become a psychological laboratory with the goal of researching the psychological reactions of individual children. The goal of making it possible to treat each child as an individual is noble, but the work is very difficult, demanding a close relationship with the children and, from the educational side, the obligation to remain on the job for many long years.

Writing about my views on the "Special Issue," I have one reservation. I am personally against listing the children leaving the institution, writing them into the walls of the institution. The reader cannot be sure if the letter reflects the real feelings of the child or if the child is able to express what was actually felt. Publishing these letters conflicts with the goal of the "Special Issue," which is meant to offer the image of the child's intellectual development as a result of the institution's educators. This "Special Issue" offers a model for other institutions of how to lead discussions, how to direct discussions, and how children can be taught to think independently and to express their thoughts.

It should be sincerely wished that each institution in its own time realizes its work in this way and makes such progress with the youth.

Childish Stubbornness: Notes of a Teacher

Tsvi Tarlovski

Nothing is known about the author Tsvi Tarlovski, apart from a note in his byline in the original source that indicates he is from Dąbrowa (Dombrove in Yiddish). Tarlovski describes well the contact between teachers and children. This selection appeared in two parts in *Dos kind* 4, no. 7 (July 1928): 25–26 and *Dos kind* 4, no. 11 (November 1928): 14–16.

A.

The last days of the school year are upon us. There is a strange, nervous mood in class. The children squirm constantly in expectation of the "decree" from the exams. The teacher, not willingly, makes a kind of examination of conscience. Various thoughts bring to mind the strangeness of the child's world; it seems to the teacher, who spends all year with children, that all of a child's virtues and flaws are already well known. The teacher has penetrated the child's very being and psychology. But then facts come and unsettle any certainties.

Today I had such a situation in my class: E. Z-k, a student in the second grade, a very pleasant boy, raised well, who never showed any extra curiosity at play, was distracted during a lesson. Today he suddenly sprung up at the end of the lesson and grabbed a friend's left ear and twisted it . . . as always I thought the teacher's glance would stop the behavior but this time he just twisted the ear with more strength.

I yelled—but it didn't help. After that, I thought a bit and called on him to let go of his friend's ear. But he didn't let go. I tried to pull him by the ear, forcibly, but he pulled, too, holding tight with both hands . . .

I reacted strongly and grabbed the ruler. E. Z-k's face became red. His black eyes were wet with tears. He looked at me again, his eyes filled with tears, begging for mercy but, at the same time, with stubbornness, and the other boy was screaming and bawling from a distance . . .

What to do? How to break such wild stubbornness?—A thought came to me. I took out my watch. It was time for a "break."

And soon the entire class was back out in the schoolyard—of course, everyone except the "two," whom I told to stay behind. In a few minutes when I looked back in on the classroom, I saw both of them sitting there in anger, one moved far away from the other.

And the boy that had been hit said to me, "Teacher, when the class went out on break and no one could see, E. Z-k pulled my ear . . . "

What do you call such stubbornness? I think it's psychological – to be continued in a second essay.

B.

In the process of working out a child's inclinations, desires, and passions, in a word, his "will," often the child's negative traits also arise, which must be eliminated or at least minimized.

It is difficult to describe exactly what is meant by the concept of "stubbornness" and its development. But one thing is clear, the stubborn person never accounts for the effect of his stubborn behavior on himself, though he understands that the consequences of his deeds can be unfavorable both for him and for those around him. In contrast to common sense, he tries with all his might to get his way.

Let's turn now to the case of stubbornness I touched upon in my earlier article.

What is this stubbornness, how do we recognize that it is psychologically grounded? According to my information about the boy and my observations over the course of a longer time, the boy E. Z-k never displayed such stubbornness before. His attitude was always good and his character calm. His little friend, as it was shown, did not do anything to him, he just did not want to whisper an answer to him. This kind of behavior should not have elicited any kind of anger or spoiled their relationship.

What was the cause of such sudden stubbornness and anger? I am convinced that the last days of the school year and exams were the only reason for such a strong psychological change in the child at a certain time.

It was just twenty years ago that the French pedagogue Binet made a careful study of the mental and physical changes in children and youth during the "high holy days" of exams.

Since then we see many of Binet's claims confirmed by many different scholarly facts, which we even see reflected in the daily press when students commit "acts of terror" during examination days. From this we can understand psychologically that the more cheerful, healthy, and capable child is not affected so strongly by the examinations. In our case, as I said earlier, the child was quiet and calm.

The fear before exams, and, in general, the nervous mood in the class, the other embittered students, who perhaps know more and have better chances to move on to a higher level—this all came together in the heart of the child, and, when he had the least opportunity, he lashed out at his friend's ear, calming the anger around him . . .

I see no other recourse to calm such a stubborn child and to free him from his situation, from the teacher and other students. In such upsetting moments there does not exist for the child any teacher, only a tyrant who gives out "bad grades" and yells about exams. Surrounded by his schoolmates, his feelings of stubbornness and ambition are just strengthened.

And, of course, when nobody was in the classroom, he let go of the ear.

If educators and teachers paid more attention to the psychology of children, especially during examination periods, they would handle cases of childish stubbornness and children's misdeeds in a completely different way. And we would come to the conclusion that it would be worthwhile to make a radical change in the system of our "exams."

But this is another topic that should be treated separately.

Pen Strokes (From My Inspections in the Provinces)

A. Goldin

A. Goldin (Aron Goldin) was an employee of the JDC. These short summaries of his inspections in the provinces offer important details about orphan care in small towns. Summaries of inspection reports appeared often in the publications of CENTOS, and they are perhaps the best source for changes in the leadership and activities of the association. The existence of the reports is proof of the bureaucratic nature of the work of the JDC. The relief work sponsored by the JDC was an investment, and the inspection reports were evidence, or lack thereof, of the progress of that investment. Records from the JDC reveal that Goldin lived in Warsaw at Nowolipie 14a in the mid-1930s and that he was the Warsaw representative of the JDC.[1] At the outbreak of the war in 1939 he was acting as general director of CENTOS, according to Barbara Engelking and Jacek Leociak.[2] He appears to have been in Israel during the war and to have tried to go back to Poland in the postwar period. This piece originally appeared in two parts in *Unzer kind* 3, no. 1 (January 1930): 30–34 and *Unzer kind* 3, no. 2 (February 1930): 69–72.

I.

Biecz (western Małopolska).[3] A little *shtetl* with about three hundred Jewish families. About twenty children in private care. The work is hard,

---

1   With thanks to JDC archivist Abra Cohen for this biographical information.
2   Engelking and Leociak, *The Warsaw Ghetto*, 317–18.
3   Baytsh (spelled Bietsh in the text) is located in western Kleyn-poyln in southeastern Poland, 174 miles south of Warsaw, between Gorlice and Jasło. I have used Polish names in the text and given Yiddish transliterations in the notes.

Aron Goldin, Secretary General, CENTOS, Warsaw (American Jewish Joint Distribution Committee Archives)

done in the old way. At the meeting of the general assembly the elderly long-serving chair was selected as a lifetime honorary member of the society. The intelligentsia has joined the new board: the town doctor, lawyers, etc. The Orthodox will also be represented but the elderly former chair stresses that this is not a question of an honor, but a question of work, and the young people will work harder.

Jasło.[4] Also private care but another approach, another appearance. Adorable children, clean, neat, educated, just a few bad children and the chair of the committee yells at them like a real father. But the children must have a room where they can do their lessons and the older ones must learn a trade with good masters. For a hundred *zloty* deposit one can buy for sixty thousand *zloty* over ten years a large house in cooperation with two other groups. And the house can be renovated. They are now restoring it, construction is going on. A celebration: there will be a workshop, a study room, dining hall, and movie theater.

---

4   Yasle (spelled Yaslo in the text) is a larger town in southeastern Poland between Nowy Sącz and Rzeszów.

Descriptions of Homes for Children

Children in the dining hall, summer day camp organized by the Association for Jewish Orphan Care, Kraków, 1930 (Narodowe Archiwum Cyfrowe, Warsaw)

A great faith and ideals help to educate the neglected child.

Nowy Sącz.[5] A larger town. Up to twelve thousand Jewish souls. A lot of intelligentsia. An energetic and indefatigable chair. There is no dormitory. There is probably no need for one. There is a very nice half-dormitory, located in its own building. The financial situation is difficult. They would like to establish a workshop, but they're looking for a new trade for the workshop.

Tarnów.[6] An orphanage for twenty-five children. There is no private care. The board consists of prominent persons who are involved in various party, political, and community affairs. There is never any time, and so the orphanage itself is orphaned. The *kehilah* will perhaps take over the institution. The situation will not improve because those in charge there are the same people, and they are always busy.

---

5 Ney Tsandz (transcription as it appears in the text) is a larger town in western Małopolska.
6 Tarnov (transcription as it appears in the text) is a larger city between Kraków and Rzeszów.

Children playing board games, summer day camp organized by the Association for Jewish Orphan Care, Kraków, 1930 (Narodowe Archiwum Cyfrowe, Warsaw)

Rzeszów.[7] A legacy gift was made. A share of a house. A trial with the heirs is ongoing. In the meantime the orphanage rents space, which is not very comfortable. Crowded. The space is too small; a tailor's workshop is located in the same building. There is a considerable deficit. This is rare in the Kraków region. The central office is engaged with their situation.

Bochnia.[8] Private care. Four full orphans live in a small room. All were under care. Today three of them are already independent and only the youngest sister is still under care. The little room serves as a bedroom, dining room, and tailor's workshop. Behind the curtains is a kitchen. The space is clean, the children are happy, and they are thinking about an intellectual profession for the young girl.

The chairwoman is very energetic. She works like a bee. Modest and serious.

---

7 Reyshe (spelled Reysho in the text) is the largest city in southeastern Poland.
8 Bokhnye (spelled Bokhnia in the text) is a small city between Kraków and Tarnów.

Descriptions of Homes for Children

Wieliczka.[9] The chair is the committee. A young doctor with a kind smile. The city hall helps secure the budget and this works well.

Kraków.[10] An orphanage with a hundred children. A magnificent building. All the necessary facilities. Strong management and educational discipline, but already a little gentler and more Jewish than in years past. There is still the possibility that the institution should rejoin Kraków Central. Some of the reasons that led to the separation have already disappeared. Private care is concentrated in a half-dormitory at the school, which the majority of children attend. There are also two dormitories for sixty boys. There is a plan to combine the two dormitories and, in the space that becomes available, to organize a dormitory for girls. The half-colonies, organized for several hundred children, are also very good. This year the local committee will receive from city hall a long-term lease for an appropriate site that will allow the committee to organize a half-colony for a thousand children. The committee has begun to build the necessary facilities.

The management is in the hands of the aristocracy, with the exception of the dormitories and the boards, which also includes the participation of the democratic element.

Równo.[11] The children, *borukh hashem*,[12] are already living in their own homes, the local dormitory for girls and the dormitory of the central office. It is said in Wołyń with pride that Równo is a little Warsaw. *Nu*,[13] the buildings were built not with money from the local wealthy but, for the most part, with money from the Central.[14] The association stands off to the side and a couple of women bear the burden, God should give them strength. Who is responsible for this? Is the situation in Równo so bad or is it perhaps just that good people have not been found?

---

9   Velitshke (spelled Velitshka in the text) is a smaller town just outside of Kraków.
10 Kroke (transcription as it appears in the text, the Yiddish for Kraków). For additional information on Jewish child welfare in Kraków, see Sean Martin, "Future Generations: Associations for Jewish Children in Kraków, 1918–1945," in *Polin: Studies in Polish Jewry* 23 (2011): 291–320.
11 Rivne (spelled Rovna in the text) is a large city in Volhynia, today western Ukraine.
12 Thank God, blessed is the name of God.
13 Well.
14 Referring to the central office of CENTOS, in Warsaw.

FOR THE GOOD OF THE NATION

Children and their counselors, Pesl Barenholts and Ayzengart, sitting in a circle on the ground in a CENTOS summer camp for orphans, Vladimir-Volynski, 1937 (I. Czterna, photographer, YIVO)

On the walls around the bunks are written inscriptions in honor of the donors. In Kraków there are bricks with the names of donors in the hallways and little tombstones as memorials in the bedrooms. For what? Everyone asks the same thing. One waits for someone bold to take them straight to the administrative office to be written in the *pinkas*.[15]

The central office is noisy and boisterous. They are buying a printing shop to establish a printing school.

Kowel.[16] A former nest of war and pogrom orphans. God sent them an old father and a young mother—and it is all right. Raytse Levin's children, so they call the older children of this professional "parent." She arranged small dormitories in private homes and the children live there as families in modest circumstances. The orphanage was a ruin. It has been talked about, written about, fussed about. The father, the old chair, Mr. Epelboym, considered the situation at length and appeared

---

15   Book of records, or register.
16   Kovle (spelled Kovel in the text) is a larger town northwest of Rivne (Równo), today western Ukraine.

one fine morning to build a home at his own expense. A beautiful building—a worthy thing. Meanwhile he has taken some of the children to his own home.

Włodzimierz.[17] The orphanage is located in an old home that belongs to the *kehilah*. It's a ruin, and it costs much money, effort, and energy to keep it clean. Very crowded. Some children sleep two to a bed. A lot was purchased and brick has been laid. But the construction plan is not approved yet. But in spring the work was begun. Fortunately the board is very close to the children and knows all the details of their lives and needs. The teacher is very devoted and always interested in new thinking, a conference, an outing. She is concerned about the question of qualifications.

In Włodzimierz the caregivers are already working, and they have a lot of money. It seems that next year the caregivers will succeed in pushing through a larger sum for a dormitory.

Uściług (Wołyń).[18] A small little town. They had the ambition to open a day-care facility.[19] A big clean room with a kitchen. The staff—an educator and a woman who cooks. Everything is primitive. Meanwhile ten children have been accepted. If the city will pay out the entire subvention (fifteen hundred *zloty*), they will take in another ten children. Membership dues and other activities are in order. A large committee with a doctor and a school representative at the head. Winter clothing?—old things have been gathered and given to a tailor to work them over. They ask us to visit more often.

Wilno.[20] The city is serious and worried. The people in charge are the same. Poor but proud. The orphanage for girls is located in the cheap apartments of the ICA (International Colonization Association). Everything makes a grave impression. The apartments, the environment,

---

17 Ludmir (spelled Ludmir [Vladimir-volinsk] in the text) is known in Ukrainian as Volodymyr Volyns'kyi, center of Ukraine's Volyn district. It is located east of Zamość, between Lviv and Kovel.
18 Nestile (spelled Ustilug [Volin] in the text) is known as Ustyluh in Ukrainian. It is a small town just west of Volodymyr Volyns'kyi near the contemporary border with Poland.
19 *Halb internat* in the original text, or *półinternat* in Polish. This was a facility for children during daytime hours; children would return to their families at night.
20 Vilne (spelled Vilna in the text).

far from the city. The efforts of the staff are wasted because the office is neglected, cold, and, according to plan, appropriate for a prison. But the board relates that everything is already a little easier: they have already bought a house and will move there in the summer. They will be going into debt, and they will have to pay in installments, and make renovations, but it will bring an end to the suffering.

The way of life—very modest. Every *groshn* is accounted for. The children do not hold it against anybody—What is to be done? They live the same way as everyone else in Wilno.

The institution in the name of Golda Marks (a private home) makes a rare impression. There is no disorder like in a barracks. The darling of the committee. A few animals in the courtyard. Two dogs on chains. The only disruption to this respectable coziness.

The Talmud Torah (an institution for boys) has more than a hundred children. In the institution is a school. A magnificent building. The children are already hardened a little too much. Who is capable of bringing in a little warmth to such a large building?

Infant home. Belongs to TOZ. From the home for infants the children go to the Golda Marks orphanage.

YEKOPO[21] is a separate chapter. YEKOPO concentrates its relief activity on the Wilno region. In Wilno proper they have no institutions for orphans. Only sixty children there are under their care, studying in different trade schools and with private masters and supported by them. The children are from the small *shtetlakh*. Orphaned children from neglected *shtetlakh* and villages.

Nowogródek.[22] A children's home. They become angry when one says "orphan house." The children are happy and energetic. Speaking, smiling,

---

21 YEKOPO is the Russian acronym of Yevreyskiy komitet pomoschi zhertvam voyny (Jewish Relief Committee for War Victims). YEKOPO was formed shortly after the start of World War I as a relief organization. By the early 1920s its work had been absorbed by another organization in the Soviet Union, but the organization still operated as YEKOPO in the provinces of Wilno and Nowogródek.

22 Navaredok (spelled Novogrudek in the text) is a town in the Grodno region of Belarus, between Białystok and Minsk. E. Yerushalmi, ed. *Pinkas Navaredok*, (Tel Aviv, 1963) includes a few pages on both the orphanage and the trade association mentioned here, 107–16.

working, eating—they do everything with courage and energy. Perhaps they have been infected with the energy of the teacher and the goodwill of the chairman.

Two dormitories. One for boys and a second for girls. There is a celebration in the town. Today is the dedication of the new building for the dormitory.

The "Shokdi Trade" Association (Hardworking Trade Association, a trade school) supports the dormitories. They were established in 1872, fifty-eight years ago. The goal—to offer the children of Nowogródek an education in a trade. A type of sponsorship, but more substantial. For the opening of the building an assembly was held in the theater and a banquet in the dormitory. Guests came from Warsaw and Wilno. It was really wonderful! A society, established fifty-eight years ago, carries out constructive relief! Today, its own building, built with miracles and the energetic work of a few community leaders!

In Nowogródek no one knows anything of deceit or trickery. And when the representatives of organizations came to greet us they brought checks for as much as God could help them, which with God's help became a couple of thousand *zloty*. It will of course be put to use: four bare walls—and in a new building everything will seem nicer.

II.

Międzyrzec Podlaski.[23] After the war an American *landsman*[24] purchased an ammunitions warehouse where a place for the orphans was organized. Not considering that the building is a very bad one, the orphan house nonetheless was considered a fine institution among those in the provinces and the education there was completely acceptable. The board manages with the funds from the American *landsmanshaft* and does not need to turn to the city for support. After a short time the *landsmanshaft* took a majority of the children to a farm in Canada. The weaker children remain in the orphanage.

---

23 Mezritsh, a small town north of Lublin, east of Warsaw, and west of Biała Podlaska.
24 A fellow countryman, someone from your hometown or surrounding region.

Corner view of an orphanage in Brest, a two-story building with many chimneys, run by the Organization for Children's Welfare and Orphan Care of Polesie, CENTOS, Central Committee in Pinsk, undated (YIVO)

No money is sent from America now, and nothing is collected from the local community (they live off of reserves), and the orphans live a miserable existence. Of the hundred requests received by the Committee,[25] twenty children are qualified to be taken in by the orphan house, but the board is afraid to do this because America does not send money and they do not trust their own resources. Eight children live now in the large building, in God's care at the edge of the city, miserable, without a teacher.

The representative from the Center made a fuss, appealed to the *kehilah* and the city—perhaps this will change the situation.

Brześć.[26] In the time of the war Brześć was completely destroyed. After the war the population began dying. The misery and need was terrible. Thousands of children were in need of care. Consequently, the number of such children today is still very high.

---

25 The local committee of the CENTOS association in Międzyrzec Podlaski.
26 Brisk (Brest in Belarussian) is a larger city northeast of Lublin, today in southwestern Belarus, close to the Polish border.

Descriptions of Homes for Children

An orphanage for a hundred children. Bought with American money in the name of Rav Soloveitchik.[27] In the orphan house something is lacking, it's hard to say what. Constant renovations and constant moving from one location to another, looking for a solution . . .

A few children are in private apartments under private care and there is a half-dormitory for thirty-five to forty children.

The central office in Polesie supports a dormitory in Brześć for boys who learn a trade in the ORT vocational school. The dormitory has existed for seven years and has strong traditions.

Pinsk.[28] An orphan house and private care. Once there were three orphan houses; today, only one remains. The house was donated by local donors. The institution is reputed to be one of the best. The education of the children is in steady and devoted hands. After a long effort there was success in getting the city to cover the costs of the Pinsk children according to the ministerial norms. The efforts were stubbornly led through the course of many years, and now there is already no distinction between Jewish and non-Jewish children; the Jewish children receive what the law says they should receive.

Because the buildings are old, they are now building a new house. The roof is already on.

A central dormitory for girls in a separate building was opened this year in Pinsk. Very *heymish*.[29] Small rooms for two, three, or four children.

The central office for Polesie is also in this building. There is a strong tie and constant contact with the departments. The authorities take care of all matters related to Jewish orphan care in Polesie through the central office.

Białystok.[30] An exemplary organization. All institutions are managed through one city committee. Great deficits—but the children lack nothing.

In the small rooms of the central office come together the threads of all of the departments of the *województwo*.[31]

---

27 Rabbi Hayim Soloveichik (1853–1918), also known as R. Hayim Brisker, son of Rabbi Yosef Dov Soloveichik. Rabbi Hayim Soloveichik was known as an outstanding Talmudist.
28 Pinsk, city in the region of Polesie, southwest of Minsk.
29 Familiar, welcoming, cozy, intimate.
30 Byalistok.
31 Administrative division, sometimes rendered in English as voivodeship or province.

The organization is led with a sure hand.

Lwów.³² A lot of institutions. Each institution has its own office, which is tied directly to the central committee. Bad times, the shiny appearance seen from the outside is already gone. Above all the situation of the dormitories, in which are concentrated many children from the provinces, is difficult.

Private care is very well established. A special office oversees the work.

The central office concentrates the work of three districts: Lwów, Stanisławów, and Tarnopol. An enormously large region. Most of those working are intellectuals with diplomas. Many children's institutions. The vocational schools and workshops that arose through the initiative of the central office for orphans are mostly under the auspices of the Union for Trade Education in Galicia (Farband farn fakh-shulvezn in Galitsie).

The central office publishes the monthly *Przegląd Społeczny* with the support of the all-Polish union of central offices.

Żółkiewka.³³ An average *shtetl*. A beautiful little orphan house, a tailor school for girls. It is not necessary to search for the chair; he is always in the institution from early in the morning. I met him during his work: he was arguing with a master who had not required an orphan to fulfill the terms of the orphan's duties.

Stanisławów.³⁴ An orphan house, a foundling house (just recently opened), a boys' dormitory, a girls' dormitory, a farm for girls, and a tool and die workshop. Each institution has its own office. Tested community leaders. Separate buildings. It is not known how all of these institutions will be supported.

Dębina.³⁵ A sanitarium for children with lung illnesses. Children from Lwów and Kraków, Bielsk Podlaski and from Włodzimierz, and from

---

32   Lemberg, L'viv in today's Ukraine.
33   Zhl'kefke (spelled Zshulkiev in the text) is a small town southeast of Lublin.
34   Stanisle (spelled Stanislavov in the text) is today Ivano-Frankivsk in western Ukraine, southeast of Lwów and northwest of Chernivtsi.
35   Dembine (as spelled in the text) is a village in the region of Lwów. For a brief description of the sanitarium, see Anna Jakimyszyn, "Organized Recreation-Curative Stays for Adults and Children: An Analysis of Cases from the Lvov Area from the Interwar Period," *Scripta Judaica Cracoviensia* 12 (2014): 94.

Warsaw and Pruzhany. In the mountains, far from people, there is a staff that sacrifices its time and efforts for the Jewish child. And you go away from there with a blessing on your lips.

Złoczew.[36] It is very cozy in the orphan house. An energetic chairman, knows all the details. Six children work on tricot machines in the workshop of the orphan house. The machines are getting old, and they are looking for money to get new ones.

The children in private care live in terrible conditions. Such poverty, for which the commission can offer no advice, is seldom seen.

---

36 Zlotshev (as spelled in the text) is a small town southwest of Łódź.

Images of Youth in School Publications

Leon Gutman

Leon Gutman worked with the JDC, but further details of the nature of his role with the JDC are unknown. This Polish-language review of Yiddish-language publications reveals connections between Polish-speaking Jews and the Yiddish speakers they served. This selection originally appeared in *Przegląd Społeczny* VII, no. IX–X (September–October 1933): 212–14.

Since the time school ceased to be the site of the mechanical transfer of a greater or lesser measure of knowledge from the older to the younger generation, the school publication appeared, alongside other products of the independent work of youth. The founding of these publications was not so much for didactic reasons, or for reasons of style or imagination, but to get to know the psychology of the child who found the publication an instrument to express thoughts and feelings. The most honest school writing, written for a grade, naturally could not include the experiences of the young person—mainly because of a lack of freedom and feelings of fear. And in addition to classroom work the educators have the opportunity to observe during adventures on field trips, in evening activities, etc., how great the difference is between students in class during lessons and students understood as individuals. Completely different criteria for the evaluation of a given individual can be seen then, criteria that in the end can lead to a reevaluation of the school's direction and goals. This beautiful collection of excerpts from the institutions of the Białystok Association for the Care of Jewish Orphans (published by the Central Pedagogical Council in Białystok in 1932) confirms our conviction that to get to know and evaluate a child, an official classification on the basis of assigned lessons is not enough. An educational examination must go much deeper. Reading the numerous statements of the children, we are aware that the period of youth cannot and should not be just an introduction to the life ahead. Youth itself is the end. Thoughts about the future should not keep the children from fulfilling themselves today or cut them off from contact with reality. This mania about the future, seen in the workload, in the grading scale, etc., is expressed bluntly in the seemingly satirical confession of the thirteen-year-old girl Cipa F., who uses the phrase "who by water, who by fire" (mi bamajim, mi baejsz).[1] Others complain about "difficult studies, I study all day" (szwere limudim, gance tejg lern ich), and so on. One student emphasizes the stress before a meeting reviewing his work: "my heart was beating like a clock" (di harc hot mir geklopt, wi a zajger), though from the result of the review we learn that he was a good student. The mood in the classroom awaiting a new teacher is always fearful: what will she be like? The children sense that dangerous bureaucracy has crept into the school here and there—and even infected their colleagues on duty, who, to serve the city, surrender to the obligation of "the custom of bureaucracy" (den minhag fun biurokratizm). The student Geir (seventeen years old) obligingly relates that even small children take their turns on duty, in order to develop a feeling of responsibility and respect for a given thing or idea. The youth have an advanced understanding of the concept of social obligation, of working for others. The awareness that someone leaving the walls of the school and going out into life has a serious battle ahead ("a wek tif in leben" in the midst of life) is a "general fact." The child then examines his conscience and is aware of his fate and that society is proud that he will be training as an apprentice, proud that he was raised to work (Eli Warszawiak, eighteen years old). Much space here is devoted to descriptions of nature and the love of nature. We are pleased to see that Jewish youth have come to love and become intimate with nature, that the fear of nature and excessive love of

---

[1] This Hebrew phrase is taken from "U-netaneh tokef" (Let us cede power), a prayer for Yom Kippur, the Day of Atonement. It is derived from a poem written by an unknown author in northern Europe about a thousand years ago. The poem is about how we might die, by water or fire, and the fate we might suffer in the next year; prayer and righteousness may mitigate this fate.

books in the diaspora has passed; we do not think badly of Bergman who was distracted from his lessons by thoughts about the hill in the forest (F. Berman, fourteen years old).² And there are sincere descriptions of how much the children are cut off from experiences of the natural world, such as the description of the *kheyder*, where the *rebe* continually threatens and the child "cytert," trembles, during "ferheren" when he is asked a question, and the child is grateful that "I am already over that" (abi ech bin szojn aryber). Among the descriptions of nature are hymns in praise of the sun, squirrels, the forest, rivers, birds, etc.: "it's a shame to go away from the hill" (a szud awekcyfuren fun den bergel) and "when we walked away we turned our heads in order to catch another look at the beautiful hill!" (wen mir zenen wekgegangen, hoben mir gehalten yn ajn ausdrajn di kep, kdej noch chapen a kuk ofn liben berg!). This youth who embraces such signs of life knows that he lives and will certainly not suffer in sickly dilemmas about himself, but he will find his life's goal in work and in his social obligations. And for this his teachers deserve thanks and wishes for having fulfilled the difficult educational task of leading children toward the sun and to work for others.

---

2   The inconsistency in the spelling of the name, Bergman or Berman, is in the original text.

The Strike: An Image of Dormitory Life

Yakov Sarner

Yakov Sarner illustrates the tension that arises when adults attribute to children a measure of self-rule. He depicts children wishing to go on "strike," illustrating the tension between the desire to let children make decisions for themselves and the authority of adults. Conceptions of self-rule and children's courts were common in many of the associations of CENTOS. There is no indication given of the location of the school.

Nothing is known of the life of the author. This piece originally appeared in *Dos kind* 11, no. 4/5 (April–May 1934): 10–12.

The children have just finished breakfast. Some gather together for school, some prepare to tidy up their rooms, but a small group of children of preschool age get together in the corner and begin to play eagerly.

"Children!" sounds the call of the teacher, "Pair up and go down to the school." (The institution has its own preschool in the same courtyard. The children go to it but not gladly.)

"We don't want to go!" screams one of the children.

"We want to play by ourselves!" calls out a second.

"It's boring there!" adds a third.

"Khevre Pletzl" (Pletzl Group), the teacher complains again, "If you do not go to school again today, you will not get a roll for a snack as your punishment." The threat works a little, and the group of youngsters pairs up and goes into the preschool.

Going through the empty courtyard, some of them forget the way to the preschool and stop by the bench between the big chestnut trees. The spring warmth and freshness of the early morning air overcomes the teacher's warning and the promise made to her. It doesn't take long before an entire dormitory is created among the benches, with bedrooms, a storage space, and with women as teachers and educators. The roles are divided up, some call out, others stand with uncovered heads, others spin in a circle, and life in the dormitory is copied with great similarity in the play of the children. About ten minutes later, when the teacher goes to the courtyard to check if the children are already in school, she sees that they are so engrossed that they do not even notice she is there, so she observes them closely several minutes longer.

The teacher decides not to disturb their play. They don't notice as she leaves and she starts preparing bread instead of the roll the children are supposed to get for a snack.

At eleven o'clock one of the children shows up with a demand: we want rolls! "The children who are in preschool have already gotten them, the children who are not in school will not get them," answers the woman in charge. With no alternative, the child inevitably moves to the bread. The bread is devoured, and then a second child comes, and after him, the rest. Quietly, a little ashamed, they eat quickly and run off to play some more.

Lunch came and went as usual, the children leaving after eating. Only those whose duty it was to return to the dining room to clean up remained. Blimke and Perel from the preschool were on duty to tidy up the dining room after the first lunch (not all the children eat lunch together, a larger part of them are still in school). This is the chore assigned to them, an assignment they achieved with great effort, after passing an exam. But Blimtsie roams around the room and Perele doesn't move from her spot. "Blimtsie," calls the teacher, "start cleaning up, it's getting late." But Blimtsie doesn't think about starting to do something. She just screams out: I want a roll! "Perele," the teacher interrupts again, "maybe you want to get to work?" But Perele answers simply: "If Blimtsie doesn't want to, I don't want to, either. We want a roll." "Are you hungry?" asks the teacher. "No, but we want a roll." Three children from the preschool group say the same thing. And, even more, they are all sitting on one bench, with stretched out hands, crying, "We want a roll, we don't want to sweep, we want a roll."

The original strike interests the teachers and they wait for the end with curiosity.

When the foolish Dvora shows up, wanting to clean up the room, the teachers dismiss her, not wanting to allow any strikebreakers.

The clock strikes three. The teacher M. gathers together the older children and goes with them to class to help them prepare the assigned lessons in school. She warns the striking children they should not disturb her, because she will not give them a roll. They should clean up, because they have not kept their word and, even more, have not gone in to school.

In ten minutes the classroom door opens. Blimtsie's head can be seen in the doorway, and a cry is heard: "We want a roll!" M. goes out and warns them not to disturb their work; if they do, she will make them stand in the corner. The other children stand looking perplexed and begin to wonder about seeking advice on how to get a roll.

When the manager shows up, they all run to her crying, "We want a roll!"

"Go and ask M. if you can go to school tomorrow!" the manager advised. The group likes the idea. They line up and march like soldiers into the classroom to talk to the teacher. But M. just becomes angrier because the noise they make disrupts the children who are working, and she shows them the door. The group goes back with downcast heads, not knowing how to end their fight for a roll. They turn to the manager again, telling her that her first advice failed and asking what to do next.

"You know what, children?" the manager advises, "clean up the dining room together and put it back in order, and I will go in with you to the teacher. Everyone should be very quiet."

The dining room was cleaned up right away. The group, with Blimtsie in the lead, went with the manager into the classroom.

Blimtsie, ashamed, moves ahead and makes her claim, "We have cleaned the dining room, we will obey, we will go to school, but we want a roll."

The manager confirms that they have cleaned everything up and everything is in order.

In a few minutes the group is sitting by the table and heartily eating the rolls and screaming triumphantly, "We have rolls! We have rolls!"

The next morning before eight in the morning the group is ready and marches straightaway into the school. They are looking forward to their rolls.

III

Home for Jewish Children and Farm in Helenówek

Education or Crime? From the Diary of an Educator

Yekhiel Ben-Tsiyon Kats

In *Education or Crime? From the Diary of an Educator*, Yekhiel Ben-Tsiyon Kats presents a series of vignettes focusing on the interaction between educators and children at Helenówek, an institution for Jewish children on the outskirts of Łódź. Kats is most concerned with what he identifies as the hypocritical nature of the work of Jewish child welfare leaders, especially those connected to Helenówek. In his telling, these leaders of Polish Jewry want to show that they care about children and the poor but, in his view, they are not genuinely concerned with efforts to help. Working for an institution such as Helenówek is simply a way to showcase their supposed charity, not a sincere attempt to change the living conditions of those in need.

Kats made an effort to disguise the identity of Helenówek and its location in the city of Łódź, but this effort was only half-hearted. The details describing both the institution and city lead the reader to conclude, definitively, that Kats is describing Helenówek. He mentions the industrial nature of the city, the neighborhood of Bałuty, and a hospital named after Izrael Kalmanowicz Poznański (1833–1900), a prominent textile manufacturer and philanthropist.

Kats's intent was to shame some of the Jewish community's most important leaders in childcare and education. But the subjective nature of his work makes it a problematic source and—other than the text's publication by CENTOS in *Dos kind*—I have not found that his critique of Helenówek found an audience and resulted in substantial reforms. I have included the translation of his text in this volume because his extended

Helenówek, Łódź, before 1939 (Massuah Institute for Holocaust Studies)

descriptions of life in an institution offer us a look inside a significant Jewish institution in one of Poland's largest cities. Moreover, these descriptions are not entirely dissimilar from those presented by other authors, writing about different institutions in different places.[1]

Kats describes how the institution operated. For example, he relates how storeowners supplied the orphanage with different products. He claims this system was abused, that storeowners offered the institution the worst products but charged exorbitant prices. He describes how the custodial staff destroyed tables to use the wood for fuel. While this is only a portrayal of one institution, Kats's text suggests the necessity of determining if similar incidents occurred in other institutions. Kats also addresses the issue of children coming into and leaving the institution. He is most concerned with how the children will fare outside of Helenówek.

---

1 For an overview of other institutions in Łódź, see Nella Stolińska-Pobralska, *Instytucje opieki nad dzieckiem w międzywojennej Łodzi* (Łódź: Wydaw. Wyższej Szkoły Humanistyczno-Ekonomicznej, 2002), and Teodor Sujczyński, "Szkoły specjalne i internaty dla dzieci moralnie zaniedbanych w Łodzi w latach 1921–1939," *Przegląd historyczno-oświatowy* 31, no. 4 (1988): 465–83.

The text is unusually frank in its description of children's sexual development. Kats recounts his perceptions of same-sex behavior among girls, his observations of the teenagers' sexually charged play, and incidents of masturbation. He also includes the stories of others who accused Khayim Rumkowski, the director, of sexual assault and other physical abuse. Kats's candid portrayal of these issues reveals the issues teachers and workers had to confront. To buttress these claims, Kats includes testimonies, awkwardly presented, at the conclusion of the text. They appear to come from the conversations of other teachers or workers at Helenówek with children who are no longer at the institution. Kats has compiled two statements from another teacher at Helenówek, Franka Oksenhendler. She has passed on statements of former residents and, it appears, asked them to confirm the truth of these statements. Two additional statements do not give full names of the former residents. He then cites statements from other former teachers at Helenówek and juxtaposes them with the glowing statements from guests and community leaders. Kats describes these children as having "escaped," terminology that itself reinforces his view of the institution as more like a prison than an educational facility.

This exposé of Helenówek, clearly one-sided, nonetheless offers readers a comprehensive look at the various activities taking place in a home for Jewish children before the war. *Education or Crime?* was published separately by Farlag "Dos kind" in Warsaw in 1933. As Kats mentions in the introductory material, portions of this text appeared separately in *Dos kind*. The subheadings, breaks in the text, italicization, and changes in font appear in the original.

Foreword

The education of the young, growing generation is one of the most important tasks for which society is responsible. The tiniest mistake, the least detour from the right way may yield difficult, even dangerous results for the child, for the child's education and spiritual development. Therefore, the relationship between the teacher and educator and his tasks and duty regarding the child demands special care.

Unfortunately, we do not encounter examples of this relationship, even among teachers and educators, let alone those culture workers who may certainly not know what to do or what not to do when working with a child.

Both men and women involved in community service think that if they are not professionally involved with children then they are not obligated to learn what is helpful and what is harmful for the child.

Very often the result is that, instead of being useful for the child, these men and women create only misery and pain, and the good intentions of those who want to create only the best and most beautiful for these children become a source of unnecessary moral misery for everyone and difficult psychological experiences for the child, whose soul is crippled and mind is dulled. In this way a situation is created, often against the will of the child's caretaker, in which the caretaker's work becomes destructive and harmful both for the child and for society. The educational work in this case is not useful at all, just the opposite—it is a criminal act, criminal toward the child and toward society.

The worst is that the majority of people who commit these crimes refuse to give any kind of account of their actions, because they are not aware that what they are doing is wrong.

Yekhiel Kats deserves praise for this collection of lively facts from an orphanage, revealing life behind the scenes at such an institution. He does not show us the external, attractive side of the institution, which is easy for everyone to see. Instead, he uncovers for us the inner side of the institution, usually covered up for outsiders and not visible to the casual visitor.

As a thoughtful teacher, he also penetrates the secrets of the children's souls, uncovering for us their experiences, their joys and sufferings, in relation to the "regime" which prevails at the institution and the educational methods used there.

It is important that the educator, teacher, and intelligent community leader involved in child care should get to know the contents of this interesting book. This will protect more than one of them from harmful and painful errors or mistakes, which, unfortunately, occur mainly when working with poor and defenseless children.

Dr. M. Peker

How Long Can We Remain Silent?

It has already been some time since Yekhiel Kats printed a series of revelations in *Dos kind* about an orphanage. Kats was once a teacher in this orphanage and he is an eyewitness. He describes what he alone has seen, and what he has seen is terrible, horrific!

We return to the topic not out of any pleasure but to disturb the "ideal" silence, even great peace, which was in no way disturbed upon the publication of these gruesome deeds, which cry to the heavens!

The children in the institution—the most miserable of the miserable poor little orphans and "throwaways"—have gone through hell in the "caring" home for orphans.

When a child comes to sit quietly to eat after being in the field where he has been singing and jumping, and he does not follow the orders of the director, he gets slapped . . .

The educator and the teacher are on the side of the director ("Feliks is good for nothing . . .").

A mentally retarded orphan lies with a high temperature and howls in misery—and no one looks in on him, no one helps him, no one goes to him.

And later a poor girl is convinced that she will find work in town. She is given a few rags and left in the care of God—to get rid of her ("Gutshe can dance and sing . . .").

When an eleven-year-old boy forgets what the teacher has said and runs again to see how the older children draw, the chair singles him out and slaps him loudly in the presence of the children and the entire staff.

When a young boy answers the chair's question about whether he has relatives in town by saying no, he has no one, the chair delivers him a terrible blow to the head.

A deathly silence follows. Some on the staff agree with the given judgment; others stay silent out of fear ("Josek's Court Martial").

There is one especially cruel example from all of these awful misdeeds which makes one shiver:

The question of children wetting the bed at night is a real issue in the orphanage. At a meeting of the educators, teachers, director, doctor, and chair, it was decided . . . in the case of one child, to not allow him to eat and drink on a regular basis; in the case of another, to allow the child to eat just once a day; and for a third, to allow the child to eat twice a day or only to drink.

When Kats turned to the teacher and said that the three-and-a-half-year-old Liltshe should be allowed to eat and drink, that she should be cared for and kept warm, she said that the chair singled Liltshe out and threatened her with the stick, saying he "will break her of this" (*a three-and-a-half-year old!*).

When a starving child does not work, the chair cruelly takes a stick to a three-and-half-year old child . . .

The girl was so tortured that she got a fever and was sent to the city hospital . . . ("Liltsha's Father")

This is not a chronicle of times long past, this is not occurring somewhere in Honolulu, in deepest Asia or Africa. This is a part of the daily practice in a Jewish orphanage in Poland, which is under society's "supervision."

In September 1926, when the Polish press printed revelations about the institution for delinquent children in Studzieniec, public opinion was outraged because of the misdeeds that occurred there. A trial was conducted against the guilty, who were punished harshly.

This case does not even concern "delinquent" children—the only "crime" of these children is that their parents died before their time . . .

The facts, as Kats has published them, call for a strong reaction, especially in light of the article published by D. Khoynik about the terrible conditions in the orphan homes in Wilno (in *Dos kind*, No. 7 from 1931).[2]

Can we overlook such deeds in complete silence?

Sh. Z. Vulf[3]

(*Dos kind*, No. 2/3, 1932)

---

[2] This issue of *Dos kind* is not included in the collections of YIVO or Biblioteka Narodowa in Warsaw.
[3] Sh. Z. Vulf was a pen name used by Shmuel Vulman (1896–1941). He served as editorial secretary of *Dos kind*. He was a popular Yiddish-language poet and prose writer. See the entry on Vulf in *Leksikon fun der nayer yidisher literatur* ed. Shmuel Niger and Yankev Shatski (New York: Alveltlekhn Yidishn Kultur-Kongres, 1956–81).

Introduction from the Author

I arrived to work in an institution for abandoned children. As a teacher, I began to keep a diary, as usual, so I would be able to keep track of and analyze my work and the work of others. This diary has fulfilled its task. It grew into an accusation against those working in the orphanage, who directly and indirectly defend everything that occurs with the orphans in this institution. It is not my fault that the role of accuser of all those who abuse the abandoned children has fallen to me. I would be happy if my accusations would, at last, resonate appropriately and save all of the unfortunate abandoned children who find themselves in the hands of the *kahal*[4] "fathers."

Naively, I tried to publish excerpts from my diary in the daily Yiddish press—to no avail. I later sent the editor of *Unzer kind*, the organ of CENTOS, the article I published in *Dos kind*, No. 4, 1932, "A Guest is Coming," but they did not publish it.

I was convinced that if the first part of the diary appeared, showing the hell in which these abandoned children live, the first to try to save the unfortunate children would be those working in the orphanage.

But nobody reacted to my revelations. They remained a "voice in the desert."

I then put a notice in *Dos kind* that I was prepared at any time to give statements and to work with others to eliminate the wrongdoing on behalf of the abandoned children, but our "society" was not at all interested.

Furthermore, the orphan remains an object, the same as other goods, for those who work with institutions for abandoned children. Some seek honor there. Some have businesses and have found there a market for their goods. An engineer, lawyer, or doctor is favored by the chair of such an institution, others in turn want to be his secretary, in order to collect a salary from the budget they collected for the abandoned children; others want to find a job for a spinster daughter, a son, or an impoverished brother-in-law who has no livelihood.

---

4 The committee that served as the Jewish community council or the smaller committee that governed the *kehilah*.

The majority of the orphan caretakers are not suited to community service or the work of education—a lot of them simply hate children—and they make decisions about educational matters!

Most of the board members with pedagogical qualifications in the field have almost no authority over the child; authority is in the hands of the storeowners who deal with herring, leather, iron, or who have a tavern or a bar . . . When "patrons" from the free professions, such as doctors and lawyers, find themselves among the representatives on the boards of the institutions, they are mostly there just for decoration . . .

The personnel accepted for work in the institutions are primarily older women and men or young women without any employment. Having the patronage of a woman or man on the board of an institution is enough to become a teacher. The teachers who come with qualifications must very often give up their positions in the workplace because they have no authority in the institution. The teacher who does something for a neglected child out of love and devotion will be removed from his position. It happens that teachers who do not allow abuse of the children by the trustees, or the beating or demoralization of the children, are thrown out. Qualified teachers who are not "servants" of the board are very few.

The men and women who "care" for the neglected children hold to the rule that a well-raised child is one who kisses the board members on the hand upon greeting them and on saying goodbye, tips his cap and bows to the ground, and knows all the "fine" manners that are accepted in "better" society. The child may hate these women and men or do the things demanded to be a "well-raised" child and to win the favor of his masters . . .

The "caretakers" of these neglected children demand that the floors and shiny brass door handles of this luxurious institution should always be clean. The main entrance must always be closed and opened only for guests or board members. If a chair should see that a child throws a piece of paper down or plays with a ball on the floor or cuts out a doll and leaves some cloth on the table or carves something with a stick—danger! The child comes to his attention and the child's teacher is seen as "worthless" because he lets the child move freely and develop according to his will and play when he likes. There are even institutions where the children can play and participate in sports in special recreation halls, but not when the child wants, only according to a specific schedule. These "caretakers" have heard something about modern pedagogy.[5] And they try it out. One can even find in these institutions specially designed workshops. But these workshops are mostly nothing more than advertising. These workshops are cleaner and more "orderly" than the office of a director of a ministry . . . The workshops and sports halls exist in the wealthier institutions only to show the various guests that the institution is directed in line with new pedagogical norms, the "modern" norms of the "intelligent" people educating the neglected children.

At the end of the book I offer a few opinions from authorities, pedagogues, community activists, editors, and journalists who have visited the home I describe in my diary.

These people have written about the institution without knowing the actual situation. They have indirectly helped the "trustees" to advertise, to gain others' trust. The honored guests who come to visit as researchers or as devoted community activists unwillingly bring the greatest misfortune to the neglected children who find themselves in the institutions. I am certain that many of them will be filled with regret when they read what I have written. But they can make up for their transgression when they devote themselves fully to their work and help to save thousands of children.

I believe that then the neglected children of this and also of all other institutions will be saved and one will no longer need to write articles but only to do the practical work on behalf of the helpless children.

If this will happen, my book will have served its purpose.

The Institution at a Glance

Six kilometers from a large industrial city is located an institution to protect and educate, supported by the community. Officially the

---

5 Articles in *Przegląd Społeczny* and *Dos kind* often refer to the leaders of "modern pedagogy," for example, the Italian physician and educator Maria Montessori (1870–1952) and American philosopher John Dewey (1859–1952). They also refer to historical figures such as the Swiss educational reformer Johann Heinrich Pestalozzi (1746–1827) and his student, Friedrich Froebel (1782–1852), who is widely regarded as the originator of kindergarten.

Home for Jewish Children and Farm in Helenówek

institution is a special organization with a board, the head of which is a chair, R., who moves in "better" society as a man of "distinction."[6]

Most of the children there are from L. and the surrounding region. They are, for various reasons, without parents or the care of a family. Half and full orphans, older children found spending days, weeks, or months on the streets between the factories and courtyards, or children brought from the municipal home for foundlings. Some have parents who are chronically ill; others have parents who received long sentences for political or criminal acts or other reasons.

The voivodeship, city hall, the Jewish community, and wealthy people who had to take in orphans send children to the institution. These groups support sixty percent of the children in the institution; the institution itself pays for the remaining forty percent from inheritances left by the rich.

The children, 120 boys and girls, can be divided by age into the following groups: a "day care" for two- to four-year-olds; a pre-school for four- to seven-year-olds; and a separate four-grade elementary school for children from ages seven to sixteen. There are also youth from sixteen to twenty years old who no longer attend school but work in the administration of the institution. The institution owns thirteen acres of land and woods. There is a luxurious four-floor house with all the amenities, including four bedrooms, a dining room, a theater room, bathing facilities, two storage areas for food and clothing, special rooms for workshops (tailoring and shoemaking), a separate one-floor building for the school and its workshop, and another separate building for a children's hospital. In a fourth building can be found a *shul* for prayer on Shabes and holidays. The institution has its own generator to create electricity. There is also a laundry.

---

6 This description fits Helenówek, located just outside of Łódź and led by Rumkowski. Kats seems to have wanted to disguise the identity of the institution, yet he is not consistent throughout the text. Other identifying details, such as the name of the Bałuty neighborhood and street names, give away the identity of the city. This thin disguise mars Kats's credibility. The institution is not identified clearly, but, in the end, it is unmistakably Helenówek. In spite of the strength of his rhetoric, Kats does not make his accusations about Helenówek or Rumkowski as directly as possible. Perhaps this is why his accusations did not evoke a more significant response from the officials of CENTOS.

There is also a separate wooden building for other inventory, both living and dead: a coop with a larger number of poultry of different types; a beehive; a stall for horses and cows; a barn for straw and hay; a greenhouse; and their own bakery.

Twenty-two people work in the institution: directors, teachers, educators, an agronomist, preschool teachers, a tailor, a cobbler, nurses, washerwomen, servants, a doctor, and an agronomist-engineer.

This is the impression made by this splendid institution when one sees it from the outside, superficially.

We will soon acquaint our readers with the *inside* of this same institution. Readers will see that this institution was not built to aid the abandoned children. It does not serve the needs of society. It does not educate. Rather, everything it does is against education, against what is beneficial.

A senator from America, on a visit to the institution, said to me:

"If it were half as luxurious, if there were simple buildings and more care for the littlest children—the institution would be a blessing. As it is now, it is, for the abandoned children, a curse."[7]

The Children Arrive . . .

April 4, 1930[8]

A little man, drenched, skinny, with a beard, a big hat on his head; on his feet a pair of large, heavy army boots; a three-year-old child in his arms, wrapped in a towel that was once black but now has the colors of the rainbow . . . holding by the hand a pale six-year-old girl with a head of unruly black hair and shoes that are dirty and torn and too big for her feet.

He had received a letter from the institution's chair that his children would be accepted.

Why does he bring his children here? What does this little man have to do with such "high ranking people"? Maybe he will pay for the children. If there is money, everything is okay . . .

---

7 I have not been able to find another reference to this visit of a United States senator.

8 Kats does not present these vignettes in chronological order.

When this little man put the children on the floor, he sighed and barely stood on his feet, his face lit up with joy, finally his children will be happy . . .

He answers my formal questions about the children he brought.

"One child," he says, "is already here with you, Ester-Malke."

I mention that he brought her here three months ago, in a jacket that was torn and thin, without any shirt. Her face was white as chalk, no trace of blood in the face at all. With time she has fit in with the other children.

The father of these three children tells the following story:

"It's already been nine months since their mother died; the oldest," he points to Ester-Malke. "the city hall in L. sent me to you. She did not want to go without the two young boys. She cried . . . I am a porter of factory boxes. Since my wife died, I earn barely nothing, one *gildn* a day is a lot. This is mostly because of the crisis, the main thing is that I have to stay at home with the children. They are still just little kids, babes."

"And who cooks for them?" I ask.

"Sometimes we eat dry bread, sometimes the neighbors give us a bit of something cooked."

"Who makes their beds?"

"I do."

"If you're not working, what do you live on?"

He sighs, deeply.

"Yes, food, about food I said earlier, I get a little help from the city, from the *kahal*, and sometimes I have the chance to go out in the street and earn a few *zloty*. Now, after nine months, I have gotten the city to take the two children from me and to support them in the institution." He smiles, pleased, and admits:

"Now I will be able to make some money more quickly, because at home I will only have the boy." (He points to a pale ten- to eleven-year-old boy.)

When all the children are gathered in a group, the father and his children in the middle with Ester-Malke, the little man takes a string of large, black wooden beads from his pocket and places it on Ester-Malke's neck. The six-year-old girl cries out, Ester-Malke lowers her head, and the tattered little man with four children stands with tears in his eyes . . . The ten-year-old boy goes to his father and hugs him . . .

I interrupt the silence and say to the father that wearing black beads is not allowed in the institution.

The father answers me:

"She understands some things already, for a year a daughter without a mother must wear black beads . . ."

Ester-Malke is glad her siblings have come. She smiles to them, caresses them, the little man takes his companion by the hand, his only *kaddish*,[9] the ten-year-old boy. He cries and kisses the other children and goes "home" to Bałuty,[10] to carry his packages among the tall smoky chimneys of the factories . . .

The newly arrived children already officially belong to the community—the community fulfills its duty. The conscience is clean . . . The city pays for the children. For the older girl, a hundred *zloty*, and for the younger girl, up to eighty *zloty* a month. If the father got this money in his hands, he would be able to hire someone to help and he could live well. The father could live from this money, too. But the father does not deserve such trust. The money cannot be entrusted to him to take care of his children. And the institution that protects and educates can do whatever it wants with the money!

The fate of the children now depends on the mercy of the "trustees," "merciful people," "fathers of the orphans," and "goodhearted women" . . . The community has little to say about it and says nothing, although it pays the price.

Now the father must stand behind the office doors, or behind the door of the private apartment of the chair or other board members, and ask for permission to see his children.

The answer is always: This is a closed institution. "Shlepers"[11] are not allowed to come and go.

---

9 The male heir.
10 Balut, in Yiddish. It is a village near Łódź that was incorporated into the city in 1915. Approximately half of the city's Jews lived in this area.
11 Vagrants.

On the side he asks, very naively and shyly, the teachers standing around and, separately, me:

"Watch after them, I beg of you."

The teachers answer with sympathy:

"Don't worry. Everything will be taken care of."

Purim in the Dormitory

March 13, 1930

The man in the long robe, who comes to us from the city every holiday in order to lead us through the traditional rituals, settles down in the *shul* and begins to read the *megila*.[12] The children come together and bring with them sticks, boards of different kinds that have been planed, and *gregers*.[13] Apparently, they started this earlier in the evening, before the *megila* reading, because when there is clapping at the mention of Haman, the children come in with little knives in their hands and finish afterwards with the *gregers*. Others clap holding a shoe with a wooden sole in one hand and, with the other, a wooden board, clapping them together with all their strength. And revenge is taken on Haman. Some of the children sit on the floor with a stick in their hands. They sit this way so they are prepared. When they hear the word Haman, clapping begins for a few minutes and it does not help to quiet it. An older boy stands by the reader and holds a pointer in his hand, looking into the *megila*. He gives the "command" to make noise with the *greger*s. Of course, this boy doesn't pay attention and often gives the command at the wrong time, and the group starts clapping . . . There's no way to stop them. If one of the Haman clappers becomes "hoarse," that is, messes up, soon there will be a movement to find a "master" who can hurry to take his place in the group. They switch off to see whose weapons work better. Until the last Haman, fresh clappers come with cut up boards, taken with permission from the workshops—they clap, as a "mitsva" . . . The reader does his work, singing the *nign*[14] with emphasis . . .

---

12 Refers to a scroll of the book of Esther, read on the occasion of Purim, the holiday celebrating the deliverance of the Jews from the persecution of the Persian Haman.

13 A *greger* is a rattle or noisemaker to be used whenever the name of Haman is read.

14 Melody, tune.

Feliks is Worthless

December 31, 1929

Feliks is eleven years old. He is in the second grade in the institution's school. It was very hard for him to get used to the dry topics in school. He used to like drawing and painting with colors, those things he was not usually asked to do.

When I arrived at the institution, the children in second grade told me that they have one friend who is very strong and does gymnastics, and all sports, better than all the other children. Feliks was indeed a normal, healthy, well-developed boy.

Today is a cold, muddy, autumn day. We went walking in the field to observe the changes in nature. Feliks was very satisfied with this lesson. He trudged barefoot through the field, and the peasants passing by admired him, taking him by the hand as if he was a good acquaintance.

It was Feliks's bad luck to find himself in the second grade with children who look only half as old as he is. Feliks asked his teacher if she would go to the Pedagogical Council for permission for him to attend the gym class for the third and fourth grade, starting at 7:30 in the morning (in winter). In addition, the second grade does not work in the laboratory, and Feliks roams around the hallways behind the doors and windows and looks to see how the children are working. He even shows up more and more in the laboratory, with the children from the third and fourth grades, hoping they will allow him to file a little or to bang with a hammer. In time, and as a result of my efforts, Feliks became an official part of the laboratory and was released from one of the periods in the second class.

Last week he came to me, boldly, his hands in his pockets, and said that he did not want to be a locksmith. "What then?" I ask, "a carpenter, in a painters' workshop?" His answer is a short one: "A smith." In truth, working at the anvil, he forges the thickest bars. His first work was a hammer that was included in an exhibit at the end of the year.

According to the regulations of the Children's Self-Governing Board, all children who attend school can participate in elections but only those in the third or fourth grades can be elected. How surprised I was when I saw today at a meeting of the children where they chose representatives for a Court Committee that Feliks had been submitted as a candidate, though he was still in the second grade. Feliks was not at the meeting; he was playing somewhere in a field or in another corner. It was already dark and nobody knew where to find the candidate whose name had been submitted. Suddenly Feliks crashed through the door, noisily, dancing in with red cheeks and dirty shoes, his hands in his pockets, his eyes wide open, bewildered but with a smile on his face, wondering why everyone is looking at him. His little friends from the second grade ran to him to tell him, proudly, that he was chosen for the Children's Court Committee. Tired, he shrugs his shoulders; he does not understand what is happening. One of the teachers present tells him officially that the children want to elect him for the committee. He smiles, shrugs, and runs quickly to the others sitting down, and joins them. He was selected with twenty of the forty votes cast.

When the time comes for the court sessions, Feliks sits half seriously, winking at other children from time to time and taking care of various "business." When the judges on the court go for a consultation, Feliks is again serious and he speaks his piece.

We come from morning exercises refreshed and in a good mood. We sit at the table for breakfast. Feliks sits across from me. He plays with the stool he sits on, first on one foot then on both feet, around and around, the picture of health. The director tells him to sit quietly, but it is not an easy thing to follow an order when you have just come from the field, full of excitement from singing and moving around.

The director hits Feliks lightly, telling him that he will have to eat standing up. Feliks glances at me, to see if I will help him. He does not scream or say anything, he just turns to the side with an angry face for the director and throws him a look with one eye, then says in Polish so I can barely hear: "What, you're hitting me? What have I done to you?" Children come running from other tables to express their sympathy to Feliks. Very carefully they say to me: "Huh! You didn't want to believe us when we told you they hit us?"

The children told me this some time ago, when I was still a "newbie" here.

Now, after Feliks "got it," they say to me: "That's how they hit us. If I were in Feliks's place, I would give it to him," says one of them, an older boy. But Feliks, after a few minutes of nervousness that was not noticed, becomes completely quiet and looks at me, smiling. He remains standing, eating. When the director comes around again, he feigns ignorance of the situation and seems satisfied with Feliks. Feliks's educators and teachers think he is the worst and worthless . . .

Yosek's Court Martial

March 24, 1930

During the first days of spring the fourth grade painted the outside of the house.

Children from the younger grades march through the black, plowed-up field and approach the line of "artists." I tell them to go away, a lesson is going on. But they do not hear me, because each one of them wants to look to see how the painting is going and to give their opinion about it, too.

Yosek, who looks at me with strong interest, does not hear what I say to him at times. Absorbed, he tells me what he thinks about one of the "artists" and then goes to the next one.

"Yosek," I yell, "Go away, you're disrupting everyone."

He runs away. A minute later he is there again.

The staff, children, and chair stand some distance away. It is the end of class. The children hold the painting blocks in their hands and go in the direction of the buildings. An order from the chair is heard: Yosek should go to him. Yosek is bold, his full cheeks are red, he goes in dressed well, with his white shirt collar showing underneath his clean, buttoned jacket, the socks neatly turned down to the shoes, like a sportsman. Yosek defends his rights and so is well dressed. The chair begins to question Yosek. Yosek answers.

Big and small, the oldest children in the institution, the entire staff, the directors of the *shul* and the institution, everyone stands around and sees what is happening.

The chair yells. Yosek is silent.

"Candies, eh?" the chair yells and then he yells to the teaching staff, "They punished him, he was not to go to school. I'll give it to him!" And the slaps resound one after the other.

Yosek puts his head down and cries silently. The chair continues to yell: "Who do you have in L.? A brother? Where does he live?"

Yosek answers: "I don't know."

"How old is he? Fifteen, sixteen? What does he do? Is he a tailor? What other family do you have?"

"No one!"

"It's not possible!" Everyone hears the distressed cry of the agitated chair.

Yosek begs him to believe him and says again: "I have no one . . . I don't know where my brother lives . . . He was here once in winter and he gave me a few *groshn* for candy . . ."

The chair gets up and yells: "Money for candy, eh?" And Yosek gets another slap to the head.

"He has to go to school!" the chair yells to the teachers standing around. Then he turns to Yosek: "Go to the teacher."

Yosek does what he's told. The chair looks away and does not notice the apology and says to Yosek again: "Apologize!"

"I already did," answers Yosek.

The chair yells and starts to hit him terribly on the head: "Apologize!"

And Yosek cries out and yells: "I already apologized!"

"Again! I have to hear it!"

And the chair adds: "Those are the kinds of lessons you'll learn from me when I'm here."

A deathly silence comes over the onlookers. Some of the staff are silent because they agree with the chair's judgment. Some are used to this and still others are hardened or confused.

The same with the children: some of them feel as if they themselves are punished at the same time, but others are used to receiving such "gifts."

A teacher says to me on the side: "This is a court martial! . . ."

When the teachers punished Yosek, suspending him from school for one day for answering the teacher too boldly, everybody praised Yosek, saying he is a good student, that he is the most active in class discussions, that he belongs to the institution's physical education committee, in which he participates respectfully and with great interest. In truth, this "good for nothing" eleven-year-old boy, broadly built and tall, has the physical and intellectual development of a fourteen-to fifteen-year-old.

Gutshe Can Dance and Sing . . .

March 11, 1930

She is seventeen or eighteen years old, chubby with red cheeks, and always with short, disheveled hair. She cannot read or write. All the children, from youngest to oldest, take advantage of her. The staff have the same relationship to her. The oldest children, who have been in the institution around ten years, remember her but it is hard to tell when she came to the institution or where she is from. The children and some of the staff think that she has an old, blind father somewhere who visited her last year.

After I arrived here, I enjoyed one of Gutshe's performances. She does not have a special voice, but her pitch is perfect and she knows dozens of songs. If members of the staff want to amuse themselves, they demand in a good-natured tone that Gutshe perform ballet figures. She does the figures much better than the teachers who laugh at her. Such amusements happen in the presence of the directors, staff, and children. When she doesn't know how to say something, she asks everyone, repeats it, and remembers.

Some of the educators used to understand that it was a crime against a child like the chubby Gutshe if they did not exercise their appropriate authority and prepare her for life after she would be sent away from the institution. The pedagogical council decides that Gutshe should be a helper for the teacher of the youngest children (two to four years old). A few days later I see Gutshe without anyone else around. She is serious, she avoids spending time and playing around with the children, doing all of the work with the little ones just as the educators instruct her. She wears a white apron and fulfills her functions satisfactorily. She's already not the same Gutshe as before, she is just like the others. She is occupied all the time, going for walks with the children, playing with them, feeding them, helping them wash and dress and tidy their rooms. It is true that her mental development is no higher than a nine-year-old child, but through her work and the knowledge that she is a helper to the teacher she has matured by some years (earlier she would wander without any purpose, sometimes bringing in wood or cleaning the pots in the kitchen). Why she has not learned to write or read is hard to say, but it's true.

I was accidentally going through the hallway where the bedrooms of the older girls are located; Gutshe also sleeps there. From her room I heard a cry, a howling, like that of an animal. It was Gutshe, crying in the middle of the bright day, all alone and no one taking care of her. I found out what was going on; at the same time as her period, she had come down with a rash and a strong fever. The older girls in her room had an easygoing relationship with her and used to help her at times. But what kind of supervision or help could they—shy, helpless, and not experienced at all themselves—have given Gutshe?

She was happy when she was told that she would get "a position" in the city, that she could work and earn money. She went to tell everyone about her good fortune. She made an effort to be serious with them. She did not understand that they wanted to get rid of her. Yesterday she cried when she said goodbye to the children and especially with the youngest ones. It was touching, this saying goodbye. She cheerfully told the staff, "I will have a job in the city, I will work." Some children gave her notebooks they had written in or pieces of paper as remembrances. The older girls gave her embroidered handkerchiefs and other things.

She lived there for years, raised as an unfortunate creature, thrown out with only a few rags as her trousseau and dowry . . .

The Teacher Can Do Anything . . .

January 6, 1930

Edek filed a complaint in the children's court against his teacher for not knocking when she came into the boys' bedroom in the morning and caught him doing something for which he, Edek, was ashamed. But the teachers do not allow a judgment against Mira, Edek's teacher.

"Can it be this way?" the children ask me.

I can't say anything.

Just yesterday, late in the evening, there was a meeting of the pedagogical council to discuss the issue. The chair of the pedagogical council presented Edek's letter to the children's court. The chair of the children's court (sixteen years old) naively turned to the chair of the pedagogical council for advice about how to handle a complaint against a teacher. This is the first case (because self-government in the institution has not been around for long). The children's right to accuse a teacher was proclaimed at a meeting of all the children in the presence of the entire pedagogical council and technical staff at the same time that the court was elected.

An issue arose out of Mira's testimony. We heard that she did not understand her infraction, what it was that she did. She said that she also hit Edek when he noticed her there, but perhaps not as correctly as other adult "gentlepeople." Why hadn't Edek written in his complaint that she had also hit him, and not only insulted him?

Maybe because children think that they cannot protest being hit, because they will receive still more abuse?

Apparently, Edek was certain that the teacher would be disciplined for this incorrect behavior.

The majority of the pedagogical council expressed that one should not show the children that there exists a limit for the teachers. At the meeting some of the teachers agitatedly demanded that Edek should be punished for his answers: "what chutzpah these 'brats' have to accuse a teacher?" . . . (officially, they can accuse a teacher) . . .

Before the decision of the pedagogical council the accused teacher declares that she will not appear in court with Edek, because . . . she is more valuable and more educated (in this way she refers to her position). Her "authority" does not allow it . . .

My arguments that it is wrong to treat this case so lightly do not help. An inappropriate handling of this situation from our side may ruin all of our efforts on behalf of the children, because the children will lose their trust in us. The decision of the pedagogical council is to hand the matter over to the daily agenda and to tear up Edek's letter . . .

And so Mira the teacher was not charged with any wrongdoing, only the "big mouth," the "rude" Edek. Because they did not have the courage to tell the children of the judgment, they said to them, "the pedagogical council has already taken care of it."

Two days later comes a letter to the pedagogical council not from Edek, but from the children's court: They, the children, cannot agree that Edek is guilty of anything and they turn to the pedagogical council for permission to try Edek's teacher. After a discussion it was decided that a teacher generally does not come under the jurisdiction of the children's court...

Who is Edek? When he was one month old, he was found in a Łódź courtyard; a year ago a woman came to him and declared herself as his mother. When Edek was asked if he wanted to go with her, his answer was short: "Since she did not know me and did not come to visit me until today, I can continue to go on without her."

He is nine or ten years old and in the second grade.

Liltshe's "Papa"...

February 25, 1930

When Liltshe was abandoned in the "Women's Defense Association" in L., she was seven months old.[15] The "Women's Defense Association" gave her over to a Christian home for foundlings, and from there Liltshe came to "Hilf" (Help), the girls' dormitory of our institution.

Liltshe was a subject of study in "Hilf," on which the girls learned how to take care of a small child.

Though she was "the obligatory grandchild" in the dormitory, and though she nonetheless, improperly, called the chair "Papa," she was very afraid. Several months later she was officially accepted into the institution. I do not know why Liltshe was part of the four-to-seven-year-old children's group, when she was barely two. Now Liltshe is three-and-a-half.

In the first weeks of my work here in the institution there was much talk about the children who take care of their physiological needs at night

---

15 This is a reference to the Froyen-shuts fereyn in Łódź, which could be rendered more literally as Women's Defense Union. Quotation marks in original.

in bed. The question is a real and important one for the life of the institution because it concerns the health of the child.

At a meeting of the educators, teachers, directors, doctor, and chair, it was decided not to give one child food and drink regularly; a second child was to be given food and drink once a day; a third child was to be allowed to eat or drink just twice a day. When I turned privately to the pre-school teacher and said that she should not heed this decision and that she should give the children food and drink, and take care of them so that they are warm at night and warmly dressed, the teacher agreed, but she said that the chair singled Liltshe out and threatened her with the stick, saying he "will break her of this!" (*a three-and-a-half-year old!*)

The method of hitting and starving the children did not bring about the desired result. The straw mattresses were still wet, spoiling the air. There have also been cases when the children, out of fear, flushed their underwear down the toilet or stashed it somewhere else. The chair, upon learning that Liltshe still took care of her physiological needs in bed, beat her. The teacher Sore Vaynrib said that often she could not look on the violent blows the chair gave Liltshe with the stick.

And this three-and-a-half-year-old is one of the lucky ones, chubby with red cheeks, and well-developed physically and mentally.

Liltshe received from someone a pretty little coat, but the chair ordered that the coat be taken from Liltshe and given to another child . . . Liltshe cried. But the chair showed up, and she cried because she was scared . . . Liltshe became sick. She got a fever. The institution's doctor sent her to a city hospital . . . She was abandoned again . . .

The concern that the children should not take care of their physiological needs at night in their beds remains on the agenda, and the only remedies for the issue are not giving the children something warm to eat and drink and beating them. At night it can be cold in the bedrooms.

"Your Child Will Not Know You!"

April 27, 1930

Afternoon. Lovely spring weather. I look down from the first floor through a window of a teacher's room and I see a woman roaming around in front of the house. The chair appears and yells at the woman, asking: "What are you doing here?" In a trembling tone, she answers: "I beg you, I want only to see my child." "Your child will not know you!"—and the chair continues on his way. Choking back tears, the woman begs: "Just to see . . . nothing more . . . I cannot rest at home until . . ." "Stop walking around here!" the chair yells furiously, "If you will not go away from here, I will split open your head!"

The woman, stunned, trembles in fear. She stoops down, wrings her hands, and begs, "I will sit here on the steps and wait . . . you will bring me my child? . . . I cannot bear this . . ."

The answer comes back: "I'm going to give it to you!"

The woman: "I've brought a couple of caramels and a roll with butter, for the child. I don't have more to bring . . ."

Finally her two children show up, accompanied by another young boy as guard, in order to ensure that the mother does nothing more than see her own children.

The Qualifications of a Director . . .

April 22, 1930

It's the middle of the day. Three hours ago I returned from my Passover holiday. All of the children sit in the big dining room, where the Seder[16] was held. The preschool is in the same room. Some of the children are already eating. Many of them are not at the table.

Yosl Bikhbinder comes in. Rusak, the director, asks: "Why are you late?" and slaps him on both sides of the head. He does the same with Shlomele Mints (eleven years old) and Aharon Zshak, a young boy from the second grade, and others.

I had not seen such incidents for several days, and I reacted strongly. But one cannot say anything, because the director (a gardener) got a message from the chair that these are the methods at this institution and that he has to apply them if he wants to stay around. (He is new to the job. Almost all of the employees, regardless of their qualifications, go through the test of being a director of the institution.) A director has to remember

---

16 The ceremonial meal on the first two nights of Passover.

to hit, to have a "strong hand." The person acting as director knows this and, knowing this, he will be able to manage the "nice" position of director. It seems Rusak wants to stay around in the job. He hits everyone, from the small children to the eighteen-year-old boys.

But Rusak, too, did not know how to stick around in the end and some time later he has left the institution . . . even his "qualifications" were not enough . . .

The Sexual Moment

The sexual moment plays one of the main roles in education. During the years of sexual maturation, education depends on the development of the character of a youth and, to a certain extent, his physical and intellectual development. This issue is not considered at all in closed institutions, because it is not considered proper.
April 3, 1930

During class I see two girls, Rive, about thirteen or fourteen years old, and Gute, about fifteen or sixteen years old, clinging to each other. They begin to kiss on the face and bite the neck. They are embracing each other under a shawl, ostensibly because the classroom is cold. None of the children noticed; they were completely silent while I was talking, and they were paying attention closely. At times I noticed their movements. The eyes of the girls at last grew dreamy and unfocused, and the older girl pressed the younger one to her, placing her hands on her naked body . . . Seeing that they had gone too far, I suddenly asked the older girl a question about the lesson.

And so the scene in front of my eyes came to an end.

It is not easy to come in and manage the children. They have to get up at seven for their morning exercises. Until I arrived they got up whenever they wanted. The staff was "forced" to agree, and the teachers significantly delayed the start of their classes.

Little by little the children got used to it. The boys more quickly, the girls not so easily.

Hele (fifteen years old) comes to morning exercises sleepy, not well rested, calm. She is always still and speaks little. Very often she lies in bed until breakfast with different excuses: a headache, she doesn't feel well, and so on.

From time to time I inspect the bedrooms very early, just as the bell rings. On the first floor, by the little children, everything is usually in order. There is always a little noise with the boys. Some are sleeping. On the second floor, where the older girls sleep, it is quiet. They are still sleeping soundly. When I knock, there is no answer; when I go in, I see most of them sleeping two to a bed (though each girl has her own separate comfortable bed). The blankets cover them, enclosing one and the other; they are snoring. Hele sleeps alone and sighs (this is not by accident . . .).

I also make similar inspections in the bedrooms in the evening around eleven or twelve, when the children are already sleeping for a long time. An older girl, Tole (sixteen years old), sleeps in the hallway on the first floor, where the children of preschool age sleep. She is as well-developed as an eighteen- to twenty-year-old. Tole stands in the middle of the corridor with Hele and they speak intimately. Upon my approach Hele went up to sleep on the second floor and Tole was left by herself in the room. I encountered such meetings often. This interested me. I began to ask the older girls about Hele and they told me that Hele sleeps very often with Tole. She comes up many times at midnight and sometimes not at all. I have indeed come across Hele sleeping with Tole in bed in a more inappropriate position than I observed with the other girls. It became clear to me why Tole did not speak with almost anyone else at the institution. She busies herself with the work that the preschool teacher tells her to do. She is calm, she likes to be alone or to meet to talk and walk only with Hele. Tole is very tall, and healthy. She does not go to school. She can barely read a little Polish. Hele is small, skinny, and pale. She goes to the institution's school. In general, she has no capability for learning, only for drawing. In class she is always dreamy and uninterested. I also discovered that Hele brings books with erotic content from the city and she reads them for Tole. Nobody knows about this.

The staff from the institution and school is away in the city on a holiday. I stay behind with the children. I get the children together and suggest that since it is very muddy, and the children tramp mud throughout the school, that we go into the barn, where there is a lot of straw, and weave straw doormats to wipe our feet on. The suggestion is accepted. The children from the second to fourth grades run with great joy into the barn and with the help of the agronomist we divide the children into groups of three. Each group makes one straw doormat. One holds the straw, another twists it, and another takes it under the same straw to weave it. We make a lot of noise singing, and we laugh out loud. One group cries out, "We have already woven ten meters." They call to see if this will be enough to make a doormat. "Should it be in a circle or should it have four corners?"

A little later they have gotten a little bored and are playing around. They are riding piggyback, both girls and boys. The agile children climb on the beams of the barn. They are "wrestling" on the straw—mostly boys with girls; they are growing up.

Hershl and Rifke are already tearing each other's hair out. With great laughter, of course. They're constantly hitting each other all the time. Hershl runs, Rifke chases after him. She catches him, they take hold of each other, put their arms around each other, and they're wrestling. She hits him and one wants to push the other down to the ground. She gives it to him properly and calls to me that I should see how she has beat Hershl. Hershl does not allow this. He chases her, catches her as she climbs up on the beams of the barn. She continues hitting him and she grabs him, climbing on the beams. The younger children yell out, "Good! She's not going to take it. That's the way!" Hershl wants to wrestle on the floor and Rifke wants to wriggle out of the situation and at the height of the situation, the girls cry out, "Give it to him good!" They are arguing above us, but we cannot see what they are doing. We hear crying out and laughter at the same time. They have bickered so fiercely that they have both fallen in between the straw and cannot get up . . . Listening to this arguing is very satisfying. I suggest to the children, "Come, we'll get them to make up with each other." We clambered up and tore them apart from each other. They are tired, red-faced, their hair all messed up, and Rifke is still arguing with Hershl.

Hershl and Rifke often liked to tease each other and hit each other, all in fun . . .

The Nourishment of the Children

The child's physical and mental development depends on nutrition. So does the child's mood, whether the child is cheerful and in good spirits. The sexual development of the child, which determines the character of the future adult, also depends on food. Whether a child eats meat, greens, pastries, dairy, sweets, or pickled foods is important, because each organism demands something different.

Therefore, when an educator cares for a child in an institution, the concern is not simply to satisfy the needs of the child to maintain strength, but also to remember about the normal and appropriate nutrition that can aid, and not impede, the child's physical and mental development.

Nutrition is a pressing concern in closed educational institutions. The human heart is tender; even in the worst times we make sure abandoned children have food to eat and do not die of hunger. But when food does come into the institutions, the child has only enough for minimal needs in comparison to what the body requires. In one institution there is sometimes too much to eat, more than in luxurious restaurants, but in another one the children go hungry or eat what should just be thrown out. The storeowners give the institutions the worst products, because the buyers only care about a low price. But they often actually pay more than the normal cost.

This is not because of a lack of resources, or because they cannot get better products, or because of not knowing or not understanding or because of irresponsibility. For most, it is of primary importance that one gets the invoices from the stores. God forbid one should be suspected of anything. From the other side, no one demands an accounting of what becomes of all of the products. There are no such controls. The children do not sign that they have received adequate food in amount and quality.

I want to bring up a small fact about an institution where I recently worked:

This institution, on one of the main streets of the city, is very solid and has its own splendid building.

And what is the situation with nutrition there?

There is bread lying around behind the oven, under the beds, in the courtyard. When I started my work there, I arranged for the baker to send

Children and staff posing around a table at an outdoor meal, at a CENTOS-Polesie day camp, Shereshevo, 1936 (YIVO)

eight to ten kilos of bread less, for seventy children, every day. But the baker had influence with the board, and the children could have as much bread as they wanted...

The butcher sends seven kilos of meat for seventy children. When I inspected the meat, I became convinced that there was a half kilo missing each time and that two and a half kilos were bones. All told, the children and staff received four kilos of meat. When I decreed that no meat should be ordered again from that butcher, it was quietly arranged that the butcher should deliver the meat. I had made the butcher into an enemy.

A Christian brings the milk. The milk measures up to what it should be and everything is in order. There's a guaranteed ruckus in the morning: the cocoa, the children claim, tastes like soap. I tested the milk with a lactodensimeter, and it turned out that it was seventy percent water. But I could not get rid of the Christian who brings the milk, either.

Before I arrived here the institution used to receive twenty to twenty-eight kilos of butter a week. I realized that this was only about half of what was needed. No one knows what becomes of the butter. The children do not get it.

The products for the colonies used to come from a business that belongs to a board member. I was naive and wanted to reduce the unnecessarily large amounts of sugar, rice, *kasha*, flour, etc. When I began to inspect the quality of the products in comparison with the invoices, it turned out that they (the products, not the invoices) were of the worst kind.

Nutrition is not just a matter for the cooks or the housekeeper. The provisions for the upbringing of the child, for the child's intellectual development, also come out of the kitchen. The "good-willed orphan workers" know nothing about this, because it serves neither their prestige nor their other interests . . .

Vandalism

February 20, 1930

From my first moment in this institution, there has always been fighting between the children and the technical staff. When the servant Wincenty and the washerwomen need to make a fire, there is no wood. To my astonishment, Wincenty quietly responds, "Sir, I have no other choice."

Another time I had to take a new door out of Wincenty's hands; the door was left over from a new building and was already half chopped up.

A good, large table stands out under the open sky next to the generator. I decided to take it into my private room. But it was too big, so the next day I wanted to take it into the workshop so the children could use it for their work. But the electrician Heniek and his assistant Berg explained to me that it had already been taken for the fire.

On February 10, 1930, I walked very early through the barn where the wagons are. I noticed a long table. I casually asked Wincenty what the table was doing there. His answer was cold as always: "The washerwomen have thrown it out of their room in order to chop it for wood—because they will give them a second table, but they cannot get wood . . ."

I went straight to Shoykhet, the administrative director, and made a fuss. Only then was the table saved. The little schoolchildren in the first grade stand around it now, pasting, drawing, and working on it.

You can use more than just wood to light the ovens, according to the staff and the children, who look at me and teach me, for the first time in H., that one can also melt candles, they burn pretty well . . . One can get candles for this purpose from the pantry, as many as one wants, whenever, even a seven-year-old child can get them. But there are many ovens, and if there are no candles, the children use crude oil from the generator as fuel for their lamps. Wincenty, with the children, uses a water pitcher to pour the oil into the ovens . . . When the very little children cannot reach the pitcher, there are small bowls for food that they can use to pour the oil in the ovens. When I say something about this, because, apart from the neglect, a catastrophe may occur, my colleagues answer me: "Otherwise they are sitting in the cold."

The children will not break this habit easily, because they have been doing this for some time.

They take the wood from the barns and stalls and fences. When I tell this to Chair R., he smiles and continues on his way.

It's difficult to let this kind of economizing go, but what can one do? Everything happens with the knowledge and at the orders of the director, which the children carry out.

When a fifteen-year-old boy chopped up a good long bench, just for fun, the staff did not want to punish him. First, it would not help; second, we want to have wood . . . Rich Jews will give away a foundation's money for armchairs and marble tables . . .

What kind of relationship can the children have to the people and to the institution when they are being raised that way? There can be no discussion about appreciating what is valuable, about what belongs to them and what belongs to society.

This is how the children are prepared for life before they leave the institution. The abandoned children take revenge on all that lives around them—taking revenge is the only goal that is rooted in the children who leave this "educational" institution meant to "protect" them.

Home for Jewish Children and Farm in Helenówek

Guests Are Coming . . .

January 19, 1930

There's a holiday atmosphere in the institution today. Guests are coming. Doctors, wealthy men, eminent pedagogues, representatives of government. They are coming for the reception for the Zionist leader N. Sokolow.[17] An arch of triumph and nationalist flags blind the eyes. All kinds of good things are being prepared in the kitchen. The children worked like donkeys for a few days, cleaning until the eyes of the guests would be blinded, so they would be fooled at a glance and give the activities of the institution "caring" for the "poor orphans" a good evaluation . . .

The children are in their "dress clothes," which are hidden away for months at a time and wait for such a celebration. They usually go barefoot, naked, and dirty . . .

The automobiles rumble up to the house. The guests are coming, I take a look through the window and my heart explodes suddenly, seeing that some of the children are being led to a separate room, to shut them off from the guests. Some of them do not have very good clothes, some of them are not good-looking, and some are impulsive and cannot stand calmly and helplessly, as the leaders of the institution would like them to. They must be put in a prison and look on through the bars of a window. An older boy stands guard in the hallway, making sure the children inside are still and quiet so the guests will not be able to hear them. And outside it is more like a holiday than ever. The little ones cry out and sing songs they have written in honor of Sokolow. Hundreds cry out, "Hear! Hear!"

And how they, the sentenced, went to their prison! Heads down, crying, despondent . . . An older boy and an older girl urge them into the room (the staff refused to carry out the Inquisition).

---

17 Nahum Sokolow (1859–1936), a Zionist leader and Hebrew-language journalist, replaced Chaim Weizmann as president of the World Zionist Organization in 1931. I have not found another description of his visit to Łódź or Helenówek, but a photograph from this visit, can be found at "Mordechai Chaim Rumkowski in visit by Nahum Sokolow in Łódź, Jan. 19, 1930," Massuah Institute for Holocaust Studies, accessed June 1, 2016, http://www.infocenters.co.il/massuah/notebook_ext.asp?book=56449&lang=eng&site=massuah.

Mordechai Chaim Rumkowski (far left) during a visit by Nahum Sokolow (second from left, to the right of Rumkowski) in Łódź, January 19, 1930 (Massuah Institute for Holocaust Studies)

Outside there is singing and commotion. Respectable men in top hats, journalists, community leaders, everyone has come to take pleasure in the day.

N. Sokolow, with his daughter, writes in the institution's golden book that they are astounded with the reception . . . they thank the institution's "orphan workers" . . .

This is not the first time. Many guests have already been here. I keep hoping that maybe someone will notice the situation of the orphans, but . . .

They have come and gone in their luxury automobiles, coaches, bikes and horses. And we are back to our usual weekly routine. Everything has disappeared like a dream. But the impression will certainly be a good one: The orphan is doing well. "Prepared for life. Healthy, cheerful, happy. A future builder of Eretz Israel," etc., etc.

At a meeting of the entire staff a few days earlier, someone brought up for discussion the chair's suggestion that some of the children should be isolated, because they are impulsive, not good-looking in appearance, or because they do not have the best clothes. We went to the chair several times and suggested that we could give our spare clothes and shoes to the older boys. All of the teachers, both men and women, agreed to sit day and night to mend the clothes of the younger children and to make slippers from rags. But it did not help. Lack of money was not the reason, because the internal and external appearance of the institution is more than luxurious.

Only Nine Years of Life in the Institution . . .

November 19, 1933

The departure of three youths aged seventeen to eighteen from the institution made a strong impression on me. They had lived in the institution for eight or nine years, they received an elementary education, learning to sign their names and to read something. Most recently they worked, cleaning the courtyard, a little in the fields, and taking coal and wood to the kitchen. I had been told that they were the oldest in the institution and that they would leave shortly for Eretz Israel.

The children were sometimes cheerful, sometimes diffident; by their faces you could tell that something was not completely right with them . . . They did not receive any physical or intellectual education; they did not know much of life, what to strive for when they would leave the home; they did not even know what awaits them in their future lives. The expression on their faces was the result of the new feeling that the time was coming when they would have to go away. They lived here eight years, not knowing anything better. What happened to them here was, for them, a "natural, happy" life . . .

And now the question comes: Where will we go now? To whom?

This question had to come up sooner or later. And now, at the last minute, this consciousness dawns on them, when the chair of the institution tells the three youths that they have to leave the institution, today, in the afternoon.

This heartbreaking scene played out yesterday. They left in the evening. Cold, rainy weather, dark, they were afraid to go into the city, they slept secretly in the institution's barn . . . After half the night we, the teachers, offered them the possibility of sleeping in a room. But it was forbidden to see them . . .

They ate breakfast secretly and were given a few pieces of bread for the pockets and sent out into the world . . .

Adele Granek

When a young person leaves the institution for abandoned children, that child is soon forgotten by everyone (the staff, the board, the other children). When an abandoned child dies in the institution, it is as if one throws a stone in the field.

Adele Granek is a victim of philanthropic "protection" and education.[18] As a teacher I dedicate these few words to her memory and the circumstances in which she died.

May 8, 1930

It finally happened today. After a few weeks of awaiting her death, a message from the hospital last week reported that she is significantly swollen, but because her heart is strong, she wrestles with death and suffers . . . The children and some of the staff no longer recognize her.

A yellow skin covers the bones of the *wychowanka*[19] (and later also the skin of the institution's nurse in the isolation room), the sixteen- to seventeen-year-old Adele Granek, who is sick with consumption.

Around July 1929 she had her first hemorrhage and was sent to Poznański's hospital.[20] She lay there for three months. The administration of the hospital let her out only on the condition that she be sent immediately to Otwock.

When she returned from the hospital, she was not sent anywhere; she was given a separate room, the so-called isolation room, so she would not

---

18   The original text includes Adele Granek's name inside a black box, the usual practice to indicate a person is deceased.
19   Kats uses the Polish word for a girl being brought up in an institutional setting. He italicizes the word to stress that she is not being cared for properly.
20   The Izrael and Leona Poznański Jewish Hospital, founded in the 1880s by Izrael and Leona Poznański. Currently Samodzielny Publiczny Zakład Opieki Zdrowotnej Uniwersytecki Szpital Kliniczny Nr 3 im. dr Seweryna Sterlinga. See Joanna Podolska, *Spacerownik: Łódź żydowska* (Łódź: Agora SA, 2009), 110–11.

Home for Jewish Children and Farm in Helenówek

meet with others from the institution. But this was only for the sake of appearances. In fact, she met often with the staff and children. Everyone visited her and she visited other buildings and rooms of the institution. It's not surprising, because how can you lock up a young person in a room and command her to stay in bed, just so visitors to the institution can see that children can be isolated in a separate room, when she can move and walk around and feel better? In fact, Adele Granek and the other chronically sick children were not isolated. It was not Adele's fault that her illness made her presence harmful for the environment, that she was lonely and helpless; she spoke of this constantly. She understood everything, she was very quick and clever. She used to say that being in the institution is not desired by those around her, that being in the institution will lead to her death.

Adele's friend Ruzhke Itskovitsh (who was subsequently Adele's nurse), another resident in the home, used to joke with her about eating. Ruzhke used to give her food that she bought with her own money. Adele was given the same sour, meager, bland food as the other children, like in a barracks. So she used to not eat the whole day. From time to time Ruzhke used to ask for things to cook up in the kitchen, so Adele would not die of hunger. The little nine- to thirteen-year-olds often asked me: "There are so many chickens and turkeys in the courtyard, why not slaughter a chicken for Adele? Such meat and protein is certainly good for the sick?!" A twelve-year-old boy who used to eat the chickens came to me and said: "No one will know, I will take fresh eggs from the hens and give them to Ruzhke, she can give them to Adele to drink..."

But both the eggs and chickens were only for the visitors and not for the sick children—I had to remain silent...

That one should send Adele to Otwock as the hospital specified was forgotten. Boymats, the former *melamed*[21] at the institution, now an employee of the *gmina*[22], came to visit us. He could not bear to see how Adele had changed and to witness her torment. He tried in the Marpe

---

21 Teacher in a traditional school; tutor.
22 Local government in Polish, here referring to the *gmina żydowska*, the self-governing body of the Jewish community.

(Treatment) association to send her to Otwock.[23] But it was already too late. Two days later she got a hemorrhage again and it was thought she would die then. No hospital would take her, but with great effort the hospital for those with tubercular and venereal infections at Aleksander 115 was forced to take her.

Two to three weeks ago, when Esterke, the clerk in the institution, shared with the chair by phone that Adele is not doing well, the chair cold-bloodedly asked if Adele's birth certificate was in the office? Because if not, he, the chair, will have to take care of it for the burial . . . (after this conversation she lived another three weeks . . .)

During the time of Adele's sickness, Ruzhke was closest to her and Adele told her everything. Among other things she told Ruzhke was that when she was just out of the hospital, the chair asked her to go into a separate room of the "Hilf" dormitory and cautioned her there. He said that she was sick and would have to live separately, far from the children and others.

Adele told Ruzhke about this conversation with tears in her eyes, and she asked Ruzhke: "How does the chair have the heart to foretell death? . . ."

Ruzhke said that when the chair came to the dormitory later to visit Adele, she reproached him; he had apparently already sentenced her to death and would not save her.

Such scenes happened often.

Adele always complained, "Why is the board so indifferent to the children? Why don't they care even when one of them is in very dangerous circumstances?"

Ruzhke says, "When I mentioned to the institution's doctor that I could easily be infected, because the air is suffocating, that I was already exhausted and that I thought I was already sick (later, when she was no longer at the institution, she had to go for a cure), the doctor did not respond, he just took from his vest pocket some kind of pill and took it himself . . ."

---

23 Established as a kitchen for the poor in 1907, Marpe functioned as a sanitarium in 1913 and began treating Jews with tuberculosis in 1924. Sebastian Rakowski, ed., *Aby ślad nie pozostał: Żydzi otwoccy—zagłada i pamięć* (Otwock: Towarzystwo Przyjaciół Otwocka, 2012), 15; Jacek Kałuszko and Paweł Ajdacki, *Otwock i okolice* (Pruszków: Oficyna Wydawnicza Rewasz, 2006), 56.

Adele died today.

Few accompanied her to her final rest. Only a few women from the board were willing to come. It was easier to take her to the cemetery than it was to take the train that would have taken her to Otwock . . .

There was no lack of candidates for Adele's place in the isolation ward.

Large rooms, terraces, summer colonies, chickens, and turkeys, fresh eggs, a special doctor, a separate isolation room. Even a room for each child—everything needed is there, but only for the outside world, for an advertisement, not for the miserable orphaned children.

What Escaped Children Say

Unemployed
June 4, 1930

By chance I ran into Dzialoshinski. To my question about what he remembers from life in the institution, he responded:

> I was born in 1912. I went into the institution in February of 1928. R. hit me often. He also hit others. I remember when most of the staff was not there and the Children's Committee found itself with all the authority. At that time R. used to come and go around with a thick, knobby club and, when something was not in order, he would hit everyone he came across. I remember once someone sent Rozen to buy an apple. In the meantime R. arrived unexpectedly and told Rozen to leave the shop. To his questions whose apple it was and where he got the money, he did not get an answer. He then flew into a rage and beat Rozen in the institution's dining room in front of all the children. Chair R. ordered him to turn in his shirt (which was just a rag) and—to go . . . Where should he go? What is he supposed to eat?—This was of no concern to him. Now, this boy, just four to five years old, sells bagels on the street . . . There was a girl with us, Andzhe Zelikhowska. She was sick; she had been neglected. She was also treated badly. I don't remember if she left the institution alone or if she was sent to her sister's. She died shortly after . . . There were

many cases of beatings. This happened often. Calculating just how many is not easy. I am at my sister's now. I am a tool and die maker without work.

Franka Oksenhendler, teacher
I attest that the above statement is my own and further attest that it is a true statement.
   Israel Dzialoshinski

Brutality, Blows, and a Purpose . . .

June 12, 1930

   Borukh Rosen, born 1913. Came to the institution in 1917 and left in 1925.

   This happened on Pesakh. His mother came and took him home, with the permission of Chair R., of course. But after the holiday, Chair R. did not want to allow him back into the institution. He said that if that boy can stay eight days at home, he can remain there permanently. The mother claims that when she gave up the boy to the institution that she also gave one hundred *zloty*, bedding, underwear—all the gear necessary. Space at the institution was tight, but there was room for a hundred *zloty*. One thing the mother cannot forget: they did not want to issue a birth certificate for the child. The boy Rosen says that when he asked Chair R. for a birth certificate, the chair grabbed him by the shoulder and threw him down the steps.

   Rosen remembers once that they gave clothes out to the children. But Chair R. thought that not everybody needed new clothes. He chose "the worst" and ordered the children not to go out from the institution because they could not represent it in this way . . .

   "Once I went into the kitchen. I wanted to get a little water. Chair R. came in, threw me out, and hit me. This was when the institution was still in L."

   In H. one was also beaten like this. He was hit several times. Once because he was speaking too loudly when Chair R. was sleeping. Once he had to buy an apple for a boy. Chair R. told him to give the apple back, threw it away, and hit him. The boy claims:

"There is no school for me, no trade, he made a thief of me . . ." (This is in fact his "profession.")
Franka Oksenhendler, teacher
I have said everything that is written here and I confirm again that it is correct.
Borukh Rosen

What an Escaped Girl Says

L., May 11, 1930

I met by chance with X. on May 11, 1930, in the apartment of the Blokh family in Łódź, on Kilinski Street, No. 19.

I talked with my girlfriend Blokh, who a few days earlier had run away from the institution, where she worked as a preschool teacher. She could no longer stand to see all the troubles of the children.

Also at the table was a girl of fifteen or sixteen whom I did not know. Hearing us talk about the institution, she started to tell us, unasked, what she knows about the place. Her eyes burned with rage when the institution in H. was mentioned.

"When I finish school and will be more grown up and independent," she explains, "I want to take revenge on Chair R., for all the children who suffered under his 'protection.' For now I still cannot say anything."

When I tell her that my impression of the Hilf dormitory is not a bad one, she responds:

> How can it be good when there is no one who can understand and empathize with us, no one to advise us? Mrs. P., the "head matron," can only be a housekeeper, not a close companion of the girls; she is certainly no teacher. When the chair comes up to the dormitory, he beats us mercilessly. I remember a gruesome case. It's already been three years, but I will never forget it . . . Before Lotka Plum, a three-year-old child, was taken from the institution in H. to the doctor, we lay her down in one of our beds for a while to sleep. When Lotka was woken up, she began to cry the way a small child cries, especially one who is sick.

Chair R. was right there. He ran to the three-year-old and hit her until her dress was torn . . . I had only just arrived with one of my girlfriends to see that the chair was in the hallway with my little sister. It was not good when I saw how my sister turned as pale as chalk, seeing her "father" . . .

. . . I do not know why he chose me to go to D. in the *vursht* store in L. for the bones for the soup and carry them in a basket every day. I am used to crying in silence sometimes because I can't carry the heavy basket with the bones . . . Once I came without bones because there were none. Chair R., our "father," asked me:

"Where are the bones?"

Trembling, I answer: "They didn't give me any because they didn't have any."

"Why do you say such lies?!"

"I'm not lying," I answer.

He came at me with a thick club and I, afraid, was beaten. After the beating I was sick for several days . . . After considering where I could run away to, I was forced to decide to stay longer in the "Hilf" dormitory, but a few weeks later I left. Several times I decided to take my own life. I thought about getting revenge and even came up with the wild idea of burning his house down . . . I still remember the effect of this wild idea today and I will not forget it my entire life . . . I was then thirteen years old . . .

The scenes that we used to see through the windows of the dormitory demoralized us children. The chair used to sit on a chair and an employee in the office sat next to him at a table . . .

She blushed, lowered her eyes, and finished: "He played with her . . ."

"This Happened to Me . . ."

L., May 4, 1930

Working in H., I very often heard from the female teachers and older girls about drastic instances of sexual encounters between the "head" of the institution and the female staff and children. I became especially interested in one case and researched it. This particular case became an open scandal, in which, after a time, the community took an interest.

I will call her X., though she is not against my giving her initials. She is even prepared to tell her story to anybody who asks . . .

She was seventeen years old. She was sent to the institution in Helenówek[24] for summer rest as a child from the "Women's Protection"[25] group.

I invited her to the room of a friend of mine. I asked her if my friend and his wife, who also lived in H. as a child and was a friend of hers, could be present. She agreed.

She told her story:

It happened in 1927, in the summer. I liked him—he was like a real father who takes care of us. On a beautiful summer day when all the girls from the "Hilf" dormitory (they also leave the city during the summer) were standing in the courtyard with Chair R., Chair R. asked where the nurse was. He meant me, though I was not a nurse. He convinced me I was a nurse, saying I could certainly stay on at the institution and he will give me a good paying position as a nurse. He asked me to take out some pills, because he did not feel well, he had a headache. My friend Tole and I went to get the medicine and a glass of water; already at the door of the house I saw the chair going behind us. He approached, poured out the glass of water, and put the medicine in his pocket. He took me by the waist and like a father with his child took me to walk in the garden, which had just been purchased by the institution. We sat at a bench near a table. He began to speak to me, saying that I should accept the position in the institution as a nurse and then he stroked me affectionately and started teasing me . . . I sensed something was wrong and began to be afraid that he was not sitting with me as a "father of an abandoned child," but as an old man who caresses me as a

---

24 Kats spells out the name Helenówek in this instance.
25 The Froyen-shuts fereyn, or Women's Defense Association.

woman and not as a child . . . In the end, he did everything against my will . . .

To my question about specific details, she answered: "You can imagine everything that one can imagine in such a situation . . ."

"And why," I ask, "was none of this ever talked about, even though 'Women's Protection' intervened?"

Her answer: "It did not lead to any consequences . . ."

She continued: "The same evening and day after he wanted me to calm down, but he saw that it was not possible because I was still completely shocked. He began to yell at me, why am I not working, though I had not come there to work, but to rest . . . I ran away from there. After this 'encounter' I was sobbing and I fainted. I went right away to a friend of mine, Fela, also brought up in H. She testified to this in 'Women's Protection.'"

The young woman X. and her girlfriend mention that when the chair used to go with the older girls from the "Hilf" dormitory to a doctor to be examined when they did not feel well, he used to stay when the girls were standing naked in front of the doctor—a "father" can do anything . . .

What Do the Institution's Teachers Say?

It is hard to forget that which causes such real pain. My work in H. belongs to those memories that cannot be forgotten.

What really happened there?

In order to answer this question, I have to characterize the way of life and organization of the institution. Its center, master, and ruler of everything was "the chair." He was not only the guardian, but the almighty master over all the poor and unfortunate creatures who had fallen into his hands and were dependent on him.

The way of life? How should I answer this when there was no system at all in the institution? One never knew what would happen at midday. The atmosphere of the institution depended on the mood of "the chair." The children shuddered at his glance and hid in the corners. "The chair" hit the children with a thick club, without mercy, at his own discretion.

Mendle Kau. and Gutshe Br., two poor, mentally backward children, were his primary victims during my time there; the teachers had no right to get involved. "The chair" rules and decides. The children, constantly frightened, in rags, filthy and hungry, beg the teachers to help them run away.

But the chair is not bad at all when he is expecting guests. He comes earlier then and passes out candies (given free by a company) and the children are happy that the chair is in a good mood . . . The chair orders them to sing, and the children, "satisfied" that they can do something, sing, until the chair and his guests leave. And so the guests, charmed, leave the institution filled with impressions of the children.

R. Zaydler
Former teacher from the institution in H.
April 1930

I received a letter from Mira. Awful things are happening there. One is in a war. The fight goes on. The Old Man does not want to pay them. In such chaos F. L. engages in double-sided politics. Working in the school, apart from F., is a very good educator, but he could not endure the "delicate" demands of the Old Man and he demonstratively left H.

Where is the beautiful Helena, whom Solokow mentioned when he was in H.? She certainly lost her soul among the evil spirits there in H. I admire his power. The revolution brought down such a powerful tsar, but R. still reigns in his "kingdom." I truly do not understand the power the man possesses . . .

Sore Vaynrib
Preschool teacher
Zamość, January 20, 1930

I have read several of the descriptions of Kats's time at H. As a former teacher at H., I can confirm that such events as he describes occurred.

Sore Vaynrib
Warsaw, April 21, 1930

I left Brześć for two reasons: First, I said that I would not work there long, and second, I was physically and mentally exhausted. Working in H., I had lost faith. I do not believe anyone. The figure of R. (the chair of H.) does not leave me. I think that I will be cheated and that all people are bad.

The Old Man still pays nothing for his actions.

Sore Vaynrib
Zamość, October 10, 1930

After reading most of the excerpts from the diary of Y. Kats, I can confirm the details of all of the incidents in H. that happened in my presence or in the presence of my other coworkers.

Knowing the institution longer (having lived there as a child), I can confirm that more such incidents happened between children and staff. The "authorities" reacted very badly to these incidents, as did the children.

Franka Oksenhendler
Resident and then teacher in the institution in H.
Warsaw, May 21, 1930

I thank F. Oksenhendler for her cooperation on my work with this book.

As a former resident, she knows the institution and her information is the best and most certain.

One should note that as a teacher, she displays a great love and devotion to the orphaned children.
Y. Kats[26]

I have read several chapters from the diary of Yekhiel Kats, and I recall similar incidents, some exactly the same, from the time when I was an instructor and Hebrew teacher there in 1927.

Such incidents were part of the daily agenda. The images Katz depicts reflect the morass that is Jewish philanthropic activity. There is a vulgar trade in Jewish children. Mismanagement, abandonment, and the

---

26 Italics and reduced font size appear in the original.

destroying of children's souls—this I experienced and saw during the course of my time in H.

I. Rozental
Student at the university in Berlin, philology faculty
Mlawa, April 15, 1930

As I was leaving the institution in H., where I worked from 1930 to 1931 as a teacher and educator, I embraced the desire to lead the children out of the jungle disguised as the institution known as H.

The institution is a home for orphans and abandoned children only during the visits of guests. At other times the orphans in this so-called "home" go hungry and suffer from cold and other problems...

Sh. Finkelshteyn
Teacher in Tarbut
Shedlets, September 3, 1931

As a former *feldsherin*[27] in H., I can confirm after a year of work the authenticity of the facts related to my work given in Y. Kats's diary. I noticed that incidents of beating and simply inhumane treatment of the children occurred often. In my opinion Chair R. is the one guilty of these actions.

Ruzha
Former *feldsherin* and, earlier, resident
Łódź, May 12, 1930

As a former teacher in H., after a year of work, I assert that the children were beaten for the slightest transgressions. They were physically and morally crippled, and, in my opinion, the cause was Chair R. The images of life in H. outlined by my colleague Kats, a teacher in H., in his diary are in full accordance with reality.

P. Brifman
A teacher in H.
Varshe-Grochov, January 13, 1931

---

27 Unlicensed medical practitioner.

What Do Guests, Pedagogues, and Community Leaders Say and Write?
If the prophets of modern pedagogy Pestalozzi and Froebel and the great Leipzig reformer of the German school, Gaudig, would rise from their graves and come to H. together with still-living significant pedagogues such as Professor Georg Kerschensteiner of Munich, the great American professor John Dewey, and many other leaders of the new education, they would take great pleasure in seeing how their great ideas have been realized.[28]

The children in H. always have the possibility to work physically and mentally and this gives them the best opportunity to develop their bodies and minds to the greatest satisfaction.

The children not only learn in H., they also live.

It is interesting to note that the chair of H., the known community leader R., has certainly not immersed himself in the work of the great educational reformers. Rather, he follows his love and sympathy for the child and his understanding that his own talent will lead him to the goal . . .

A. Perlman
Gymnasium director

The institution in H. strives to give its children what a wealthy community at a high cultural level can give them. H. has an established approach which distinguishes it from a range of philanthropic institutions.

The institution's educational program is clearly established and without ambiguity.

Whoever gets to know H. recognizes its true nature—and is dazzled by its greatness, its beauty, and its size . . .

Sh. Riger
Gymnasium director

---

28 Johann Heinrich Pestalozzi (1746–1827), Swiss pedagogue and educational reformer; Friedrich Froebel (1782–1852), German pedagogue and student of Pestalozzi; Hugo Gaudig (1860–1923), German pedagogue and educational reformer; Georg Kerschensteiner (1854–1932), German educational theorist and professor at the University of Munich; John Dewey (1859–1952), American philosopher.

I understood that this is neither a game nor the experiment of a dilettante, but that it is there simply to create new educational possibilities for Jewish youth.

There are two great treasures in the institution in H.: (1) The youngest of the Jewish children are raised in an atmosphere of productive work; and (2) the interest in, protection of, and support for the Jewish community.

A new valuable generation is growing up in H.

Michał Brandstätter[29]

Distinguished pedagogue, gymnasium director

The young Jew who learns in H. to observe directly the phenomena of nature and to create new worth from the strength of one's own work learns at the same time to understand the world in context and to love its internal harmony.

H. serves to prepare the young Jew not only economically but also nationally.

Dr. M. Braude[30]

Everyone who visits H. sings the praises of the institution and its director. I find no reason to doubt what they say.

Dr. Y. Frenkel[31]

---

[29] Michał Brandstätter (1882–1943) was a well-known teacher, educational administrator, and journalist from Łódź. He helped to establish Jewish secondary schools in the city, and he also worked as a language teacher in both state and private schools.

[30] Marcus Braude (1869–1949) was a rabbi and innovative educational Zionist leader. He became head of the progressive synagogue in Łódź in 1909. In 1922 he was elected a Senator of the Polish Republic and in 1924 he became of member of the Łódź Jewish Community Council. In the 1910s Braude created a series of secondary schools that stressed fluency in Hebrew and Polish.

[31] Jeremiasz Frenkel was a contributor to *Miesięcznik Żydowski*, a Polish-language Jewish academic journal, and *Opinia*, a Polish-language Jewish weekly focused on political, social, and literary issues. See Eugenia Prokop-Janiec, *Polish-Jewish Literature in the Interwar Years*, trans. Abe Shenitzer (Syracuse, NY: Syracuse University Press, 2003), 20.

IV

CENTOS in Otwock

The Therapeutic and Educational Institution in Otwock (Three Months of Activity)

Zofia Rosenblum

Otwock developed as a resort town in the late nineteenth and early twentieth centuries. Many found the climate of Otwock conducive to good health and went there for the treatment of tuberculosis. By the 1920s, the small town had acquired a reputation for its medical facilities, and its guesthouses and treatment centers attracted thousands of visitors, many of them Jewish. The oldest Jewish health care facility in Otwock was known as Zofiówka, a facility for mentally ill Jewish adults established in 1908 and led by the neurologist Samuel Goldflam.[1] Other institutions, such as Marpe and the Jewish Anti-tubercular Association Brijus (Health), contributed to the town's reputation as a health resort and treatment center.[2]

By 1939, over ten thousand of the town's nearly twenty thousand residents were Jewish. Jews owned over eighty percent of the businesses in Otwock and were active in the town's leadership.[3] The guidelines established for the city council in 1919 called for the mayor of the town to be Christian and the deputy mayor to be Jewish.[4] This small town became host to a unique CENTOS institution. In 1927 Mendel Sznejerson, the director of CENTOS, asked Zofia Rosenblum to create a special institution for children who could not manage life in a children's home.[5]

---

1 Mary V. Seeman, "The Jewish Psychiatric Hospital, Zofiówka, in Otwock, Poland," *History of Psychiatry* 26, no. 1 (March 2015): 98–104.
2 Marpe was established in 1907, and Brijus was established in 1901. Rakowski, *Aby ślad nie pozostał*, 15. These other Jewish institutions did not have a direct connection to CENTOS, though their work is sometimes mentioned in the sources for the CENTOS institution in Otwock.
3 Rakowski, *Aby ślad nie pozostał*, 13, 17.
4 Rakowski, *Aby ślad nie pozostał*, 11.
5 Szymańska, *Byłam tylko lekarzem*, 114.

The request surprised Rosenblum because she did not work exclusively with Jewish children and she did not know Yiddish, but she recognized the need. Rosenblum came from an educated family. Her father, the owner of a dress factory in Łódź, was a Polish patriot. Her mother had studied music in Dresden. She told in her autobiography of how she was taken by her nanny to be baptized; only the chance return of her parents from the theater prevented the baptism. Her grandfather founded a home for the elderly and a home for children in Białystok. Artur Rubinstein's aunt taught her German, and the pianist's cousin was a close friend. Rosenblum studied medicine in Paris, finishing her doctoral work just before the outbreak of war in 1914. She spent the years of World War I in Russia, studying in Kharkov and later working in a psychiatric clinic for children in Moscow, with the neurologist Grigory Ivanovich Rossolimo (1860–1928), and later in Mińsk.[6] She founded a pedological[7] clinic in Warsaw in 1923. It was these experiences that prepared her well for her work with CENTOS.

Rosenblum's desire to fight for poor children stemmed from her dream as a young teenager. As a fourteen-year-old girl, she dreamed of being a doctor, not one for whom patients paid, but a doctor paid by the state.[8] She recognized that many could not pay for the services the wealthy could afford. She achieved her dream in 1924, when she went to work for the Kasa Chorych (Health Insurance Fund) in the Warsaw neighborhood of Wola. She did not approve of the fact that the Jewish proletariat could only turn to *feldshers*; in her new position, she was able to address their needs more professionally. She worked in this position until 1933.

A villa in Otwock that could accommodate thirty-five children was rented in 1928.[9] Rosenblum recognized early on the need to assess the varying levels of the children's skills and intelligence, and she oversaw the selection of children for the institution and the care they received. The initial goal was to help those children in smaller towns and cities with less

---

6 A Russian neurologist. Rossolimo's conception of the psychological profile emphasized an individual's strengths and weaknesses.
7 Pedology refers to the study of the physical and psychological development of youth.
8 Szymańska, *Byłam tylko lekarzem*, 101.
9 Located at Glinicka 4. See Pękowska, "Organizacja Zakładu Leczniczo-Wychowawczego 'CENTOS'" and Szymańska, *Byłam tylko lekarzem*, 114–30. Rosenblum names Horensztein as the steward, or supervisor. Horensztein's daughter also worked with the children. This chapter of Szymańska's memoir details her work at CENTOS in Otwock.

access to specialized care. Most of these children came from Yiddish-speaking families. As the institution developed, the leaders found they were accepting more children from the cities, and the language of the institution changed to Polish accordingly. The work of the educators in Otwock was demanding, not least because of the specialized needs of each of the children. Kalman Lis referred to this as "intimate education"; Rosenblum described it as "individualized education."[10]

This piece originally appeared in *Dos shutsloze kind* 1, no. 6 (June 1928): 25–29.

The Therapeutic and Educational Institution in Otwock must fulfill two tasks:

I. Accept from educational institutions those children who are not suitable for cooperative living in an educational setting with normal children;

II. Guarantee to the mentally retarded children who have shown explicit signs of a psychological constitution such conditions for an education that will favor their intellectual development and help them to further develop their ability to behave appropriately in society.

With this purpose, before the opening of the institution, the association sent the directors of the institution abroad, to visit similar institutions in Germany and Austria. The association also began to carry out, as far as possible, an expeditious selection of the children.

The selection of the children took place in the institutions where the children were staying, on the basis of surveys that were filled out by the teaching staff and inspected by the director of the new Therapeutic and Educational Institution. The teachers, who have some preparation in psychology, possibly through a master's degree, assessed the children, along with specific research in the intelligence level of the children and a determination of the index of intelligence (in numbers) according to the Binet-Terman method.[11] An evaluation from school, a pedagogical exam of

---

10 Szymańska, *Byłam tylko lekarzem*, 127.
11 Alfred Binet (1857–1911), French psychologist and pioneer of intelligence testing; Lewis Terman (1877–1956), American educational psychologist. Terman revised Binet's

the children, and a long conversation with the teacher and the child were also used to select the children. The goal was to gather together the material necessary to get to know the inclinations and mood of the children of the institution. Such research was conducted for about two hundred children. After some consideration forty-five candidates were selected, with the aim that the intellectual level of the children would be more or less uniform. One young boy with lower than 0.4 was accepted. Two boys with higher scores, 0.73–0.68, and clear psychopathic constitutions were accepted. The index of the children's intelligence ranges between 0.5 and 0.65, which corresponds completely with the level of a *special school*.

The ages of the children range from thirteen to fifteen years old, with few exceptions (three children of nine to eleven).

From this schematic overview we see that the institution has not fulfilled its first task completely, that is, it has not freed the orphanages and dormitories of the most difficult children, such as idiots and hopeless fools.

The management has already given up on the idea that in a small institution (amounting to only fifty beds) there should be no differentiation of types of children, and so the goal of the institution is to teach the children to adapt to a practical, and, to the extent possible, an independent life and to train them as soon as possible in the different artisans' trades. That's why accepting children who are not able to work would be contrary to the goal and could be very damaging to the life of the institution.

The institution opened on March 12, 1928, in the building of the former institution for orphans in Otwock. It was specially rebuilt and refitted for its new purpose.

The staff of the institution consists of a director who drives every week from Warsaw, a special education instructor, a doctor, on-site directors, a manager (a representative of management), a male teacher, three female teachers, and a trainee.

The educational personnel and local doctor have only worked in therapeutic pedagogy since the opening of the institution. They work in

---

intelligence test and called it the Stanford-Binet IQ test (here apparently called Binet-Terman). See Paul Davis Chapman, *Schools as Sorters: Lewis M. Terman, Applied Psychology, and the Intelligence Testing Movement, 1890–1930* (New York: New York University Press, 1988), 27.

special schools and they have become acquainted with the appropriate methods and pedagogical consultation.

In a series of meetings with the director, the issue of the spirit in which the institution should be led in order to fulfill its tasks was discussed, and the educational and cultural program was determined. In the course of three months, thirty-five children came into the institution; of these, three were sent back as inappropriate (seventeen years old, deaf and dumb, and the like). Today there are fifteen girls and eighteen boys. In the course of the first three weeks the teachers became acquainted with the types of children, which they categorized as following:

1. Mentally retarded (passive type)
2. Mentally retarded (active type), with no specials signs of psychopathology
3. Mentally retarded, with evident psychopathology
4. Mentally normal, but psychopathic

Soon after coming to the institution the children underwent a physical and neurological examination. The children were generally weak and poorly nourished.

In the course of the first month, the teachers made significant efforts toward controlling the group of upset children, who had lost their equilibrium because of the changes in lifestyle, new conditions, and new environment. Thanks above all to free movement in a large park, great patience, a mild approach, and far-reaching individualization, the teachers succeeded in building a closer connection with the children. It also helped that the teachers were also the teachers in the classroom, and so they had the opportunity to become well acquainted with the minds of their students in the entire environment. The life in the institution will be structured, as far as possible, to have the character of a family life; each teacher will be together with a group of children, in school and for excursions. Common games, amusements, and work in the workshop make it possible for the teacher to get to know each child under her care. Thanks to the small number of children in each group, there is a favorable personal influence of the teachers on the children, which helps each child fight against feelings of worthlessness and aids in bringing out the child's positive traits and capabilities, according to the principles of Adler.[12]

The rooting of certain principles of the institution's life in the consciousness of the child, such as, for example, teaching the children to wash their upper bodies, to clean their bedrooms, etc., has become much easier since the beginning. The children consented to the duties placed upon them, and they do not violate these duties. The children's support for solidarity and cooperation and their feeling of responsibility, their behavior fulfilling their duties in the dining room and bedrooms, became an important factor.

In the course of three months, the group of children, which at the beginning was enormously spoiled, has been controlled to the extent that, today, on their own initiative, the children do not have to be called to the table and, after eating, they do not leave the table until they hear the bell.

An enormously important factor in the self-control of the children was the work in the workshops. Because the workshops were just built, only three workshops have been opened, provisionally: shoemaking, basket weaving, and linen making. The children's great zeal and desire to work and the joy the children show with each item successfully made are the clearest signs that the vocational education of a mentally retarded child is not only desirable, but simply a necessity of life. Even if this vocational education is not entirely satisfactory and cannot guarantee that the child will be able to take care of himself, it will strengthen the child's self-esteem. His ambition and his will to reach the goal will make him partially capable of taking care of himself. The children work in the workshops of the institution four hours every day.

Our children go to school less willingly. For nervous, upset children the obligation to sit even a short time during a lesson is sometimes very painful. The school is led according to the principles of a work-school with as much participation from the children as possible: we strive not to stuff the children with books but to strengthen their memory and to teach them to observe, to see, and to think.[13]

---

12 Alfred Adler (1870–1937), physician and psychologist from Austria.
13 This conception of the school is in line with the tendency of the leadership of Jewish children's organizations to stress the importance of vocational education. In spite of its importance, this topic has been little explored by historians of interwar Poland.

To a great extent, the choir (formed a month ago) and gymnastics have helped to discipline the group of children, who had become terribly wild and out of control. We do not have the right to draw conclusions at the end of three months of organizing, but we will present the results of our work objectively:

1. The health of the children is splendid. All of the children have developed physically, become strong, gotten color in their cheeks, and their eyes shine brightly.
2. The children accept the influence of the teacher not because of a fear of punishment (which in general is not used), but because, more and more, they have developed their will and inner restraint, due to the teachers' effect on their ambition and the teachers' display of trust and faith in the students. A warm, generous relationship between the teacher and the children will make possible a deepening of this trust and strengthen the ties of sympathy.
3. Movement play and sports, though not in a sufficient measure, are also excellent ways to strengthen the children and to develop in them a sense of discipline.
4. The work in the workshops has moved the children to a healthy competition and kindled in them a love for physical work.

Can one foresee what will be the educational consequences of this work? It is difficult to answer this question: one cannot determine the answer in advance. As it will be with the teachers, so it will be with the children. The more faith in the purpose of the work, the more love the teacher possesses, the deeper the stamp of influence on the strongly suggestive and impressionable spirits of the children. This difficult work is enormously demanding, and often does not succeed. It requires much patience, love, and intelligence.

Awakening in an Institution*¹
(Images of an Institution for Defective Children in Otwock)

Kalman Lis

Kalman Lis (1903–42) was a social worker and children's writer. He worked in the Therapeutic and Educational Institution in CENTOS in the late 1930s and he was there when war broke out on September 1, 1939. Seriously injured, he recovered in Warsaw and then returned to Otwock, where he was killed with children from the institution after the city was attacked by the Germans in 1942.[2]

The asterisked note indicates that this text is a fragment from the book *Di kleyne melukhe tsentos* (The little kingdom of CENTOS), but I have not been able to find any other reference to this publication. CENTOS did publish *Der heyl-pedagogisher anshtalt "Tsentos" un zayn dertsiungs-sistem* (The therapeutic-pedagogical CENTOS institution and its educational system) by Lis in Warsaw in 1937. This publication, a thin volume of less than fifty pages, appeared originally in the Polish-language *Szkoła Specjalna*, a journal of the Union for Polish Teachers, edited by the well-known pedagogue and leader in the field, Maria Grzegorzewska (1888–1967). The book, which included the observations of other teachers and psychologists, is only a part of what Lis planned to write. A prefatory note to the text indicates he had two other titles in preparation, *Dos silvetl fun a gaystik-opgeshtanen kind* (A profile of a mentally delayed child) and *Der hayl-pedagogisher anshtalt "Tsentos" in reportazh* (The therapeutic-pedagogical institution

---

1 *Fragment from the book *Di kleyne melukhe tsentos*. This asterisk and accompanying note appears in the original text.
2 See the entry for Kalman Lis by Khayim-Leyb Fuks in the *Leksikon fun der nayer yidisher literatur*, ed. Shmuel Niger and Yankev Shatski (New York: Alveltlekhn Yidishn Kultur-Kongres, 1956–81).

"CENTOS" in reportage). The latter proposed title is another indication that this institution attracted significant attention among those interested in child welfare. I have not been able to locate either of these texts. This piece originally appeared in *Unzer kind* 3, no. 10 (October 1930): 420–24.

 The sun comes up. The children in the institution get up earlier than I do. Yosek's singing reaches me from the three rooms for the children. Yosek is the institution's cantor, who gargles upon waking and before going to sleep. When Yosek is stubborn or will simply not agree to go in to wash up, the only way to get him to do something is to let him sing. He smiles to himself and strides into the washroom, gargling. From a nearby room comes a fresh complaint of the so-called manager of the institution, the tall, thin Zalmen. The squabble is on account of a shovel that Yosek's friend intentionally hid from Zalmen. Yosek wants to show him its hiding place only on the condition that he, that is, Zalmen, should give him a piece of thread that he can use to sew up in a hole in his summer pants. After the first ring of the bell, the entire group, apart from the abovementioned manager, is still in bed and they're waiting for me to personally show my face in each room separately. I start with the first room—the parliament of this enclosed kingdom.

 The president, Itzik, a disheveled boy with brown hair and an almost childish face but a pair of darting eyes that look out mischievously from under his short brow, sleeps in one bed with his favorite, the dog "Aza," and, when I wake up, I have to first of all wake up Aza and only afterwards, when Itzik gets up, will the other boys get up, too. But Itzik cannot tear himself away from Aza. He pets him on the neck, cuddles him to his thin body, and in exchange gets from him a wet lick of the cheeks and a kiss on the lips. When I tickle Aza under his leg, Aza jumps up, dances over the frame of the open window, and disappears. By that time Itzik is already in his shorts and in the next minute he's already lying down with Aza next to the doghouse. And the hungry puppies come one after the other to Aza's dripping teats.

 Sobotski is the president's right hand when it comes to a matter of something on the left hand, like stealing a couple of pieces of bread with butter from the kitchen for Aza or hiding a couple of cups of coffee in a box on the table. The little, lively Sobotski, who slips out of your hands like an eel when you think you're just about to catch him stealing, lies down as if he's innocent and pretends that he doesn't even notice that I came in and that I am holding half the blanket in my hands. That's when I notice that he has tricked me. Under the covers, he is already in his trousers.

Hershek, the prime minister, when he needs some kind of help in an emergency—for example, getting a teacher to give permission for a game on a stormy night or to apologize to the chairman whose guests were attacked with a hail of pine cones, or to allow or not the playing of *klishes*, or to get from the manager the boards and tools needed to fix the doghouse, and so on—Hershek, the rascal with the impish eyes of a fox, rolls himself three times on his own bed and the fourth time, with one try, he lands on the bed of his friend Yankl and hits him in the mouth with his bare feet ... Shimek, who just yesterday seized on a new word that pursues him with every step, greets me with a hysterical cry, "GOOD MORNING, TEACHER, *boyml, boyml, boyml!*"[3] With him it's easier. Liolek is Itzik's wingman for the dogs, and when President Itzik is at the doghouse, Liolek will not spend another moment in the bedroom.

The first room is on its feet, and in ten minutes they will start making their beds. Now I go to the second room; Povidle is up already ... Povidle is a young boy of about ten, new to the room just less than three weeks ago. The group crowned him with the nickname Povidle because soon after arriving in the institution Moyshek asked a question of each of the boys in turn: "What do you make *povidle* (jam) from?" And with each boy he answered the question himself, saying that you make *povidle* from beets, you cook them first, then put in sugar, then they have to cool, the beets, that is, then you eat it and can call it jam. And if you want to calm Moyshek during an argument with a friend, or when little Moyshek gets a smack and cries, you need to ask him the same question, what do you make *povidle* from? ... Povidle is already the first one up because he wants to get out of washing the upper half of his body, and he thinks, who knows, perhaps he will be successful in avoiding it this time ... Povidle's helper, the clever and always fiery Yosele, has already managed to have a fight with Yosl "the Cantor" on account of an "Anglas," a little picture that Yosl

---

3 Cooking oil, in Yiddish.

"the Cantor" unfairly took away from him yesterday. Now he's threatening me, the teacher, that he will not get dressed, not make his bed or Povidle's bed, and, in general, not go to wash up, if I do not recover the "Anglas" from Yosl "the Bull."

Kuba, a thirteen-year-old, deeply retarded hysteric with the movements of a bear, cannot manage his slippers because there is no way the right slipper will fit on the left foot and no way in the world the left slipper will fit on the right . . . This laborious task would be endless until the end of the generations were it not for Hershek, the supervisor, who wants to hurry up and finish with the room more quickly and puts Kuba on the bed and roughly forces the right slipper on the right foot and the left slipper on the left foot.

Yosek "the Horse," a thirteen-year-old assistant to the manager, got the nickname "Horse" because he always runs to *schlep* something, to lug something on his back, and is the first one to carry the basket with the children's food whenever they go on a field trip, has already managed while tying his shoes to make one knot in one shoelace and two knots in the other. He ties his shoes in a deadly fashion; there isn't one night when you don't have to cut his shoelaces with a knife because they are so tightly tied. Under the best circumstances you have to stop and try for twenty minutes to untie the knots, biting your lips until they're bloody and maintaining your patience and strained nerves.

With God's help the "Anglas" incident between Yosele and Yosl the Cantor is solved, Kuba's slippers were put on the right feet, and Yosek the Horse's laces were untied and tied again, Povidle's bed was made, and the second room is already in the middle of being cleaned and aired out.

On going into the third room, I hesitate, beginning to wonder if I have truly rung the bell this morning or not. The superintendent isn't even there yet. And his carefully made bed gives the impression that he did not sleep there last night and that he did not sleep there for many nights before. The boys in this group lie under the blankets, as if they don't have to get up. Across the hall in the second room, beds squeak, mattresses groan, and a young supervisor tries to mop up the floor with a heavy broom. This is a sign that I did indeed ring the bell, and so I yell out in a loud voice: "Good morning children, get up!" Khaim the Comic—the Comic, because he mimics the diction of the entire teaching staff, including the supervisor, plays tricks in the washroom, pretends like he's a gramophone, a radio, etc. From his mischievous face pop out two smiling eyes, one is covered with a blue cataract, and while this eye smiles naively, the second seems to be mocking, sticking out its tongue behind your back and whistling with a small, thin whistle, "Teaaccher, goood mooorning, why is our room so early, even before the ringing of the bell?" In the meantime he steals deeper and deeper under the covers and his left foot reaches out to the next bed, and he jabs his friend Potzi, as if giving him a prepared signal. Potzi dances out of bed, and he quickly begins to pull a long sock over a bare foot, looking at me with two dark, velvety soft eyes. His glance returns to the sock and he succumbs, deep within himself, to a not unnoticeable mocking smile: "*Aha*, foolish teacher, it says . . . I am Potzi . . . what?" As he pulls up his sock, he softly touches his hat, like an animal licking clean a shiny, matted section of pelt . . . because he, Potsi, in all of his external appearance and psychological makeup, confirms Darwin's theory in the best way . . . Nutek, always the cynic, laughs at me, right in the face, because . . . just yesterday Nutek hid the teacher's bell, as he always does with the teacher's keys, and the teacher should know that . . . The last thing he says is that if the teacher will come in two minutes, he will see what's going on! . . . And as I go out and look in through the keyhole into the third bedroom, I see nothing less than Nutek and Khaim shaking hands, Potzi neighs like a horse and bares his two rows of healthy alabaster-white teeth, like a black man, and the heavy Belgian pony Mikhl-Barabanshtshik[4]—he's called Barabanshtshik because his passion is to drum on a table, a wall, or a board whenever he hears a march, a mazurka, or a polka—this is also his only way of getting to class, singing a march to the accompaniment of his drumming—Mikhl-Barabanshtshik slides himself out of bed, dressed and ready, even in his socks . . . and this is all because of a prank . . . I am delayed a full eight minutes and I meet the group by their clean and neat beds.

The dormitory is awake . . . The sun is smiling down and laughing in all the corners of the dormitory.

---

4 Lis adds to his description of Mikhl and the other boys through a clever play on words. The Belgian draft horse is a breed of horse from the Brabant region of modern Belgium, and the Yiddish word *baraban* means drum.

Two Visits in CENTOS[1]

Helena Boguszewska

Helena Boguszewska (1886–1978) wrote for children and adults. She authored a series of biology textbooks and also wrote often about issues of social work and education. She collaborated closely with the writer and editor Jerzy Kornacki (1908–81). She and Kornacki formed the literary group *Przedmieście* (Outskirts) in 1933. The group disbanded in 1937 but was reactivated after the war in 1958. Boguszewska and Kornacki hoped to encourage prose writers to use fact and observation in their fiction, in an effort to draw attention to the social conditions of the lower classes. The group had a special interest in the experiences of other ethnic populations.

This piece originally appeared in *Przegląd Społeczny* VII, no. XI (November 1933): 240–49.

I

CENTOS is an institution in Otwock for Jewish orphans, those who are psychopathic and delayed in development. I visited the institution twice. The first time was four years ago. The second time recently, in April, before the Jewish holidays.

---

1 The following appears in the original text as a footnote: "The following report, about the educational and medical institution for Jewish children in Otwock sponsored by the Union of Association for the Care of Jewish Orphans of the Republic of Poland in Warsaw (CENTOS), is printed with the permission of the author and the editorial board of *Wiadomości Literackie* from No. 36 (507) of that publication."

CENTOS in Otwock

Helena Boguszewska, 1938 (Narodowe Archiwum Cyfrowe, Warsaw)

I arrived the first time in the afternoon, on a winter day. The wooden gate with the inscription "CENTOS" leads to a large area surrounded by pine trees and buildings. It looks like a typical Otwock villa. I went to the nearest building, with steps and a veranda; children crowded the hallways. I did not observe them closely, but at first glance everything seemed normal. Then the bell sounded, and everyone sat down to dinner at long tables in the glass veranda. Beyond the windows were frost, snow, and pine trees and inside were the hubbub of voices, the press of bodies, and good, abundant food. The teachers spoke and laughed with the children, everybody talked of the goings-on in the institution, of matters important and urgent that everybody knew about, and the bread disappeared from the baskets surprisingly quickly.

It has been said that the children do not eat much soup and meat, that they just "stuff themselves with bread" and use their napkins for their noses. How to fix this? Everybody was talking, joking—it was a happy atmosphere. Lejzor, the twelve-year-old on duty, passed out the plates of barley soup—everything was normal.

He was passing out the plates, then suddenly, without any reason, he said that he would no longer pass out the plates. Why? Because there was a line? After he had demanded for so long to take his turn on duty? Yes, yes, this is all true, Lejzor does not say no, only that he will no longer pass out the plates. The puzzling grimace of his bittersweet mouth, the fleeting glance of his reddened eyes beneath long eyelashes—no, he will no longer pass out the plates, that's it. He disturbed the rhythm of the meal and in the air was an atmosphere of tension created by Lejzor—already things are not normal.

No, this time Lejzor doesn't make a fuss; the doctor puts his arm around his shoulder, whispers something to him, and the mollified Lejzor again passes out the *kluski*. The dinner continues in the usual rhythm, at its own pace, the children "stuff themselves with bread," and the teachers speak merrily with the children—again, everything is normal.

"Our Lejzor is a nice, good boy," they say cheerfully, "only he has such moments . . ."

Let's hope that these "moments" do not become worse . . . because, as I found out later, Lejzor is not easy to manage. But I have no idea what it could be like: Do I know what Lejzor's life was like when he came into this world? Perhaps he came from a small town where, when there is an outbreak of typhus or cholera, Jews make a match of two of the poorest children, for example a young girl and the most troublesome boy, and take "the couple" to the Jewish cemetery, at the cost of the community, as an offering to fate? From such macabre events come such boys like Lejzor . . .[2]

I survey all of the children, and some strange things strike me in the midst of this ostensible normal scene. For example, right in front of me, my neighbor at the table, Sura. She is probably sixteen years old, red and fat, with thick, full lips and unruly hair. Where have I seen her before?

Oh, I have seen her, I've seen her dozens of times, and not in the same place: in Zdołbunów, in Prużany, in Rożyszcze, in Kowel, in Parysów, and

---

2 For an explanation of Jewish wedding customs, including examples of *shvartse khasenes*, when a wedding for two of the area's poorest individuals was arranged as a good deed to end the crisis of an epidemic, see Barbara Kirshenblatt-Gimblett's entry in *YIVO Encyclopedia of Jews in Eastern Europe*, s.v. "Weddings," accessed May 26, 2016, http://www.yivoencyclopedia.org/article.aspx/Weddings, and Nathaniel Deutsch, *The Jewish Dark Continent: Life and Death in the Russian Pale of Settlement* (Cambridge, MA: Harvard University Press, 2011), 263.

other places, too . . . bedecked in colorful rags and baubles, flying along the filthy streets of small towns, squatting along the walls of the market square, dressed in rags, laughing, jostling, pushing, throwing stones in the manner of a classical "foolish Sura," and now she's sitting here next to me, quiet and cheerful, having a conversation with me at the level of a polite nine-year-old—this is "our Sura," with the unruly hair tamed by the teacher—"our Sura, the perfect hostess" . . . Because though her reading in school is poor, she likes to cook and iron and, now, when the teachers praise her, she laughs with a normal smile, happy and sheepish . . .

My eye falls now on a small boy, ruddy and fat, with pronounced facial features and the face of a half-idiot. In the most quiet whisper I ask about him. "Oh, him?" smiles the doctor, "This is our Abramek, our "calendar child." Abramek . . . Think of any date from your life, and he will tell you what day of the week it was. He likes when people ask him . . ."

And the eight-year-old Abramek, looking like five and having the sense of a two-and-a-half-year-old, answers after a moment's thought: "Wednesday."

"And July 25th, 1917?"

"Thursday."

And I know that this was a Thursday, because I remember.

But he is not able to put on his hat, to get himself dressed, or to do much of anything else. There's no question of reading. He's not able to speak properly. He says "Thoisday." And when he is asked, even in a childish way, if this is a leap year, he is filled with terror, like an angry cat or stuffed owl in the hallway. This is the calendar child! One needs to treat him as if he were only a year old.

And Mosiek? Such a Mosiek I do not wish even on my enemies. The doctor is able to pull Mosiek out of his dark madness with just a glance, but no one is able to handle Mosiek when the doctor goes on vacation. Appeals to honor, calling on all of Mosiek's hidden virtues, with all kinds of entreaties and suggestions do not work: "Mosiek, you are a sensible boy, you can be trusted?" Mosiek carelessly breaks windows with stones, pulls plants in others' gardens out from their roots, curses the other children with the most inventive curses on the street, and does many other things I cannot mention here . . .

"How do you stand all of this?"

"Oh, this is nothing," they respond cheerfully, "really nothing, if you only knew what happened here eight months ago, how everything fell apart..."

I can imagine: children like Sura and Lejzor gathered from the streets of the small towns, halfwits from the roads of villages, wretched heroes of scandalous big city incidents. Thrown out of homes and shelters because nobody could deal with them—they fly here now in the snow between the pines, normal children, happy, "free" after the lunch recess until they begin work in workshops, and we look on them through the windows from above, from the doctor's office. For example, Boruch: his uncle, an old Jew, brought him here, a poor shoemaker with a white beard and reddened eyes, saying with a sniveling voice:

"Doctor, if you do not accept him, I will probably drown the snot-nosed brat, because I can no longer..."[3]

We look on from above, as Boruch chases a ball. "This Boruch, he has organizational abilities," the doctor suddenly explains. "But, necessarily, he must govern them, control them... he organized entire gangs, took them to market stalls, to neighboring orchards—but here he is directed otherwise. He treats the animals well... we'll see what becomes of him... And Ryfka?"

They show me the daily logbook:

"... today Ryfka has been very excited all morning. She did not want to do anything in class, she left the classroom, she threw rocks...

"... Ryfka again had an attack of madness, she cried, she demolished the garden..."

Two more pages on Ryfka. Constantly Ryfka. Always Ryfka. She's a nightmare, the terror of the institution.[4]

What makes Ryfka so awful? Show me this Ryfka...

... "Ryfka again very excited"...

---

3 Compare to Kats's description of a man bringing his children to Helenówek. These descriptions are most certainly stylized but they do point to a real need for child care.
4 In the chapter of her memoir describing her work at CENTOS, Rosenblum describes a young girl, Rywka, who was especially difficult to handle, "our most difficult child." The Rywka described in the memoir entered the institution in 1928 and was there for at least nine years. It is possible that this is the same Ryfka described by Boguszewska. Szymańska, *Byłam tylko lekarzem*, 115–16.

Will she be in the workshop?

She will be. It's already started. We can go.

So we go through the darkened courtyard in the direction of a row of windows, all lit up. The whole building resounds with children at work. Workshops, workrooms on both sides of the hallway. Shoemaking, carpentry, basket making, a tailor. I recognize that I already know something about those whom I see working: Lejzor hammers into a soft sole crammed with wooden pins, Boruch planes a wooden block. Sura sits bent over, clumsily, with some needles. Everyone is important, occupied, useful. Is it easy to encourage them to work? It's not easy. It takes much patience from the masters and the educators. But patience is not something that is lacking in CENTOS: it is in the air. Somebody doesn't want to work? They wait cheerfully and patiently until he does. And, more or less, everybody is already doing something. And this is good when someone turns to work. This is holding on to the edges of the world of normal, everyday people. For example, just look at Boruch: how he loves his carpentry . . .

In the preschool by the little table, Abramek labors away over a piece of clay, drooling stupidly, plunged in the unlit darkness with no news of any calendar. I squat down next to him.

"You don't recognize me, Abramek? We spoke earlier, for a moment after lunch. I asked you about July 20, 1925 . . ."

Only after this kind of mysterious approach does Abramek "understand," "Wednesday," he lisps delightedly "Wesday" . . . and again plunges himself dully into the lump of clay, from which he cannot form anything . . .

And Ryfka?

The eight-year-old little girl with the round innocent face, puffing with excitement, plays with a little cart made from a cigar box, with bobbins as wheels. She will show me, she says, if I want to do it. We play for a whole hour, we talk. She is cheerful, almost normally developed, calm, and terribly attached to the teachers. If she falls into a rage, this torments them. And then she says: "If I knew where my parents that rejected me are buried, I would stomp upon this earth, stomp, stomp . . ."

Or she wrings her hands, "Can I help it if I'm crazy?"

But Ryfka isn't crazy. She's had such a life . . . The doctor says that Ryfka will be okay. But he knows what she's saying . . .

II

When I visited CENTOS for the second time after four years had passed, it was a blue April day, with an icy lining but heated a little by the sun. Suddenly there was sun on the square before the main building, where boys, already unknown to me, played ball and ping pong on a wooden table they themselves made. They boasted of their new carpentry workshops. Earlier there were only five and now there are nine. They themselves made several small tables for the bedrooms, for the entire institution, but the little tables are still not finished—Do I want to see the tables? Of course, I want to, we go there after lunch, but where are the little girls? Why do I see here only boys?

The girls are upstairs, they're making order in the bedrooms for the holiday the day after tomorrow and they asked that nobody go there until they finish. Only one girl spins around the house, she traipses behind each and quietly looks on a few steps from those conversing . . . this girl is "cataleptic," she drags one leg and constantly holds her hand suspended in the air, as if she intends to do something. But she does nothing, just stands there quietly and looks on with her sweet loose smile, glued to her face.

The bell sounds and everyone hurries home to prepare for the holidays. The home is full of the sounds of people making order, of steps on the stairs, people rushing with buckets and rags, with the legs of furniture out of place, temporarily exiled from their corners. For the holiday "there dare not be" even a crumb of bread, piles of *matse* lie in the pantry . . .

And again, as before, we sit down at long tables on the glassed-in veranda, again it's crowded and there is the buzz of voices, as always, but even more so, because of the holiday. But before there was frost and snow beyond the windows and now it is a lousy, chilly April day, and there is talk of gardens, vegetable patches, and who is planting what . . . and the child on duty distributes the potato soup, and then the barley soup—the child on duty is someone else, and again the teachers say that the children do not want to eat *kasha*, they just put the meat on bread and eat it that way, they "stuff themselves with bread" and use their napkins for their noses. "You haven't solved this problem in the past four years?" We laugh and the teachers again return to their own concerns, that is, to the concerns of the institution. Lejzor comes tomorrow for the holiday . . . Lejzor? The boy who four years ago was on duty, who passed out the barley soup but didn't want to and almost made a fuss? Nobody remembers this: so many children passing out barley soup and not wanting to, so many fusses, though in general they like being on duty very much and there are those who make a fuss when their shift ends. But Lejzor, from the Jewish cemetery? "Ah, yes, our Lejzor . . ." "So where is he now?" "Lejzor is already on his own, independent, a normal person, he is a shoemaker in a small town, he's coming tomorrow . . ."

"And Sura?" I suddenly remember my neighbor at the table years ago. "Where is Sura?" Sura also works: she finished fourth grade, she grew up and is a housewife. Chana makes linens, Leja does embroidery, they all stay in touch and everyone's coming . . .

Mosiek is coming for the holiday, too. "He's completely changed, he is simply completely different since the time the doctor found his mother." "How? He found his mother?" "Yes. It turned out that this was just trauma, Mosiek was just tormenting himself, thinking he was just simply thrown away and that he knows nothing about his mother. Ach, it wasn't easy to find this address, on the strength of only one letter from America, to trace Mosiek's wanderings from one shelter to another, thrown out each time because he was "impossible." Well, in the end the doctor found Mosiek's mother. And it wasn't easy to convince her, the mother of the illegitimate Mosiek, to accept that it was up to her if Mosiek will be a normal, healthy person or a troublemaker without sense . . . Well, it worked out. She came, was persuaded, here in the office she waited for her son, she brought him even some small package with candies or something . . ."

"Well, and was Mosiek very happy about it?"

"Well, yes, certainly he was but it didn't look like that. Actually, he didn't want to even see her. He was silently huffy, as if offended. But he ran to the bedroom, to his teacher, whom he always loved, and he threw himself around her neck: 'Do you know that I already have my own mother?' And then he again returned to the office and said nothing to the mother, again completely as if he didn't want to see her . . . That's the way he is, our Mosiek. But he calmed down completely, so that now he is in a home for normal boys, he works with great fervor, simply is a fanatic at work, will be an excellent carpenter and manages everywhere, just like Boruch . . ."

We're silent for a moment. We sit by ourselves on the empty veranda, over undrinkable tea, we can see through the big window that the children are already running around outside the home, because today is a bright, clear day . . . I look at them and think: they are already adults, they will be here tomorrow for the holiday, all dressed up, and they will talk like average, normal people. Is this what will give the staff strength, when they meet the next wave of children in awful misery, with schizophrenia, hysteria, or imbecility? Because not everyone can triumph over this suffering, even with goodwill and talent . . . for example, this Abramek, he was a complete idiot aside from his calendar obsession, wasn't he?

I was right on the mark: Abramek actually pulled himself up to almost normal, he is in the first class at the gymnasium, his secret calendar skills are at the same level but all his other talents are very much developed. There is a new boy here now, as young as Abramek was then, barely five years old . . . Do I want to see him?

"This one . . ."

"Dressed in corduroy? But he's not doing anything?"

"No, indeed . . . he has rather too much going on, he's able to open all kinds of locks with a skeleton key, to steal everything. So there's no place that will take him. Shmulek, come here, Shmulek!"

The boy is ruddy and fat, with wily, squinty eyes the color of his brown jacket, he cuddles up to the teachers, smiling and satisfied with himself. "I'm not a 'thief'" he cries out suddenly and aggressively, almost threateningly, in the direction of those looking on him from afar, and he looks grimly upon his colleagues, those he stole from, whose suitcases he broke into not long ago.

"No, Shmulek. You are not a thief. You are . . . no, you will be . . . a good boy . . ." a teacher tries to calm him down.

Well, when Shmulek was sick and in the hospital, he said such awful things to the nurses that after three days they begged that he be taken away. Boruch used to be just like him, and Mosiek, too . . .

"It's nothing. From this, they will become people, the doctor laughs." Have you seen our Ryfka?

Ryfka? I recall a winter afternoon and early twilight and how we struggled in the snow in the direction of the lit-up windows, and the cart made from a cigar box, to which bobbins were supposed to be attached as wheels. I look out the window: it's still a clear day, and the workshops are apparently closed because they're cleaning there for the holiday. The older boys have run off somewhere. A tall girl in a thick gray sweater drills the entire team of the youngest, organizes some game, places them in fours, some in pairs, or other way around . . . to see how she commands: one, two, and three! And everyone runs somewhere and again they gather together and make a circle, they sing, they march . . . how she rules over them, how she holds the group in her hands. "This cannot be easy, especially if the little ones are just like Ryka was?"

"There are some like her," the doctor admits, "here actually are some like Ryfka, as Ryfka was before. You don't recognize her?"

"No, really?" Ryfka, a born organizer, Ryfka, a caretaker of children, Ryfka, leading a group, substituting for the teacher who went on vacation? Again she puts them all in pairs, she starts them singing a round, in places breaking the rhythm from leg to leg, clapping in time as each little pair takes its turn, with the rhythm, in the spirit of the march and the group . . .

They go under the window singing *tadorot-katakamalusia-tańcowała-rannąrosą- i tupałanóżką bosą, nóżkąbosą . . .*[5]

She leads them to the vegetable garden, they have to see to something there before the holiday . . .

A small parade disappears behind the azure fence, over the gray vegetable gardens, still barren from the winter. I pull away from the window: a garden? I look at the shelf . . . was the institution's logbook here, or was it in the doctor's office upstairs?

". . . Ryfka again very excited. She demolished the garden . . ."

The logbook was already sent to the archives. How many logbooks have there been since then, how many children have demolished gardens . . . But the garden is always fixed somehow and is actually better each year. Now, for example, fruit trees have been planted. And as for Ryfka, we already have another "story" about our Ryfka. Let me show you how Ryfka answered one of the questionnaires about interests, worked up by the

---

[5] The children are singing "Dorotka," a traditional Polish lullaby. Boguszewska writes the words as the children would have sung them.

educational psychology group. But we have to go to the office upstairs, because all the responses are there.

". . . I like best to play with small children, because it's very pleasant and they listen and in general are better and more pleasant . . ."

". . . I think the most virtuous quality is a liking for the poor and for those who are mute and blind . . ."

". . . I would like to know how the blind and mute speak and to know where they have books and how they read . . ."

". . . My dream is to be a teacher and to work in a kindergarten . . ."

". . . If I had a lot of money I would give it to the poor, I would build a large house and give it to poor children . . ."

". . . If I would have a lot of free time, I would go to the magistrate, I would ask that an orphanage be built for the children . . ."

". . . When I have a lot of time, I think about poor people, because they don't have anything to eat or anywhere to sleep and they don't have the comforts that I do . . ."

Dusk falls outside the window, it is cold but the clarity of spring is already here. I hear singing—the children are returning. Outside the doors the rhythmic stomping gets louder and at the threshold the chaotic sound of small shoes on a newly washed floor inside and the authoritarian sound of clapping hands:

"Careful! Take off your shoes! Careful!"

Somewhere a door slams. The doctor listens and smiles.

She took them to the room. There are no workshops today because they're cleaning but she's already gathering them for supper. The children are with Ryfka already, so they will be quiet. Do you still want to still see the school? Ryfka is already out of this school, because it's a special school, and she's moved up to a normal city school.

In the last moments of the day I see classes, drawings, exercise books, schoolwork like in a normal school, as if the work is just done by younger children. In the entrance hall the older girls replant the window boxes into pots—for tomorrow! In the courtyard the little ones finish cleaning shovels in the sand—for tomorrow, for tomorrow! I wait for the "doctor," who is going to Warsaw with us tomorrow, there isn't much time before the train. A crowd gathers around me. We're talking about tomorrow, the holiday, who is growing what in the vegetable gardens, and if it is better to sow patches of cucumbers or onions, and about the "big lions" in the Warsaw zoo. The cataleptic girl stands quietly in the corner a few steps away, her hands always suspended in the air, patient and listening.

"Is it true that the Hitlerites in Germany are beating Jews?"[6]

Who is asking this? Is it possible that the cataleptic girl asked this? She repeats this not loudly, mildly but insistently:

"Please, is it true?"

I tell them that it's true. And everybody is quiet. Only after a moment one of the boys pulls out a small dirty hand and strokes my fur collar.

"Is this fur 'from a lion'?"

The door opens, the doctor comes with a suitcase, still speaking with someone, recommending something to someone . . . Light bursts out from the hallway, and only now do I see that it is already late and dark outside. Ryfka sings with the little "mountaineers," someone calls out to the boys to wash their hands because soon will be the bell . . .

We go. The train is at 7:50, there is still a lot of time . . .

---

[6] Boguszewska's article appeared in November 1933.

Five Years of CENTOS Activity in Otwock

Zofia Rosenblum

Zofia Rosenblum published reports on the CENTOS institution in Otwock in both *Dos kind* and *Przegląd Społeczny*. This section consists of two reports, the first published in *Dos kind* and the second published in *Przegląd Społeczny* in three parts. The first report appeared in *Dos kind* 11, no. 1/2 (January–February 1934): 15–19. Rosenblum did not know Yiddish, so this must have been translated from a Polish-language original for publication. There is no indication of the translator or the location of an original text in Polish.

A report in three parts appeared in *Przegląd Społeczny* VIII, no. I–II, III, and IV (January–February 1934, March 1934, and April–May 1934): 23–31, 49–57, and 89–93. Each of these parts appears in translation below, after the report from *Dos kind*. The report from *Dos kind*, covering the same time period, is included here because it differs substantially from what appeared in *Przegląd Społeczny*.

Five Years in Otwock

I. The Difficulties Confronting the Institution

From the first moment that the institution opened, there have been many difficulties to overcome.

1. The living conditions. The buildings of the institution, which seemed very developed five years ago, are too small and not suitable for their purpose. These are wooden buildings which are difficult to heat in winter, in addition to the great quantity of coal needed for heating and

which therefore takes up a large part of our budget. In spite of our significant material difficulties, we have twice made fundamental renovations to the buildings. In the course of five years we have constructed a building for workshops, an isolation building, a laundry, and a cellar. And there is still a need to expand the institution by constructing another building with bedrooms and a dining room.

2. Health conditions. There has not been one instance of an epidemic in the five years of the institution's existence, with the exception of the flu epidemic of 1931–32. Almost eighty percent of the children and all of the teachers had the flu. This drastically affected the educational work of the teachers in the two winter sessions.

3. From the first moment we were established we have had to fight increasingly greater financial difficulties. We do not have a fixed budget and we were forced after some time to accept children from private families.

From the beginning of 1931 the Warsaw magistrate,[1] just as other magistrates, (mostly) sent us children, reimbursing the institution for the costs of the children's maintenance. The costs of keeping a child today (maintenance, learning a profession, school instruction, medical care, clothing) run to 3.75 daily.[2] Though this institution is the only one of its kind in Poland, the Jewish community does not properly appreciate its need. We have heard more than once: "Why lose money on an abnormal child, when there are so many normal ones? They were born idiots and they'll remain idiots."

The results the institution has achieved contradict these claims. It seems that it is more economical to prepare a retarded child for life by learning a profession than to maintain a helpless idiot at the cost of the community. It seems that everybody understands that it is better to educate a morally depraved child and to not allow him to become a criminal than to lose money on an arrested child in prison. It seems that the community will learn to appreciate how important it is to educate psychopathic individuals and teach them to adjust to normal society. In Western Europe

---

1 *Magistrat*, in Polish. The administrative body of a given territory, equivalent to a city council.
2 Presumably 3.75 *złoty*, though no unit of currency is given.

they stopped discussing this long ago. Individuals differing only in small ways from the average are taught in a variety of well-established, first-rate institutions. The problem of prevention and mental hygiene interests the most serious thinkers in the world. In Western Europe, institutions such as ours do not need to fight for the right to exist. We won recognition for our work only very slowly through laborious and intense effort. Even medical professionals in the field complained to the leadership of the institution when a child unsuitable for the institution was turned down. "Who is the institution for, if you do not take any idiots?" Meetings with teachers, psychologists, and medical professionals helped them to understand why the selection of children must be strongly enforced and why the institution has such importance as a center of therapy and education.

With the growth in the number of children, the institution must be further developed. An observation building is needed, a site where, for scientific and research purposes, a child can be placed for a short time.

It is absolutely necessary to find a patron who will be concerned about the fate of our children after they leave the institution. The institution is in close contact with children who live nearby and invites them for holidays. We want to find a patron to ensure that each child has appropriate supervision and work after leaving the institution. We wish to remain in contact with our children in other cities because only then will our work not go to waste.

These are future problems. The problems are important; the obligations are great. But we are certain that the institution will receive authorization and that it will succeed in attracting friends, people of good will, and professional colleagues. We think we can make a modest but worthy contribution to the great work in the field of the mental health of the Jewish child.

II. "The Day of Independence," as Described by a Teacher

The general assembly of children decided to organize a "day of independence."[3] The discussion during the assembly was very stormy. The older

---

3 Another "day of independence," when Janusz Korczak and his children from the Home for Jewish Orphans showed up as unexpected guests, is described further below.

children stressed the importance of the day, as a sign of their domestic independence and that they could manage on their own. Everyone accepted the test with great enthusiasm. The night before the day of independence a lively commotion reigned throughout the institution: children gathered in small groups and hotly debated the distribution of the next day's tasks. There was another meeting in the evening that seemed very impressive. In the fourth grade classroom the tables were arranged in a square and Sheyne, who had arranged the meeting, found a place by the window with pencil and paper in hand. Teachers were not allowed to attend the meeting. The meeting proper did not last long. The children went to bed quietly. I stood off to the side during the meeting and observed everyone separately. The older youths were quiet and serious, thinking about the tasks they would take on tomorrow.

They did not forget to take the bell from me. Around five in the morning I heard children's voices. Some of them thought that it was already time to get up, others thought there was still time. Every minute someone went to determine the time. When six thirty finally arrived, the bell sounded and almost in the same moment all of the children jumped out of bed and got dressed in a flash. One did not have to prod the children to get up. There was a feeling that a sense of discipline dominated, a strong but comradely discipline: "We have to show the teachers what we really are." There was no teacher supervising the cleaning of the rooms this time, only Frida Pelts, the incessantly screaming girl who always made a commotion, known by the nickname Frida the Blockhead, a real punishment from God and a plague on the institution. Her gait, which resembles that of a duck, was today imposing and dignified. Mendl, a terror to the children and, more than that, a master rascal, oversaw the order in the washroom and led the children to the showers with a rare tenderness, with a smile on his lips. It was later related with pride: "The children did not even need to be told to brush their teeth, they did it on their own." They did not wake me up. I heard that when Potsi (Mendl's wingman) suggested waking up the teacher in order that he should see "what he sees by us," he got an answer: "Oh, better to let him rest." When I wanted to leave the room, I saw that they had locked me in from outside. I knocked. In about a minute there was the squeak of a master key, a very widely distributed tool among our children, and a bowl with water was brought into the room. The girls explained to me: "There's nothing for you to do today in the bathrooms." Through the window I saw a group of children playing ball. Of course, according to the distribution of the work, the supervision of the younger children before breakfast fell to her. I tried to leave the room, but the boys forcibly pushed me back in. It did not help at all to say that I wanted to take a walk before breakfast: "You will certainly write about all of this, and we don't want that." The children prepared breakfast half an hour earlier than usual. For breakfast, Sheyne, our noble one, who thinks that physical work is beneath her honor, dusted the tables and benches in the dining room. Potsi, a *freser*,[4] who usually sneaks into the dining room through the window and lies in wait for the appropriate moment he can pinch something unnoticed, solemnly placed himself by the door so that no one would go into the dining room before the bell. The teachers lined up together with the children. Yosek watched over the behavior of the children during breakfast.

Ten minutes after breakfast, two groups were organized. The older children chose to go on a small excursion, and the younger children went to the park under Perele's supervision. At ten thirty, peace reigned in the dormitory. There were no children to be seen, no children to be taken to the woods, there were no voices to be heard and no arguments. The teachers rested.

At precisely one o'clock the children themselves made lunch. This time the teachers traded places with the children. They stood in line at the door of the dining room and let control of the dining room be taken out of their hands.

During eating there were none of the usual arguments and bickering, those children on duty calmly waited their turn. The children talked quietly among themselves at the tables. Mendl, the older boy on duty who usually fights with everyone, today helped the others on duty with a friendly readiness. After lunch the tables and dining room were carefully cleaned. Everything was done swiftly and energetically. It should be noted that in the morning the children sent off Sala the cook, with a great parade,

---

4   One who eats like an animal.

dressed in her good clothes, for a longer excursion. At lunch "the teachers" changed: the children who worked in the morning now rested; some children went for a walk in small groups. The older boys and girls chose to go in the Świder, knowing that their excursion to the river without supervision would create for us—the educators—great distress, and they turned to me with a request, that I should take part in their excursion, and the girls invited the female teachers as their guests.

For the evening meal, which took place in a cheerful and happy mood, the dining room was very clean. Tsisha, always sullen and angry, supervised the hand washing. Today she patiently helped the younger children and strongly reprimanded the older children for their negligent washing. Potsi, who just yesterday had to be implored to wash his hands, checked everyone's cleanliness on their way into the dining room. After eating the children suggested to the teachers that they should go together with them to the bathing rooms. No amount of excuses or joking worked: we had to go together with the children to the showers and submit to the orders of the "on-duty teachers." Wishing the children a good night, we recognized how pleasant the day had been, proof of the children's discipline and their ability. With song, the happy and satisfied children went to sleep.

A Report on Five Years of CENTOS Activity in Otwock

Zofia Rosenblum

This three-part text originally appeared in *Przegląd Społeczny*, January–February 1934, 23–31; March 1934, 49–57; and April–May 1934, 89–93. The three parts are combined in the translation below.

The Union of Associations for the Care of Jewish Orphans, having under its care more than five thousand children in closed orphanages, decided in 1927 to create for abnormal children a separate institution, in the full understanding that the abnormal child hampers the educational work of a normal institution and does not actually receive any benefit from the normal institution.

In 1928 the Union acquired and renovated the building of the People's Educational League Orphanage in Otwock, and the creation of the institution became a reality.

We then faced the question of what type of children to accept into the institution: (1) those who would help us to relieve the institutions in the provinces, or (2) those who would ensure our effort was not wasted and yield the best results. With these issues in mind, we decided to select the children very carefully and not to accept such varying types of children that additional educational difficulties would be created.

The institution has as its goal the adaptation of the abnormal child through an appropriate education, special instruction, and work in workshops, with the goal of coexistence in society and the ability to make a living. We decided from the beginning to accept only those children who would be able to meet these expectations, using Binet's conception of *enfants éducables*.

It was then decided that, in spite of the pleas of the local committees, the institution would not accept severely retarded children, for example, those not suitable for instruction in school because of significant imbecility or idiotism. With this in mind we decided not to accept children who were intelligent but deeply psychopathic, who would feel very bad in an environment designed for mentally disabled children, and morally neglected children who need other educational approaches. We worked from the assumption that the retarded child had no possibilities of development in the provinces where there were no special schools, and out of the obligation to first help those institutions far away from the big city and without contact with special schools.

With this goal in mind it was decided to accept the fewest children from the larger cities and to reach out to the smallest orphanages in the *kresy*.

Colleagues trained in the work of the clinic for children's mental health spread the goal of selecting children suitable for specific orphanages. These colleagues conducted interviews and submitted each potential child to psychological research with the Terman method and the short Rossolimo profile, with the goal of establishing the child's intelligence quotient. An exhaustive conversation with the child about intellectual and social interests completed the method of selection. The goal of the presence of colleagues from the clinic in individual orphanages was to get to know the children in their own space and to determine if a child was especially burdensome for an orphanage.

After arriving in Warsaw the colleagues from the clinic presented 157 carefully prepared interviews. After a joint conference and several meetings, thirty-seven children were retained, with the intelligence quotient of the children ranging from 45 to 75.

In practice, however, the child subjects arriving at the institution were incredibly varied. Mentally undeveloped children displayed certain highly psychopathic characteristics. Others had asocial inclinations; they were thieves, liars, and vagrants. Each child was entirely individual, in need of a suitable approach. This above all determined the educational character of the institution, which worked to further the individualization of the children.

In time a certain percentage of the children from the *kresy* were sent back as unsuitable for the institution, since they did not make enough progress to qualify sufficiently to work in a workshop in a normal orphanage.

Lamentable material conditions forced the institution temporarily, over the course of two years from 1930 to 1931, to accept children from private families, most often the significantly disabled, since only those who were most burdensome in the home were entrusted to the institution.

The institution created a department in a special annex for fifteen children, significantly disabled, each with an IQ lower than 40. A special educator and teacher worked with these children, who were not combined with the group of schoolchildren. The effort to educate these children turned out to be so disproportionate to the work put in by the institution, the institution had such difficulties with the parents, who did not see tangible results after several months, and the staff was flooded with so many unjustified accusations that the department was abolished after two years.

At present the institution accepts (1) mentally retarded children with an IQ not lower than 45; (2) mentally retarded psychopathic children of school age; and (3) morally disabled children who, we are certain, have engaged in asocial behavior, such as stealing, playing hooky, as a result partly of mental retardation and partly of very bad environmental conditions.

The institution has several such children, transferred by the court for juveniles, and is very satisfied with the educational results.

The CENTOS institution, as the only Jewish site for abnormal children, is forced to accept very different types. It cannot specialize in a specific direction, like institutions in the West, where psychopathic, mentally undeveloped, morally neglected, and epileptic children are placed in appropriate institutions.

The data show that 131 children passed through the institution from March 21, 1928, to March 1, 1933. Twenty of these children will not be considered in the general statistical overview of progress and results because they stayed in the institution less than an entire year.

Of 111 children, forty have left the institution. Currently the institution has seventy-one children.

Children Who Left the Institution

Fifteen boys were 8–14 years old (37.5%); six girls were 8–14 years old (15%); seven boys were 15–20 years old (17%); twelve girls were 15–20 years old (30%). In total, there were twenty-two boys (52%) and eighteen girls (47%).

Of these, ten children were in the institution for a year, nine for two years, and twenty-one for three years.

To further distinguish among these children:

I. Twenty-five were mentally retarded (62%)
   a) Twelve were feeble-minded (30%)
   b) Seven were imbeciles (17%)
   c) Six were idiots (15%)
II. Eight (20%) were psychopathic
III. One (2.5%) was epileptic
IV. Two (5%) were recovering from an operation for chronic inflammation of the brain
V. Four (10%) were asocial

Of these forty children, six (15%) suffered from difficulties with speech.

The educational results were as follows: seven (17.5%) were very good, fifteen (37.5%) were good, thirteen (32.5%) were satisfactory, and five (12.5%) were not satisfactory.

By *very good* results we understand:

a) Placement of the child in an elementary school, which is proof of the complete socialization of the child and of the child's possibility of life within the group and a guarantee of normal mental development; and

b) Training in a trade and systematic work in the trade outside of school.

None of the children who left the institution were suited for a normal school because of a low intelligence quotient. In addition, there were remarkably asocial children who were not suited for life within a group because of defects in character.

If we indicated that a child qualified for very good results, it was because the child mastered reading and writing in two languages (Yiddish and Polish) in a relatively short time and qualified to work in a trade. Many children are supporting themselves by their work in a trade and belong to trade unions. The institution maintains contact with them for three years, as proof of their complete adaptability to independent life.

Good results indicate progress in a special institutional school and systematic work in a trade.

These children are presently living with relatives, in families, where they make a living in their trade and are not a burden on society.

Satisfactory results suggest minimal progress in a special institutional school, but comparatively good progress in learning a trade.

These children are under the care of local committees, some with private families, others in dormitories. They are not independent, they are not able to earn a living, they work to the extent possible in their trade, or they learned another trade and apply it to their lives to a significantly greater degree than before staying in the institution.

An *unsatisfactory* result indicates a complete lack of progress in studies and in a trade and the inability to adapt to social life, seen in five children (12.5%).

These children left the institution because they were taken by their families, primarily for material reasons (inability to pay), or because they passed the institution's age limit, or because the institution, not being able to maintain these children for free because of a lack of funds, was forced to return the children to the local committees to which they belonged.

Children in the Institution

From these results there are seventy-one children, forty-four boys and twenty-seven girls. Thirteen children are aged five to seven, fifty are aged eight to fourteen, and eight are aged fifteen to eighteen. Time of stay: eleven children stayed less than a year, twenty-eight children stayed one year, eighteen children stayed two years, seven children stayed three years, two children stayed four years, and five children stayed five years.

Types of children in the institution at present include fifty-one (71.7%) mentally retarded children: thirty-four (47.9%) of them feeble-minded, thirteen (18.2%) imbeciles, and four (5.6%) idiots.

Also in the institution are thirteen (18.3%) psychopathic children, two (2.8%) epileptics, one (1.45%) cataleptic, and four (5.5%) asocials.

Among these children, thirteen (18%) have speech defects.

Such are the educational results, not including eleven children who stayed in the institution for less than a year.

13.3% (5% boys and 8.3% girls) attained *very good* results.

These children go to elementary school in Otwock, study a trade during free time, adapt to social life, and cooperate with officials in creating attempts at self-government, publications, a court, and a social group.

48.2% (31.6% boys and 16.6% girls) attained *good* results.

These children participate regularly in a special institutional school, make progress in their studies, and work in workshops with good results.

30% (20% boys and 10% girls) attained *satisfactory* results.

These children attend a special school, a preschool of the institution. They make little progress in their studies but comparatively better progress in the workshops and in crafts classes such as *slöjd*.[1]

8.3% (5% boys and 3.3% girls) attained *unsatisfactory* results.

These are children who are not making progress either in their studies or in a craft or handwork. The only educational result is that they are comparatively independent (they complete the same chores, they dress and wash themselves), and they live together with the group in institutional conditions.

---

1 *Slöjd*, sometimes referred to as Sloyd in English, means craft or manual skill in Swedish. The Finnish educator Uno Cygneaus (1810–88) developed apprentice programs in woodworking, metalworking, and other crafts in the late nineteenth century, and the Swedish educator Otto Salomon (1849–1907) popularized this form of education. This is another example of educators and social workers turning to the work of earlier reformers such as Friedrich Froebel. See Otto Salomon, *The Theory of Educational Sloyd* (Boston, MA: Silver, Burdett & Co., 1896).

As the statistics show, the children changed significantly in the course of two years: the children arriving in the institution are significantly younger, and more of them have a significantly higher intelligence level than the previous children. These circumstances greatly changed the character of the institution. While the greatest pressure at the beginning was to educate the children in a craft, the first priority of the institution now is schooling, because of the older age of the children.

Assisting in this goal is the institution's preschool for mentally retarded children and a three-grade elementary school.

The nature of the workshops also changed; the first workshops focused on crafts (shoemaking, basket-making, linen-making), to facilitate the independence of the older child. Currently the workshop is a supplement to the school, and handwork is one of the stages in the education and training of the child. The current workshops, carpentry, *slöjd*, women's work, and linen-making, are not intended for vocational education but rather to teach above all skills and coordination of movements, agility, and systematization. The workshops are meant to prepare the young child for the study of a craft. They are also powerful educational and medical tools, allowing the child to release energy positively and purposefully.

The Therapeutic and Educational Methods Applied in the Institution

The task of the CENTOS institution is to offer care for the mental and physical development of each child's own capabilities at the child's own pace. This goal of the educational system of the institution relies on knowing the child's mental characteristics precisely, gaining the child's trust, making contact with the child, and uncovering the characteristics and intelligence on which the child can rely as a foundation for further improvement.

The conditions to fulfill this task are exceptionally favorable at the CENTOS institution. The home, neat and tidy, makes a nice impression, in the middle of 5.6 acres of beautiful forest, far from the tumult of the streets. Most rooms are four to six beds, with the exception of two twelve-bed rooms. The children are divided into groups, corresponding to age and to common characteristics.[2]

Rooms for boys are on the ground floor; girls are on the second floor. Rooms are bright, full of sunshine and light. Children have the right to decorate their rooms with flowers, drawings, or paper cuttings. Children do not have access to their bedrooms in the middle of the day. Two bathrooms with showers allow for the maintenance of exemplary cleanliness. Children are bathed twice weekly in winter; in summer they get a warm shower daily. The dining room, kitchen, and housekeeping are on the ground floor. On the other side is a separate entrance to the doctor's office, where medical and psychological exams are conducted, and a separate adjacent room for various medical purposes.

Nearby is the so-called little house. This is a dormitory for fifteen children with glandular tuberculosis and those in a feverish state.

An isolation room and a room for the women serving as public health experts are located in a separate building. The three-grade school, adjacent to part of a park that serves as the school garden, is also a separate building. A workshop building is located further into the park. On the ground floor of the workshop building can be found the carpentry and *slöjd* workshops and a large gymnasium that also serves as a multi-purpose room. On the first floor is a workshop for the sensory training of the deeply retarded and workshops for linen-making and embroidery.

The administration and apartment of the administrative director of the institution are also in a separate building.

Near the workshop building is a large space for games and play. There are separate spaces for playing basketball and croquet in the area of the forest. An entire range of classes, especially for the youngest children, takes place in the forest in the summer. The forest is carefully maintained, the pathways planted with stakes of trees (the work of the boys), the flowerbeds very carefully maintained by the girls, who delight in each flower. These very favorable exterior conditions make the work of the staff easier. The institution's staff consists of a director, a doctor of psychopathology, a manager, four teachers

---

2 "Awakening in an Institution (Images of an Institution for Defective Children in Otwock)," the article by Kalman Lis translated above, offers a good example of how the boys experienced group living.

(male and female) working in education, one teacher for *slöjd*, a carpenter, a woman serving as a public health nurse, and technical staff, such as cooks, assistant cooks (girls at the institution for over four years serve as assistant cooks), janitors, assistants to the janitors, servants, and washerwomen.

The educational staff must be acquainted with the field of therapeutic pedagogy. The institution tries to recruit those strong in pedagogy, with a diploma from an institute focusing on special education.

About ten teachers, both men and women, have come and gone over the five years of the existence of the CENTOS Institution. It should be emphasized that their relationship to all of the children was exceptionally close and warm. An instance of bad behavior toward a child was never noted. On the contrary, the teachers' exceptional warmth, understanding, and attachment, especially on the part of some of the especially young female teachers, should be noted. This very warm relationship among the children, teachers, and director was evident to everyone who visited the institution. The children are not shy or treated roughly; they address every new visitor with confidence. The institution creates the impression of a large family.

After arriving at the institution, each new child is taken into the group appropriate for the child's age and intellectual development and from the first moment we try to accustom the child as quickly as possible to the new environment. Each child is assigned a mentor from among the group to initiate the child into the life of the institution, the child's privileges and obligations, etc. This method has given us very positive results for five years; the retarded child, shy, uncertain, often not able to speak or manage in new surroundings, more easily becomes accustomed to and understanding of his peers, and more accustomed to the new environment, than with a teacher. And among the mentors there develops a sense of responsibility and a real tie to the new child, so that instead of mocking the weaknesses of the new arrival, the mentor observes the child critically and tries to help the child relate to the group positively. For certain psychopathological children, the obligations of the mentor were an important part of their therapy; only in relation to other children were they able to tame their wild, irrepressible impulses. The greatest punishment was the deprivation of the right to care. The memory of the fourteen-year-old P. S. stands out. This girl, deeply psychopathic, spoiled, not responding to any educational influence, even from the director, whom she liked very much, experienced completely unrestrained attacks of anger. At a meeting of the pedagogical staff, she was qualified for removal from the institution, as completely unsuitable for living in a group situation. Several weeks before her departure a deeply retarded girl, a mongoloid, very helpless, arrived at the institution. P. S. asked if she could take this child under her care. With deep emotion we observed the truly maternal affection and unlimited sensitivity this poor young foundling, disabled by fate, suppressed, only to offer to another, so very injured being. She was focused, serious, submissive, completing all activities and giving in to discipline, constantly taking care that Ewusia would not suffer the least injury. When Ewusia was taken from the institution by her parents, P. S. endured a very painful period, which led to her running away.

Over the five years of the institution's existence, we never had an instance of a mentor consciously causing harm to a child, but there often occurred friction between a mentor and older children, when the mentor would heroically defend the child under care. The mentors met regularly with the director and teachers to share their observations, which were often characterized by exceptional accuracy and understanding. All minutes of these meetings are in the archives of the institution.

Independently from the mentors, of course, the educational staff conducted regular observations of the new child at school, in the workshop, and in the institution. From the first moment of the existence of the institution we have aimed to build a separate observation building, an indispensable necessity for this kind of institution. Unfortunately, because of the tight space and few staff members, we have not yet been able to designate even several rooms for this goal.

However, because of the expansion of the institution, we have no doubt that with somewhat better economic circumstances we will reach this goal in time and establish a small observation building.

School

The institutional school registered by the Board of Education encompasses a preschool for significantly retarded children, a preschool for psychopathic and mentally inhibited children, and a three-grade special school with divisions according to age and level, at present first, second, and fourth grades. The language of instruction for three years was Yiddish, as the majority of children hail from the *kresy* and did not know Polish at all. As a result, children have been recruited primarily from the city institutions of Warsaw for the past two years, and Polish was introduced as an instructional language starting with the 1931–32 school year.[3] A program of special education is used in the school. The Montessori system is used in a preschool for significantly mentally retarded children. The methods of Froebel predominate in the preschool for psychopathic and mentally retarded children, with the aim of encouraging the child toward independent work. The child acquires knowledge the natural way, taking part in life, in economic work, in the garden, etc. Play is, of course, treated as a serious area of interest for the child, and so it performs an important educational role.

The methods of Decroly[4] are applied in the special school. There is a constant effort to apply the methods about the child's centers of interest. Because of the changing group of children and the influx of new children in the course of the school year, these centers of interest have not yet been systematically introduced. We aim for the child to have an active relationship to study, so the student will acquire knowledge and not receive it. Lessons are often led in the form of field trips about nature and sightseeing. Near the school is a garden and each schoolchild cares for a garden patch and has the obligation to garden daily.

For two years the institution has been in contact with the City Elementary School and has sent eight children to individual grades (three, four, and five). The children have made good progress. The school stresses discipline, socialization, and independence.

Workshops

The institution's workshops have gone through two periods. When the institution at the beginning accepted thirty-seven older children, our goal

---

3 The question of the preferred language of Jewish educators and social workers deserves further examination. The experience of CENTOS in Otwock shows an institution that tried to serve Yiddish-speaking children but then turned to Polish.

4 Ovide Decroly (1871–1932), Belgian teacher and psychologist.

was to give the children in the shortest time possible a vocational education that would facilitate their existence. The following workshops were organized: linenmaking, basketmaking, and shoemaking. Qualified masters from the guilds led the workshops. They found there was a great interest in vocational work. While in the first period of the existence of the institution, the children had to be convinced to attend, the workshops won the initial fight for general acceptance. The linenmaking and shoemaking workshops satisfied institutional needs and even accepted small commissions from private individuals. The basketmaking workshop played an important educational role; it was invaluable for excessively active children or those with uncoordinated movements. The work of basketmaking is easy and does not demand excessive concentration of attention or great physical effort; it is well suited for the needs of significantly retarded children. The results of the progress of the children lead to some of them being designated as assistants to the masters. The attitude is always cheerful and the children compete with each other to achieve the greatest results. After two years the institution organized and exhibited the work of the children. Almost everything on display was sold, which added to the great spirits of the students and the masters and testified meaningfully to the achievement of this work. Two shoemakers currently live independently from this professional work. Ten girls also work as professionals. Because at present the children have changed and their age ranges from seven to fifteen, the workshops have of necessity ceased to be sites of vocational training but instead are used for professional work. Younger children work in the *slöjd* workshop, making boxes, beams, and in bookbinding. Twelve older boys work in the carpentry workshop, and one girl in linen-making, as part of the institution's sewing room.

Educational Methods

The goal of the institution is to make the child independent and prepare the child for life in society. With this in mind, the first educational principle of the institution is that the child will work in all areas connected to the domestic life of the institution: cleaning, laundering dresses and handkerchiefs, helping in the kitchen, working shifts in the dining room.

Each child, starting from the youngest, has chores assigned to the extent of the child's abilities. The duty schedule changes once a week. The service staff is not available for the bedrooms or bathrooms or for passing out meals. For completing chores, the child is accountable only to the educators, who take care to encourage the children to work and to do the work together with them. Knowledge of home economics (the kitchen, laundry) is obligatory for the older children, independent of their work in school and in the workshop, with the goal of wanting to inculcate in them skills for independent living.

The so-called "days of independence," spontaneously introduced by the children, are an interesting educational experiment. During these days, the director and teachers as well as technical director, at the request of the children, remove themselves from their positions and are only passive witnesses to the self-governance of the children. The older children take the organization into their own hands, assign certain children to complete various work, and even consider supervision and care for the smaller children, including walks, games, and classes in the workshop and in school.

It is interesting to note that on one such "day of independence" a group from Dr. Korczak's Home for Orphans unexpectedly visited.[5] On their own, the children organized a reception for the group, showing them around the institution, explaining to the guests the purpose of the workshops, garden, etc. The older girls prepared dinner for fifty people, while the boys organized a volleyball game. "Days of independence" occur only at the request of the children—they are never imposed on them.

An attempt to introduce self-government was made, but it was not successful in the most complete sense of the term. But some organizations remain from this attempt, including the Children's Court, which currently meets under the name Friendship Circle; this is the group that resolves misdeeds, offenses against the entire group.

All children take part in the meetings of the Friendship Circle. The liveliness of the Circle is seen in the fact that at one meeting eighty-seven

---

5 Zofia Rosenblum mentions this visit in her memoir, *Byłam tylko lekarzem*, 122. Marzena Pękowska also discusses this visit in her article on CENTOS in Otwock, "Organizacja Zakładu Leczniczo-Wychowawczego 'CENTOS,'" 151.

issues were on the agenda. The children are on the board of the Circle and, often, the director of the institution, if chosen by the children. The children always try to conduct the meetings so they can experience their independence as much as possible. Since introducing the meetings of the Friendship Circle, minor thefts, which had long occurred often enough, happen less and less frequently. The meetings of the Friendship Circle are held once every two weeks. At these meetings certain issues related to the governance of the group are worked out and the obligations and needs of the group are discussed. In this way the regulations of the institution are not forced on the children but instead submitted, to the extent possible, for acknowledgment and criticism. The first initiative of the Friendship Circle was the creation of a club of older children and a library, as well as the founding of an institutional newspaper. The institution does not use any punishment or repression in relation to the child outside of persuasion, appealing to the opinion of the group, and in emergency cases, relative isolation and excluding the child from the group. The result of this method of progress is the socialization of the child: the acquisition of confidence in one's own strengths, the destruction of feelings of less worth, and the urge to work. Seeing how, in these conditions, the intimidated, shy, and passive mentally retarded child slowly begins to display individuality and increasingly trust the teachers, the educational staff becomes more and more convinced that all punishments (of course, not corporal punishment, which is not even a consideration) only hinder the development of the child and have a negative influence. This attitude also reflects meetings of the pedagogical staff, where questions of punishments and any type of repression are frequently discussed, showing the staff's deep understanding and investigation into each individual case of a child's misbehavior and the analysis of the basis of the child's behavior to uncover any interesting manifestations of the child's psyche. With respect to the child, we use primarily the individual psychology of Adler,[6] with direct observation during classes, games and play, and consider broadly the study of Freud, with careful attention to the lives and sexual impulses of children.

---

6 Alfred Adler (1870–1937), physician and psychologist from Austria.

We ask ourselves often if we are progressing favorably, raising the child in an atmosphere of freedom, without forcing on the child strict regulations. It seems to us that we are progressing. Children, knowing that they will be strictly disciplined for playing hooky, cease to play hooky if they sense that at any moment the teacher will give the child permission to go outside of the institution.

Little Leoś W., a twelve-year-old vagrant, a typical child of the streets, ran away to Warsaw only once over the course of a two-year stay in the institution. Since this time he has not run away; he simply goes to the director and tells him that he misses his grandmother. This longing for his grandmother happens more or less once every six months. A trip to Warsaw is then arranged for Leoś, and the child returns calm and happy. ("Earlier I ran away all the time but from here I don't, because the first time I ran away, they really worried about me," says Leoś to those visiting the institution.)

Thefts among the group of children are a more difficult issue. They happen constantly, though there are significantly fewer thefts now than at the beginning. The children have individual little boxes, in which the teachers never look, even if they know that the child has placed something stolen there. Thieves are spontaneously reviled by the community, which often demands that they be strictly punished.

The affair of Hania W. is still remembered. Hania, a fourteen-year-old moron, stealing everything around her, embezzled all of the workshop funds. The children demanded her expulsion from the common sleeping areas, dining rooms, and workshops. At the meeting of the Friendship Circle there was a unanimous demand for the "death penalty" for Hania. "Why feed a thief? Pani Doktor tells us that Hania has such a need for candies that she cannot stop herself and therefore she steals. If she was given candies, she wouldn't steal. But who in life will give her candies? We don't agree with Pani Doktor. Better to get rid of her already."

Seeing this united front of the children, the administration directed the case of Hania B. [sic] to the juveniles' court and only with the court's verdict did the children capitulate and agree to accept Hania back into the community.

Some children can only be positively influenced by one individual educator. The director of the institution has an entire range of such children, otherwise very unruly, who submit only under his influence. Thanks to the positive influence of the woman who serves as the institution's public health nurse, the fifteen-year-old Wolf S., entrusted to us by the juvenile court, was saved. This habitual, very impulsive petty thief, not submitting to any persuasion, has changed completely because of Miss J., for whom he harbors unlimited gratitude. Because of her work, Wolf attends the sixth grade of the Elementary School and behaves himself both in school and in the institution in an exemplary way.

There is still one educational factor to which the institution pays great attention, namely contact of the children with families. Our children are primarily foundlings. The city orphanage, which is located here, usually cannot give us any information about the families. We try at the institution to get from the child all the information about family members and to make contact with them. The institution sought out the families of several children and encouraged them to visit the children. As long as the family itself wishes, the institution gives the child vacation for the holiday. Of course, the institution shares information with the families regarding any questions and corresponds regularly with the families of the foster children entrusted to their care. The staff of the institution makes a real effort to visit the families and to get to know personally the child's environment. We consider it very desirable to send the children to their families for vacation. The child is not isolated from his loved ones, is close to family, shares their worries and concerns, *but the family is not torn from the child and has a constant feeling of responsibility, and, with time, the family will be able to take care of the child.* Moreover, the family is the tie between the child and the external world.

Therapeutic Methods

The institution's therapeutic methods rely above all on a strict selection of the children and the creation to the extent possible of an educationally and intellectually uniform group.

The tight space of the institution does not allow us to create a section based on an established structure, dividing the children into family groups to be educated in separate buildings. Perhaps in the future, when the institution expands, we will be able to accept an established structure as the basis for the segregation of the children. At present we have created groups of fifteen children, on average, with an educator at the head of each, responsible for the group.

Children not appropriate for living in a group setting in an institution are withdrawn. This year the institution sent away a child who had not made any progress in the course of three years, returned two significantly intellectually undeveloped children to a private family, and placed two girls in Zofiówka.[7]

For psychopaths we use psychotherapy and methods of work, trying to pull these children into the rhythm of life as much as possible (workshops, organized play, sport), to give them an outlet and potential energy. Chaim K., a fourteen-year-old psychopath, is very typical in this respect. He is intolerable in these surroundings, he misbehaves, taunting children and educators—if there is no organized work. Chaim changes completely when he is given ample work. He works with determination, with fanaticism, he does not rest, he forgets even about the hours of meals: "My work calms me." He is an excellent carpenter. He painted the furniture in the institution. When the children had to leave for the summer colony, Chaim begged with tears that he be left behind: "What will I do at the colony? Here there will be the renovations of the institution, there will be so much work and I have to go," he said with deep regret.

Very passive, backward children (with hypothyroid type Hertogh), as well as children with inflamed endocrine glands, are given appropriate glandular therapy, sometimes with very positive results. In a few cases of epilepsy (three children), the usual therapy is applied, Sedobrol, Luminal, Gardonal, Brom, a sodium-free vegetarian diet.[8] These children improve significantly if the therapy is applied *very systematically*. Scrofulous children get cod liver oil.[9] All children are weighed regularly once a month and the charts of their weight are compiled.

---

7 See Seeman, "Jewish Psychiatric Hospital."
8 Sedobrol was an early tranquilizer. Luminal is used to control seizures.
9 Scrofula refers to the swelling of the neck glands due to tuberculosis of the lymphatic glands of the neck.

Physical examinations take into consideration the constitution of the child and may include an internal organ examination or neurological-psychiatric examination. All children have their eyes examined by a specialist.

In connection with the two cases of active tuberculosis at the institution, all children and staff were submitted to regular exams from the "Brijus" (Health) Association. A group of children were identified as having been affected by glandular tuberculosis and being in a constant state of a slightly raised temperature. These children are under constant care of the Anti-tuberculosis Clinic of the "Brijus" Association. Wassermann tests are done in groups to the extent possible.[10] The institution is in contact with a dentist in Otwock and with the Association of Friends of Children School Clinic in Warsaw, to which we direct children needing the care of a laryngologist, dermatologist, etc.

Each child has an individual folder, where the child's health card is kept. An institutional psychologist, who comes from Warsaw two to three times annually for a period of several weeks, conducts all psychological research at the institution. Besides intelligence quotient, determined with the Terman test, younger children are examined using the Winkler test, while older children submit to a range of testing of motor skills, attention, memory, and the questionnaire of Dr. Lipszycowa. This testing comprises a profile. The profile also includes the director's notes and the teachers' notes about the behavior of the child at the school and in workshops. Any and all reports about the child are attached, along with the child's work (drawings, compositions, letters). The director keeps an observation book, in which he notes remarks on each child.

Much attention is paid to motor skills among the children delayed in mental and social development, as is done often with the disabled. Using our own resources, we have organized a gym, which, because of a lack of funds, is still not satisfactorily outfitted with equipment. The work around the home gives the children an opportunity to practice their movements. We also try to organize the children into sports teams (volleyball, sledding, skating, croquet, ping pong, biking), recognizing that sports in an institution of this type are one of the most effective therapies.

10　The Wassermann test is an antibody test for syphilis, named after the bacteriologist August Paul von Wassermann (1866–1925).

The institution suffers from a lack of musical instruments. This is at present one of the biggest weaknesses of the institution, because we rightly think that music and rhythm are both therapeutic and educational, but, unfortunately, instruments are temporarily unavailable to us because of a lack of material resources.

Entertainment

In addition to sports, which I mentioned previously, children have several games for rainy days in the clubroom; a library, where the titles are replenished often; a Pathé Baby film projector (the film changes every two weeks);[11] and a beautiful radio with a speaker. The initiative of the children in setting up shows is very happily supported. The children express a desire for arranging events in the evening and with the help of teachers, and sometimes without, they make costumes. There is a range of evening activities in the institution, in which all the children take part, even the very young children, to their great joy.

There are also occasional field trips to Warsaw, to the zoo, to the movies, etc.

The children also take great pleasure in editing publications to which each child has the right to send an article or submit a drawing. Some young children created their own little newspaper, which hangs on the wall the same day the other, larger little newspaper appears.[12]

Accepting Children into the Institution

Before arrival in the institution each child must be examined by the Association of Friends of Children School Clinic and by the institution's psychopathologist. The children are subjected to three kinds of examinations: (1) physical, (2) psychological-psychiatric, and (3) sociological.

1. The physical examination, in addition to examining internal organs and a thorough neurological exam, includes X-rays and an examination of

---

11 The Pathé Baby film projector was designed for home use.
12 These newspapers are not extant.

the eyes for trachoma. No child can be accepted to the institution without certification from the oculist of the Health Center or without X-rays.

2. The psychological-psychiatric research includes determining intelligence quotient with help of the Binet-Terman scale and examining specific mental functions, such as memory, attention, motor skills, etc. An individual conversation with the child, touching on the child's interests, experiences, and schoolwork, supplements the examination and helps us to obtain a precise image of the child's mind. The child's former teachers at the other institution or the family share their observations about the child. If the family entrusts the child to our care, we will determine the most precise case history possible.

3. The sociological examination includes research into the child's surroundings, to the extent that we know about those surroundings, and an interview with the school the child attended previously.

Minutes from the Fourth Council Meeting on August 7, 1932[13]

Agenda

1. Election of presidium
2. Reading of minutes from previous meeting
3. Organization of teams
   A. Football
   B. Volleyball
   C. Croquet
   D. Ping pong
4. Current business
   A. Skórnik
   B. Kulawski
   C. Janek
   D. Leoś
   E. Miron-Gryluś

---

13 The spelling and lettering or numbering of names throughout this section is inconsistent, as it is in the original text. I have retained the use of the abbreviation "P." for the Polish forms of formal address for an adult man, Pan, or adult woman, Pani.

I. Entered as the first item on the agenda, the election of the presidium:

List of candidates: Fejga, Lea, Szejna, Zygmuś, Niedzielski, Różka, Doctor Brodaty, Zocha, and Natek.

Fejga, Lea, Szejna, Niedzielski, Różka, and Brodaty received a majority. A majority rejected Zygmuś. Doctor Brodaty had two votes against.

Election of chair: Różka: four, Szejna: six, Fejga: six. Fejga was chosen as chair with the agreement of Szejna.

II. The minutes were read and confirmed.

III. The organization of the teams. The doctor refereed. It happens often that children who do not know how to play any games still want to take part in a game, bothering others. When they are not allowed to play, they are ready to fight. We do not even know in what game somebody could take part. Because of this, teams should be formed, for example, a football team to which only those who play football can belong. There will be five teams:

1. Volleyball
2. Croquet
3. Ping pong
4. Football
5. Dodge ball

Each team must have its own captain, referee, and badge. The captain has a different badge than the team. The team, together with its captain, must put together the rules. The doctor introduced a motion to create a Sports Commission, which would organize the teams. The motion passed.

Several children wanted to take part in discussing this issue: Kulawski, Natek, Sobocki, Kukuś, Leoś, Salka (Gryluś: I don't know what's going on, so I can't take part), Skórnik, Abramowicz.

1. Natek: I want P. Szmul to be there.
2. Sobocki: Should be Skórnik.
3. Kukuś: Pan Szmulek.

4. Leoś: If children will have clothing, there will be no one to sew.
5. Gryluś: Brodaty.
6. Salka: There have to be three whistles: big, smaller, and smallest.
7. The doctor explained that the issue at this moment is not about the selection of candidates for the Sports Commission but about belonging to these sports teams. Because nobody spoke up, the voting was entered:

1. P. Doctor—unanimous
2. P. Szmul—a majority
3. Kulawski—eighteen
   Skórnik—a majority
   Brodaty—a majority
   Różka—a majority
   Zygmuś—a majority
   Miron—ten
   Natek—fifteen
   Sobocki—ten
   Janek—two
   Leoś—zero
   Gryluś—two

The Commission will be composed of the following:
1. P. Dr.—unanimous
2. P. Szmul—a majority
3. Skórnik—a majority
4. Brodaty—a majority
5. Różka—a majority
6. Zygmuś—a majority

Substitutes:
1. Kulawski (eighteen)
2. Natek (fifteen)
3. Miron (ten)
4. Sobocki (ten)

The first meeting of the Commission will be on Monday at ten o'clock.

Entered as the fourth point of the agenda: Current business. A) Skórnik (submitted by P. Dr. and P. Sala).

I. P. Doctor reported: The first chair committed a violation of the discipline of the institution and left the institution for the entire day. I do not know where he was, but Skórnik will probably think it is appropriate to explain himself. Because he was a first chair, who was able to come up with appropriate punishments for others during his term in office, I call for a strict punishment for him.

II. P. Sala saw that Skórnik was in the tree grabbing apples together with other boys at five in the morning. With him were Niedzielski, Abramowicz, Natek, and Miron. He also gave Różka an apple.

The chair allowed the accused to speak.

Accused: I don't have anything to explain.

Doctor: You admit your guilt? (in the first case)

Skórnik: Yes.

Dr.: Where were you?

Skórnik: In Warsaw, at my mother's.

Skórnik also admits to guilt in the second incident.

Dr.: Can you explain why you did this?

Skórnik: No.

Dr.: How many apples?

Sk.: Four.

Dr.: Who else got one?

Sk.: No one.

Dr.: Who was with you?

Skórnik: Niedzielski, Różka, Abramowicz, Miron, Natek.

Dr.: Did you do this in cooperation with the others?

Skórnik: No.

The co-accused:

Dr. to Niedzielski: You were with Skórnik?

Niedz.: Yes.

Dr.: You knew that Skórnik took an apple?

Niedz.: Yes.

(Skórnik in solidarity did not want to betray his friends.)

Dr.: Did Skórnik tell you that he took an apple?

N.: He didn't say anything.

Dr.: So how did you know?

N.: I figured it out. First Skórnik went up on the roof to see if there were apples there, and when there weren't any, he went to take some.

Dr.: And how many did you get?

N.: Half an apple.

Dr.: And it didn't occur to you that you shouldn't do this? That you should tell somebody about this?

N.: No.

Skórnik: When they went to eat the apple in the room upstairs, Niedzielski didn't want to go. Miron got an apple and wanted to give Niedzielski half an apple. Niedzielski didn't want to take it from the beginning, only later he took it.

Doctor to Natek: Were you with Skórnik?

Natek: Yes?

Dr.: Did you know that Skórnik took an apple?

Natek: No.

Dr.: How many did you get?

Natek: One and a half apples.

Dr.: Where did you eat the apples?

Natek: In Skórnik's room.

P. Sala: As I said, I will tell the Doctor that you said, "I'm not afraid."

Dr. to Abramowicz: You were together with Skórnik.

Abramowicz: Yes.

Dr.: You knew that Skórnik took the apple?

Abramowicz: No.

Dr.: You were okay with all of this?

Abramowicz: No.

Dr.: You were afraid?

Abr.: I'm not afraid of anything.

Dr.: You didn't think that whoever helps is also guilty?

Abr.: No.

Dr. to Miron: What do you have to say?

Miron: The same as Niedzielski.

Różka appears next as a witness. When I woke up after the alarm and went to Jozefów, I knew that Skórnik had eaten the apple. I thought that he found it, because the wind in the night had torn the apples from the tree. I asked him to give me a piece. He did. Then I heard P. Sala shouting that Skórnik went on the roof to look for apples, then that he climbed on the tree and took the apples, and P. Sala turned to me: "You will be a witness," and to this I said that I can only say what I heard from P. Sala.

Gryluś (witness): I saw the whole gang go to the garden. I didn't want to go with them. I didn't care about going to the garden. P. Sala came and said, look how they're taking apples. I saw the boys sitting there.

Dr.: And who was there?

Gryluś: I didn't see, they were all sitting with their backs toward me. I recognized Natek and Skórnik.

Dr.: And who didn't you recognize?

Gryluś: There are only a few children in this world?

Leoś: Niedzielski was probably afraid, he didn't want to say anything at the meeting, because Skórnik gave him half an apple.

Janek: Skórnik stood on the tree.

Gryluś: Janek was still sleeping, like an angry dog.

Zygmuś: Skórnik stood on the tree and roof and looked for apples and the rest of us stayed on the ground, Sala said Skórnik was taking the apples.

(Skórnik: What's it to you, Zygmuś? I already know this.)

The accused left the room. The Doctor spoke. Skórnik committed two crimes: First, he went to Warsaw without permission, but the longing for his mother explains that. The second case is much more serious. Nobody is assigned the chore of taking care of the garden, because the children know that nobody steals from us; the first chair comes and steals apples from the tree. But because his friends met with him and ate the apples, then they are all equally guilty. Only one, Niedzielski, had pangs of conscience, the others ate the apples in peace.

In light of these circumstances, one should consider a serious punishment for Skórnik.

Chair: For better teachers.

Różka: That he not play and not speak with anyone for two days.

(Ryfka: I think that this is too big a punishment!)

Chair: Seven days arrest.

Różka: Because he is very wise, it would be interesting to know how he would punish himself.

(Johan listens in and communicates to the accused.)

Dr.: But we as a team should have a punishment ready in case the presidium does not agree on the punishment Skórnik comes up with.

The presidium decides to punish Skórnik with five days of house arrest. He does not have the right to leave the room and in case of need must ask for permission. In addition, he is not allowed to go to the garden for ten days and he cannot be chosen as captain of any team.

Natan, Abram, and Miron cannot be chosen as captain of any team and for ten days cannot go to the garden.

The punishment begins on Monday.

The next meeting will be after the arrival of P. Doctor.

The chair closed the meeting at six o'clock.

Working with Abnormal Children: On Eight Years of CENTOS in Otwock

Abraham Berger

Abraham Berger worked with the JDC, but further details of the nature of his role with the JDC are unknown. This text originally appeared in *Przegląd Społeczny* X, no. VII-VIII (July-August 1936): 167–73.

First Special Department for "Less Able" Jewish Children

The most typical abnormal child, that is, the mentally undeveloped or impaired child, came to attention in Poland relatively late, apart from the rich tradition in the field of educating deaf, blind, and morally neglected children. (The Institute for the Deaf and Blind in Warsaw was established in 1817; the Galician Institute for the Blind was established in Lwów in 1872; and institutions in Studzieniec and Puszcza Mariańska in 1876.) Barely eighteen years has passed since the Association for the Care and Research of Children, with great effort and with the support of pedagogues around the world, organized the first special department for "less able" children, children delayed in development. The fact that teachers needed explanations for which children should be placed in a special school suggests how little was known about the issue of mentally impaired children in 1917. After such an explanation, it was usually the director of the school who chose several children from the younger grades and sent them to the administration for a physical and psychological exam, which also focused on physical characteristics, responses, and behavior. This was how the first department for so-called "less able" children began.

From this department for "less able" children there emerged in December 1917 a group of Jewish children, who, upon the recommendation of the school inspector, were transferred to a separate school building at Ogrodowa 42. This special department for mentally impaired Jewish children on Ogrodowa is today an educational institution of historic significance, the result of the efforts of our pioneers in the field of therapeutic pedagogy and their passionate work socializing and making independent the mentally undeveloped Jewish child.

The Present Educational Situation for the Abnormal Jewish Child

Regarding the present state of education for abnormal Jewish children, it must be stressed that at this time schools of this type can be found only in the largest communities in the country. To wit: there are two schools for mentally impaired children in Warsaw, on Nowolipie 18 and Świętokrzyska 16, as well as a school and dormitory of the Association for the Care of Deaf Jews at Śliska 28.

There is the Ezras-Kmim school for deaf children in Łódź. In Lwów there is the Bardach private school for "deaf children of the Mosaic faith."

The school for undeveloped children in Wilno is located in the building of the Jewish community on Orzeszkowa Street. Near this school is also a shelter for "young thieves and vagrants," street children.

In other larger cities, Jewish children study together with non-Jewish children (because the number of special schools in Poland is very small). Therapeutic-educational institutions, usually organized for more difficult types of abnormal children, make up a separate part of special education. For abnormal Jewish children affected significantly by a lack of mental development there are in Poland barely a pair of such institutions primarily of a private character (those of P. Spektorowa in Łódź and Dr. I. Twerski in Groty in Warsaw), in addition to the famous CENTOS in Otwock for children delayed in development and morally neglected, the institution for deaf and blind children in Bojanów Poznański, already liquidated and transferred to Warsaw on Graniczna 8.

One should note that the private therapeutic-educational institutions, because of their very high monthly rates (around two hundred to two hundred fifty *złoty* per month) are inaccessible even for parents from the middle class, not to mention educating the children of the less wealthy and the poor. These children are completely lost to us, increasing the cadre of underage criminals for whom the only school of life is poverty and the street—and the ranks of the mentally ill, ending their lives tragically in psychiatric hospitals such as St. John of God and Tworki, etc.[1]

The Problem of Abnormal Jewish Youth

Those also on the margins of special education include the great army of abnormal youth. From my own work in education I know the general living conditions at home and specific pedagogical conditions that exist for our undeveloped youth outside of the school system.

This is a problem deserving of attention in all respects, but especially with regard to the age of the individuals, who should be organized at the earliest opportunity into workshops where, learning a trade, they will cease to be a burden to their parents, society, and the state.

But organizing this professional education—this is the dilemma facing activists and pedagogues today. American actions in this area, moving toward the organization of special farming and gardening colonies for abnormal youth, are also instructive. Pedagogues and social activists in Switzerland are also engaging in a rousing discussion of the topic with great interest. They have established a vast network of parents' committees led by social workers to find places of work for undeveloped youth, with the goal of making it possible to teach them some trade. The

---

1 The Hospitaller Order of the Brothers of Saint John of God has been present in Poland since 1609. The Order established a number of hospitals throughout the country, including one in Warsaw. For the Order's own history, see the website of the hospital, Zakon Szpitalny Św. Jana Bożego Bonifratrzy, http://bonifratrzy.pl/historia-zakonu/historia-zakonu-w-polsce/, accessed May 28, 2016. Szpital Tworkowski is a hospital for the mentally ill founded between 1888 and 1891 near Warsaw, known today as the Mazowieckie Specjalistyczne Centrum Zdrowia im. Prof. Jana Mazurkiewicza, in Pruszków. See the history page of the website of Mazowieckie Specjalistyczne Centrum Zdrowia for a basic outline of the hospital's history, http://tworki.eu/index.php?option=com_content&task=view&id=59&Itemid=83, accessed May 21, 2016.

lack of such committees here means that the entire burden rests on the shoulders of the unfortunate parents, who have no help in realizing their goals for their children and are completely helpless.

The Origins of the Therapeutic and Educational Institution CENTOS in Otwock

The Warsaw Central Office and the Social Care Department of the city of Warsaw direct orphaned abnormal children to CENTOS in Otwock for better special education.[2] CENTOS in Otwock—this is the only significant Jewish therapeutic-educational institution in Poland for orphaned children, those delayed in development, psychopathic, and morally neglected, established in 1927. The accounts of our pioneers in the field of therapeutic pedagogy (Dr. Z. Rosenblum, B. Auerbachowa), introducing the first steps in educating the abnormal Jewish child (*Dos kind*, 1928), steps envisioned for the first time thanks to the scale of the efforts of the Central Union of Associations for the Care of Jewish Orphans in the Republic of Poland, relate the following:

> In December 1927, when CENTOS began to realize its plan for the renovation of the buildings of the orphanage of the People's Educational League in Otwock and to evaluate its suitability for institutional goals, the launching of a Jewish center for special education became a reality. At the same time the Central Office mobilized its team of psychologists, sending them to all of the Jewish orphanages in Poland with the goal of conducting research and interviews identifying children and noting the particular characteristics of each child and the child's intelligence quotient. The first group of children arrived at the CENTOS institution on March 12, 1928. They were divided into groups, furthering the goal of individualized education.

---

2 Thus both the central office of CENTOS and city officials recognized the importance of the work of the institution in Otwock.

The History of the Development of CENTOS in Otwock

After sketching the beginnings of Jewish activity in the field of care for abnormal children by looking at the establishment CENTOS in Otwock, let us turn to its history from 1928 to 1933 (see Dr. Rosenblum in *Przegląd Społeczny*, 1/2, 1934) and from 1933 to 1935. Statistics show the best picture of the current state of the institution. From its founding on March 21, 1928, to March 1, 1933, 131 children passed through the institution. Sixty of these children left the institution before 1933. Seventy-one children remained after 1933.

Children leaving the institution

Gender	Age of children from 8–20	Length of stay
Boys	22	Less than a year old – 20 children
Girls	18	1 year – 10 children
		2 years – 9 children
		3 years – 21 children

Children remaining in the institution

Gender	Age of children from 5–18	Length of stay in
Boys	44	Less than a year old – 11 children
		1 year – 28 children
		2 years – 28 children
Girls	27	3 years – 7 children
		4 years – 2 children
		5 years – 5 children

The age of the children remaining in the institution deserves attention because of the nature of the institution and its educational work. It becomes clear from the statistics that in the early years of CENTOS in Otwock an older element predominated which, left out of a general education, was able in the shortest time to train for life in society. This explains the great pressure in the area of vocational preparation and the exclusive focus on crafts in the workshops. The change in the age of children in later years (ages five to eighteen instead of ages eight to twenty) also affected the entire educational approach in Otwock. The institution's school was included on the books of the Warsaw Board of Education. Polish became the language of instruction. The number of departments has also grown, and the local features of the institution's grounds have been applied in the program of special education. But the number of workshops (shoemaking, basketweaving) has been reduced, so they are less focused primarily on crafts, and, at the present moment, the school has reached a very high educational level.

The year 1935, a year of very active Jewish organizing for the education and socialization of undeveloped youth, represents a separate phase in the development of the Otwock institution. In "Our Work," an article by P. Goldin (*Dos kind*, March 1935), we read the following: "The therapeutic-educational institution in Otwock continues to grow and in this week the number of children has already reached 120. The need for investment to reach the goals of the institution is clear. The institution has developed very well, and this has recently been recognized positively and advantageously for the institution in both the Jewish and the Polish press (*Kurjer Poranny*, January 19, 1935, "Stan—Dziecko najbardziej upośledzone"), which have treated the institution as a serious subject for reporting". One should also add that after the recent liquidation of the Foundling Home on Płock Street, the number of children in the CENTOS institution grew still further.[3] The current number of children in the eight-year-old institution is currently more than 170, in light of which the Central Office was forced to develop a branch on Zatrzebie near Falenica, in which are

---

3 This is a reference to the Dom Opieki dla Opuszczonych Dzieci Żydowskich (Care Home for Abandoned Jewish Children), located at Płocka 26, Warsaw. Construction on this building began in 1927 and was only finished in 1933. The institution was closed for administrative and financial reasons by the Warsaw city council in 1935. The building became the Instytut Gruźlicy i Chorób Płuc (Institute for Tuberculosis and Diseases of the Lung) in 1952. Jarosław Zieliński and Jerzy S. Majewski, *Spacerownik po żydowskiej Warszawie* (Warsaw: Muzeum Historii Żydów Polskich, 2014), 96.

concentrated children of preschool age.⁴ The children are divided into educational groups. There are five groups in the Otwock institution: three groups of boys, one group for older boys, and one group for girls (numbering thirty-three), each led by an educator. The fundamental slogan of the CENTOS institution is the furtherance of independence and socialization of the child under care. The institution realizes this goal through the individualization of the child's education, both academic and vocational.

After the wake up call at seven in the morning, the children run briskly to wash their upper bodies with cold water. Next, those on duty, each group in its turn, make up the beds, clean the bedrooms, bathrooms, hallways, etc. They also take care of cleaning up the classrooms and the workshops. The children have great freedom in their education and many opportunities to demonstrate their abilities and ingenuity. Classes in school begin by placing on the calendar the appropriate signs for the daily weather and the therapeutic exercises, which have a positive influence on the mental construction of the abnormal child.

The results of such methods of instruction and teaching, with regard to the future and the survival of the CENTOS students, are unusually good and beneficial. Many of them are already working with master craftsmen, supporting themselves. Some of them, after instruction in special departments of the institution, attend the normal elementary school today (eight children). Others study a trade in trade schools in Warsaw, housed in the city at the cost of the institution or still living in the institution. The best result of the independence of the boys in the institution is their own work on furniture for the institution (tables, benches, cabinets, cupboards, hangers, and other items). The linenmaking workshop for the girls also produces everything for the institution in this area. There is also no doubt that the efforts of Jewish society to socialize and normalize the undeveloped and morally neglected Jewish children under the care of CENTOS in Otwock are not wasted.

To summarize, it is clear that the current state of Jewish activity in the field of educating abnormal children and teaching them to work still

---

4 Falenica, a village immediately southeast of Warsaw, became part of the city in 1951.

awaits significant action on the part of the Jewish community. One should mention as the next task the solving of the problem of abnormal Jewish youth (by finding work for them!) and the organization of a correctional facility for children difficult to maintain in other institutions, a topic about which much has already been written in our professional journals. To realize these goals, we must interest all of the Jewish community in our work, above all, the parents of the abnormal children.

At present many young criminals and underage prisoners, as well as a cadre of mentally impaired, purposeless abnormal youth, are becoming beneficial members of Jewish society.

Afterword

The history of CENTOS begins and ends with providing assistance to children during war. The short life of this vibrant organization is inextricably tied to war and its consequences. CENTOS in Otwock was a target of bombing on September 1, 1939.[1] Zofia Rosenblum went to Otwock that day. She recalled in her memoir how the planes flew so low the children could see the face of the pilot. The pilots knew they were not flying over a military installation.[2] According to Rosenblum, the CENTOS building was the first building to be bombed. Another Polish writer, Melchior Wańkowicz, also memorably described the initial assault on Otwock and its toll on the city. Kalman Lis was seriously injured during the bombing. Rosenblum later returned to Warsaw and was cut off from Otwock.

After the start of the war, the institutions of CENTOS continued their work, to the extent possible. Aron Goldin, then general director of CENTOS, fled Poland. Briański, a lawyer, took his place.[3] The psychologist and Poale-Zion Left member Adolf Berman was Briański's deputy and then head of CENTOS during the war.[4] Rosenblum became the medical

---

1 For the best description of the bombing see the testimony of Melchior Wańkowicz, "Tragedia pierwszego dnia," in *Gazeta Samorządowa* 9 (1993): 1, 10; quoted at length in Marzena Pękowska, "Organizacja Zakładu Leczniczo-Wychowawczego 'CENTOS' dla żydowskich dzieci niepełnosprawnych intelektualnie w Otwocku (1928–1939)," *Przegląd Historyczno-Oświatowy* 1/2 (2014): 154–155. See also Adolf Berman, "The Fate of Children in the Warsaw Ghetto," in *The Catastrophe of European Jewry*, ed. Yisrael Gutman and Livia Rothkirchen (Jerusalem: Yad Vashem, 1976), 400; Józef Barski, *Przeżycia i wspomnienia z lat okupacji* (Wrocław: Zakład Narodowy im. Ossolińskich, 1986), 32.
2 Szymańska, *Byłam tylko lekarzem*, 130.
3 Engelking and Leociak, *The Warsaw Ghetto*, 317–18. Briański's first name is missing from this and other sources.
4 Bauer, *American Jewry and the Holocaust*, 83. For more on Adolf Berman and his family, see Marci Shore, "Children of the Revolution: Communism, Zionism, and the Berman Brothers," *Jewish Social Studies* 10, no. 3 (2004): 23–86.

director of CENTOS during the war, and she worked closely with Adolf Berman and Józef (Gitler) Barski, an activist who worked to feed and educate children in the Warsaw ghetto.

CENTOS was officially dissolved in July 1940, but its work continued under the newly formed Żydowski Samopomoc Społeczna-Komisja Koordynacyjna (Jewish Social Self-Help Coordinating Committee), known in Warsaw by its Yiddish name, Aleynhilf.[5] Barski described in his memoir how CENTOS was able to maintain contact with its hundreds of sites outside of Warsaw in the early months of the war, but that, as Warsaw became more isolated, so did CENTOS. The organization was, however, able to reach nearby sites like those in Otwock and Miedzeszyn. According to Adolf Berman, CENTOS served over twenty-five thousand children in one hundred institutions in the Warsaw ghetto during the war, operating thirty orphanages and children's homes, twenty day care centers, twenty food kitchens, and children's corners.[6] Yehuda Bauer has written that, from July to October 1941, CENTOS was active in 143 sites throughout the General Government, the Polish territory occupied by Germany during the war.[7]

The range of care CENTOS aimed to provide is astonishing, given the conditions of the war. In his memoir of the war years, Barski told of just one disturbing murder seen from the window of the CENTOS office on Leszno 2. A German gendarme shot a boy returning from the Aryan side with potatoes and bread.[8] In spite of the pervasive violence, the activists of CENTOS organized libraries, entertainment, and day camps, among other activities. Barbara Temkin-Bermanowa (wife of Adolf Berman)

---

5 See Olga Orzeł, ed., *Dzieci żydowskie w czasach Zagłady* (Warsaw: Żydowski Instytut Historyczny, 2014), 15; Barski, *Przeżycia i wspomnienia*, 27; and Samuel D. Kassow, *Who Will Write Our History: Emanuel Ringelblum, the Warsaw Ghetto, and the Oyneg Shabes Archive* (Bloomington: Indiana University Press, 2007), 114.
6 Berman, "The Fate of Children," 404. Peretz Opoczynski, whose reportage of the Warsaw ghetto offers an invaluable source for this history, cited a CENTOS report that twenty-six community kitchens and nine children's homes were in operation as of September 1941. *In Those Nightmarish Days: The Ghetto Reportage of Peretz Opoczynski and Josef Zelkowicz*, ed. Samuel D. Kassow, trans. David Suchoff (New Haven, CT: Yale University Press, 2015), 92.
7 Bauer offers additional numbers in his history of the JDC during the war, *American Jewry and the Holocaust*, 90, 102.
8 Barski, *Przeżycia i wspomnienia*, 43.

organized the Central Children's Library.[9] Books returned to the library had to be disinfected. The Central Committee for Children's Entertainment organized puppet theater performances and other theatrical events, including the June 1942 performance of Rabindranath Tagore's *Post Office* in the orphanage run by Korczak and Wilczyńska. Kalman Lis continued to be active during the war as a cultural leader in Warsaw, using his talents and organizational skill to organize Yiddish cultural activities. Oyneg Shabes, the Underground Ghetto Archive originated by Emanuel Ringelblum, preserved his poetry.[10] Echoing similar events such as the Week of the Orphan held in earlier years, the Month of the Child was designed to focus attention on the plight of children during the war and was held from August to September 1940 and September to November 1941. A third Month, planned for August 1942, never happened, because of mass deportations to Treblinka.[11]

The small town of Otwock, over half Jewish, was divided into three smaller ghetto districts on November 4, 1940.[12] One of these districts was the "health resort" ghetto, where the neighboring institutions of CENTOS, Marpe, and Brijus were located. A Committee for Social Care was set up in July 1940. The districts were entirely closed to non-Jews on January 15, 1941. Zofiówka and Brijus continued to operate during the war, to the extent possible. TOZ, the Society for the Protection for the Health of the Jewish People, also opened an office in Otwock during the war. The liquidation action of the Otwock ghetto took place from August 19 to 24, 1942. Some of the doctors from Zofiówka and Brijus committed suicide, and the children and staff of CENTOS were killed. The Jews of Otwock were deported to Treblinka. Some escaped and survived, thanks to the help of neighboring Poles, while others were killed or turned in.

---

9   The best summaries of childcare in the Warsaw ghetto can be found in Engelking and Leociak, *The Warsaw Ghetto*, 317–29; Kassow, *Who Will Write Our History?*, 261–63; and Barski, *Przeżycia i wspomnienia*, 28–30.
10 Kassow, *Who Will Write Our History?*, 185, 21; Engelking and Leociak, *The Warsaw Ghetto*, 663.
11 Sources related to the Month of the Child reveal both the level of organization needed for such events and the criticism that sometimes ensued. Korczak himself criticized the Month of the Child as proof of hypocrisy, as propaganda rather than actual work meant to help save children. See Engelking and Leociak, *The Warsaw Ghetto*, 328–29.
12 Rakowski, *Aby ślad nie pozostał*, 21.

AFTERWORD

The children still under the care of Kalman Lis were shot. Lis went into hiding but was soon shot and killed by a gendarme.

Rosenblum served as the medical doctor for CENTOS in the early years of the war.[13] She managed to escape the Warsaw ghetto with the help of a Polish colleague, Maria Łeszeżanka, in August 1942. Łeszeżanka put Rosenblum on the list of the city's workers in the Department of Social Care and helped both Rosenblum and her niece, Janina Magnuska, escape to the Aryan side. Rosenblum was hidden by the nuns of the Immaculate Conception in Ożarów. According to J. Włodarczyk, it is at this time that she accepted baptism and began using the name Szymańska, a name she used professionally after the war.[14]

Some of the accounts describing efforts to aid children and provide relief during the war echo prewar attitudes. For example, questions of language use were still fundamental. The Children's Corners established by CENTOS were not regarded as effective, and Peretz Opoczynski cites as the reason the fact that they were conducted in Polish.[15] In addition, the general tone of some of Opoczynski's writing betrays the author's frustration with "the community" and its lack of response to the crisis of the occupation. Opoczynski described the selfishness of "the sick, morally atrophied, and stone-deaf public," writing that their "feeling for the common good" ended at their own front door.[16] He excoriated "the community," especially its leaders, for its lack of response to the evident starvation and homelessness in its midst. At times his harsh rhetoric recalls the tone of Yekhiel Kats's depiction of Helenówek.

---

13 See *Polski Słownik Biograficzny*, v. 50, s.v. "Szymańska, Zofia."
14 The entry for Rosenblum in *Polski Słownik Biograficzny* refers to an article by J. Włodarczyk, "Zasłużeń dla pedagogiki specjalnej: Zofia Rozenblum-Szymańska (1888–1978)," *Szkoła Specjalna* 46 (1985): 6, 367–71. See also Mordecai Paldiel, *Churches and the Holocaust: Unholy Teaching, Good Samaritans, and Reconciliation* (Jersey City, NJ: KTAV Publishing House, 2006), 211. Rosenblum does not discuss the name change in her memoir. She recounts an attempted but interrupted baptism when she was a child, but she does not mention baptism as an adult during the war. For more on Janina Magnuska and her relationship to Rosenblum, see Szymańska, *Byłam tylko lekarzem*, 223–26.
15 Opoczynski, "Children in the Streets," in Opoczynski and Zelkowicz, *In Those Nightmarish Days*, 93.
16 Opoczynski, "Children in the Streets," 87.

AFTERWORD

Similarly, in their study of the Warsaw ghetto, Barbara Engelking and Jacek Leociak quote Emanuel Ringelblum's depiction of "typical prewar philanthropy." Ringelblum outlined the democratic self-help conception of philanthropy and opposed it to the bourgeois-philanthropic conception of philanthropy.[17] Ringelblum's awareness of this distinction shows that this change in how the work of social care was done had not escaped the notice of the larger community. Moreover, this division persisted throughout the war, at least in Ringelblum's view. The frustration of Opoczynski and Ringelblum is certainly understandable, given the destruction of the war. But it is also important to remember that their own work attests to the fact that there were those who continued to use their skills and talents to care for the community under the worst circumstances. A full examination of the transformation in the field of social work is beyond the scope of this volume, but some of the authors included here, such as Zofia Rosenblum and Maks Schaff, bridged the gap between the old-fashioned philanthropy of the elites and the field of professional social work.

The fate of these associations and their leaders is in some cases well known, but in others, much less so. In August 1942 Janusz Korczak and Stefania Wilczyńska went to their deaths in Treblinka with the children they cared for.[18] That their story has taken on the tone of myth makes it no less poignant. The Polish scholar Grzegorz Siwor has recently told the story of Dawid Kurzmann, a merchant from Kraków and fervent supporter of that city's Home for Jewish Orphans.[19] Kurzmann, too, went to his death with the children, along with his son-in-law Dawid Schmelkes and Anna Feuerstein, the Home's director, and her husband Leopold. Siwor also recalls others involved with childcare who went to their deaths with the children they cared for, including Roza Ajchner and Tola Minc of the sanitarium in Miedzeszyn; Anna Taubenfeld, Hanna Kupperberg, and

---

17 Engelking and Leociak, *The Warsaw Ghetto*, 292–93.
18 Olczak-Ronikier, *Korczak*, 422–33; Kicińska, *Pani Stefa*, 247–52.
19 See Grzegorz Siwor, *Enoszijut: Opowieść o Dawidzie Kurzmannie* (Kraków: Wydawnictwo Vis-á-Vis Etiuda, 2014), and "Ofiara Dawida Kurzmanna," *Tygodnik Powszechny*, February 28, 2015, https://www.tygodnikpowszechny.pl/ofiara-dawida-kurzmanna-26790, accessed September 9, 2016.

AFTERWORD

Rechman from Lublin; and Rabbi Mendele Morgenstern from Włodawa. This list is, unfortunately, incomplete.

Some of the authors whose work appears here continued their advocacy for children in the postwar period. In addition to her memoir, the postwar works of Zofia Rosenblum include *Mój tatuś pije* (My father drinks) and *Dziecko nieznośne czy chore* (The child: Intolerable or sick?).[20] Rosenblum became an important figure in public health after the war. Helena Boguszewska continued her interest in writing about children as well. The site of Helenówek itself also played an important postwar role. The facility served as the setting for the filming of *Undzere Kinder* (Our children), a Yiddish film that featured the comedy of Shimon Dzigan and Yisroel Shumacher. The film, directed by Natan Gross and Shaul Goskind, reveals the ways in which child survivors of the Holocaust attempted to heal after years of trauma.[21] Aspects of the postwar history of Jews in Poland echo the post-1918 period. *Undzere Kinder* is one example; the existence of a children's home in Otwock from 1945 to 1949 is another.[22]

Reviewing the history of Jews in Poland throughout the twentieth century, including the period after 1989, one is struck by the consistency of support from the outside Jewish community, in the form of the work of the JDC. The theme of aid from abroad in the history of twentieth-century Polish Jewry is simply inescapable. In short, the community was in crisis or recovering from war throughout the entire century. Poland's twenty-one years of independence were all too brief, but Jewish community leaders used this time well to establish the associations and institutions needed to improve their prospects.

The history of Jewish child welfare in Poland reveals how the community attempted, with a significant degree of success before World War II, to build their nation by caring for the least fortunate. The work of CENTOS

---

20 Zofia Szymańska, *Mój tatuś pije* (Warsaw: Państwowy Zakład Wydawnictw Lekarskich, 1962), and *Dziecko nieznośne czy chore* (Warsaw: Państwowy Zakład Wydawnictw Lekarskich, 1969).

21 See Jan Schwarz, *Survivors and Exiles: Yiddish Culture after the Holocaust* (Detroit: Wayne State University Press, 2015), 45–48.

22 See Franciszka Oliwa, "Dom ocalonych dzieci w Otwocku (1945–1949), Wspomnienia," *Biuletyn Żydowskiego Instytutu Historycznego* 3/4 (1986): 89–105.

also demonstrates how the Jewish community adapted to Poland's new political, social, and economic conditions. While this history is but one facet of the complex history of Jews in Poland during the war, the work of CENTOS was of exceptional importance, as it reveals the community's values and concerns for what they expected to be the future generation of Jews in Poland.

Acknowledgments

I have worked on this project for many years, and I have incurred many kinds of debts: institutional, professional, and personal. I am grateful to the United States Fulbright Commission for making possible the initial research for this work and to the YIVO Institute for Jewish Research for the Aleksander and Alicja Hertz Memorial Fellowship. This project allowed me to spend time in many libraries and archives in Warsaw, Kraków, Łódź, L'viv, Vilnius, New York, and Jerusalem. I am especially indebted to the staff of the Biblioteka Narodowa in Warsaw and the staff of the American Jewish Joint Distribution Committee Archives, including Shachar Beer, Abra Cohen, Shelly Helfand, and Misha Mitsel. Marta Ciesielska, the director of the Museum of Warsaw's Korczakianum, generously shared her work and her publications. Sebastian Rakowski from Muzeum Ziemi Otwockiej shared his research and his knowledge of Otwock.

Yeshaya Metal, Ludmila Sholokhova, and Vital Zajka of YIVO patiently answered my questions about CENTOS publications. Amanda Miryem-Khaye Siegel of the New York Public Library also assisted with her extensive knowledge of the library's holdings. Jan Adamczyk of the Slavic Reference Service at University of Illinois at Urbana-Champaign provided important information as well. At home in Cleveland, many librarians helped me to access articles and books I would not otherwise have been able to use. Carl Mariani of Case Western Reserve University, Adam Green of John Carroll University, Jean Lettofsky of the former Aaron Garber Library of Siegal College of Judaic Studies, and the staffs of the Cleveland Public Library and Cuyahoga County Public Library offered an invaluable service. Their work is much appreciated.

Ellen Cassedy told me I really would be able to translate the Yiddish texts, and Kathryn Hellerstein offered important advice about translation.

ACKNOWLEDGMENTS

The extraordinary Yiddish teacher Paula Teitelbaum provided crucial assistance, helping me with many words, phrases, and concepts. Tomasz Markiewka not only always answered my questions about Polish patiently, but he was also quick to respond and unusually perceptive. Anna Frajlich-Zając introduced me to the study of Polish, and I will always be grateful for such a model of elegance in language and instruction.

Many people have indulged my questions about sources and related topics or have provided me with opportunities to speak about my work at conferences. I am grateful to them for their encouragement: Natalia Aleksiun, Samantha Baskind, Robert Brooks, Anna Ciałowicz, Patrice Dąbrowski, Krzysztof Górny, Regina Grol, Kate Heilman, Melissa Hibbard, Beth Holmgren, Hanna Kozińska-Witt, Christine Lurz, Jenni Marlow, Mary McCune, Joanna Michlic, Paul Niebrzydowski, Annamaria Orla-Bukowska, Bogna Pawlisz, Monika Polit, Brian Porter-Szucs, Tomasz Pudłocki, Robert Moses Shapiro, Meylekh Sheykhet, Keely Stauter-Halsted, Michał Trębacz, Zosia Trębacz, Michal Unger, Leon Weisberg, Joanna Wiszniewicz, Michal Wilczewski, Jarosław Wołkonowski, and Nathan Wood. The work and advice of Michael Berkowitz, Irina Livezeanu, and Antony Polonsky often strengthened my resolve to complete this project. I am indebted to them for their support and generosity.

Józef Lorski, Joanna Kulesza, Daria Świerczyńska, and Robert Świerczyński have all acted as my hosts in Warsaw in many different ways. They made possible my research visits to different sites and, by sharing their own stories and knowledge of Poland's Jewish community, taught me about how much more there still is to learn.

My work in the Cleveland Jewish Archives at Western Reserve Historical Society impressed upon me the value of making primary sources available to the public. Sylvia F. Abrams, Margaret Burzynski-Bays, Pamela Dorazio Dean, John Grabowski, Alan Gross, and Sally H. Wertheim encouraged my interests and helped me understand the different ways historians can make contributions to our understanding of the past. I am also grateful to the staff of Academic Studies Press for their patience and assistance, including Matthew Charlton, Kira Nemirovsky, Gregg Stern, Sharona Vedol, and Meghan Vicks. Holly Schreiber's careful editing greatly improved the text and translations.

ACKNOWLEDGMENTS

Writing about orphans leads to much thinking about parenting and families. I grew up in a large family, without any of the distress experienced by the children and parents discussed in the text. I have always known that my parents, siblings, and extended family support me, though they may know little about my actual work. I am grateful for the confidence their support provides, and grateful, too, for their embrace of the family I have created. My husband Richard Romaniuk was very patient as my work on this text progressed, however slowly. He contributed in numerous ways, from assistance with translation to careful close readings. My stepdaughters, Marianna Romaniuk Dostal and Hanna Romaniuk, helped me to understand the importance of the role of the parent. Finally, I have been constantly aware of the shadow of loss that pervades this topic: the loss of the orphan's parents and the loss of lives during the Holocaust. I dedicate this book to the memory of the parents and the children and in honor of the social workers, doctors, and teachers who did so much to help them.

Index

A
Abramek, "calendar child" in Otwock, 157, 162
Adler, Alfred, 147, 185
Ajchner, Roza, 210
Aleynhilf (Jewish Social Self-Help Coordinating Committee), 207
American Jewish Joint Distribution Committee, *see* Joint Distribution Committee (JDC)
anti-Semitism, 3
Asch, Sholem, 70
Association for the Care and Research of Children, 198
Ayzengart, 80

B
Babicki, Czesław, 50
Balcerek, Marian, 7, 58
Bałuty, 94, 103, 106
Barenholts, Perl, 80
Barski, Józef Gitler, 206, 207, 208
Barwiński, Henryk, 70
Bauer, Yehuda, vii, 14, 15, 18, 19, 28, 40, 41, 206, 207
Ben-Levi, xi, xii, 25, 60–63
Berger, Abraham, xi, xviii, 198–205
Berman, Adolf, 206–207
Białystok, 35, 37, 39, 143; Association for the Care of Jewish Orphans, 88; CENTOS in, 85–86; opening of day-care facility, 45–46
Biecz, 75–76
Bielsk Podlaski, 86
Binet, Alfred, 74, 144–145, 172
Blokh family, 133
Bochnia, 78
Bogen, Boris, 34–35, 35–36, 53–54
Boguszewska, Helena, xi, xvii–xviii, 154–165, 211

Bojanów Poznański, 199
Boymats, 129
Brandstätter, Michał, 141
Braude, M., 141
Briański, 206
Brześć, 26–27, 84–85
Brifman, P., 139
Brijus (Jewish Anti-Tubercular Assocaiton Brijus [Health]), 142, 189, 208

C
Cape Town, 61
CENTOS, vii, viii, 1–59, 4, 5, 91, 94, 100, 149–150; development of, 35–49; finances, 37–39; leaders of, xviii; name of organization, vii–viii; number of institutions, 1938, 39–40; offices and committees, 37, 39–40; and Orthodox community, 49; in Otwock, 142–205; publications of, 9; and Zofia Rosenblum, 143; during World War II, 26, 211–212
CENTOS Therapeutic and Educational Institute for Children in Otwock, xi, xvi, xvii, xviii, 142–205
childhood, 4
children, abuse of, 94–141, 98–99, 116, 118–120; development of, 65, 72–74; sexual development of, 96, 113–115, 121–123, 185; stateless, 29–35
children's courts, 67, 91, 113; complaint against teacher, 113–115; discpline of children, 108–112, 184–187, 191–197
Constitution of 1921, 3
Council of Jewish Women, 30–31
Czyżewski, Kazimierz Andrzej, 67–68

D
"days of independence", 168–171, 184
Dąbrowa, 72

INDEX

Dąbrowiec, 38, 39
Decroly, Ovide, 182
Der yosem, xv
Dewey, John, 12, 140
Dębina, 86
Dos elendste kind, 9
Dos kind, xiii, xvii, 9, 50, 51, 53, 55, 56, 60, 72, 91, 94, 96, 98–99, 100, 102, 166, 201, 203
Dos shutsloze kind, 9, 144
Dubno, 25–26
Dzialoshinski, Israel, 131–132

E

education, 34, 49, 167, 183–187; equity with non-Jewish children, 85; in Otwock, 147; school publications, 88–90; Union for Trade Education in Galicia, 86; vocational, 40, 45, 47–48, 62, 83, 176–178, 182–183, 204
Eretz Israel, xv, xviii, xix, 18, 31, 55, 61, 126, 127
Ezra, 30–31

F

family (family life), 4, 10, 53, 57, 103, 146, 180, 187, 191
Farbstein, Yehoshua Heshel, 36
feldshers, 143, 139
film, 190
Feuerstein, Anna, 210
Feuerstein, Leopold, 210
Finkelshteyn, Sh., 139
Flaxman, Chaim, 34
foster care, 50–59, 78, 85, 86, 87
Frenkel, Jeremiasz, 141
Freud, Sigmund, 185
Fridman, I., 26
Froebel, Friedrich, 140, 177, 182

G

Galicia, xix, 12, 14, 19, 20, 86, 198
Gaudig, Hugo, 140
Goldflam, Samuel, 142
Goldin, A., xi–xii, 42, 75–87, 206
Goldin, P., 203
government, local, 41–43, 45, 167; state, 45–46, 56, 69

Grabiński, Stefan, 68–69
Granek, Adele, 128–131
Grundwag, Simche, 22
Gutman, Leon, xi–xii, 88–90

H

Halperin, Reb Yosef, 60–61
Hebrew, language and culture, 48
Helenówek, xi, xiii–xvi, xvii, 94–141, 158; during and after World War II, 209, 211
Hilf, 130, 133–134

I

institutional care (orphanages), 40, 44, 46, 50–59, 83–85, 86, 87, 91–93
intelligence testing, 144–145, 173–174, 189–191
International Colonization Association, 81
Itskovitsh, Ruzhke, 128–131

J

Jasło, 76–77
Jewish identity, xviii, xix, 45
Jewish Social Self-Help Coordinating Committee, 207
Jeżewski, Kazimierz, 50
Joint Distribution Committee (JDC), viii, ix, xii, 5–6, 8, 9, 10, 13, 18–35, 41, 48, 49, 56, 58, 88; ideology, 28; inspection reports, 21–28, 53–54, 61, 75–87; operations, 20; relationship with local committees, 21

K

Kahn, Bernard, 31
kehilah, viii, 5, 11, 12, 38, 42, 43, 59, 84, 100, in Tarnów, 77; in Włodzimierz, 81
Kats, Yekhiel Ben-Tsiyon, xi, xii–xvi, xvii, 94–141, 158, 209
Kerschensteiner, Georg, 140
Kępski, Czesław, 7
Khoynik, D., 99
Klaftenowa, Cecylja, 45
Kohn, Józef, 46–47
Kołomyja, 42
Konczyński, Tadeusz, 67

217

INDEX

Korczak, Janusz, ix–x, 10, 38, 168, 184, 208, 210; early career, 12–13; institutionalization of children, 51, 55, 57–59
Kowel, 80–81, 156
Kraków, x, 11, 12, 20, 32, 37, 39, 42, 43, 48–49, 77, 78, 79, 80, 86, 210
Kultur-Lige, 26
Kupperberg, Hanna, 210
Kurzmann, Dawid, 210

L
language, 2–3; linguistic assimilation, 4, 27
Lejzor, child in Otwock, 155–157, 160–161
Lifszyc, Fejga, 58
Lis, Kalman, xi, xvi, xvii, 1, 144, 149–153, 179, 206, 208, 209
London, 61, 63
Lublin, 210–211
Lwów, xi, xii, xviii–xix, 11, 16, 20, 37, 38, 39, 41–43, 44, 45, 86; Bardach (private school for deaf children), 199; Galician Institute for the Blind, 198; Home for Orphans, 64–71
Łeszeżanka, Maria, 209
Łódź, xi, xii–xvi, 102–103, 139, 141, 143; Ezras Kmim (school for deaf children), 199; Froyen-shuts fereyn (Women's Defense Association), xv, 135; Helenówek, 94–141; Izrael and Leona Poznański Jewish Hospital, 128

M
Magnuska, Janina, 209
Mały Przegląd, 10, 55
Marks, Golda, 82
Marpe, 129–130, 142, 208
Medem Sanatorium, x
medical care, issues of, 128–131, 143
Miedzeszyn, x, 207, 210
Miesięcznik Żydowski, 141
Międzyrzec Podlaski, 83–84
Minc, Tola, 210
Ministry of Labor and Social Care, 8, 30
Ministry of Religious Confessions and Public Enlightenment, 8
Minorities Treaty of 1919, 15, 46
Mława, 139
Montessori, Maria, 12, 182
Month of the Child, 208

Morgenstern, Rabbi Mendele, 211
Mosiek, child in Otwock, 157, 161

N
Nasze Życie, 17–18
nationalism, 2, 3, 16, 46, 59
nationality, xix, 29, 36, 44, 45
Neustadt, Leib, ix, 53
Nowogródek, 82–83
Nowy Sącz, 77

O
Oksenhendler, Franka, 96, 131–133, 138
Opinja, 141
Opoczynski, Peretz, 209
orphans, 4–5, 17; war orphans, 13–14; number of full orphans, 39; number of half orphans, 39
Orthodox Jews, 49
Otwock, xi, xvi–xviii, 130, 131; People's Educational League Orphanage, 172, 201; TOZ, 208; during World War II, 206, 208
Oyneg Shabes, 208

P
Palestine, xv, xviii, xix, 18, 31, 55, 61, 126, 127
Parysów, 156
pedagogy, therapeutic, 180
pedology, 143
Peiser, Simon, 19–20
Peker, M., xiv, 97
Pękowska, Marzena, xvi, 16, 184, 206
Pelts, Frida, 169
Perlman, A., 140
Pestalozzi, Johan Heinrich, 140
philanthropy, 5, 11, 12, 17, 18–19, 35, 56, 128, 209–210
Piłsudski, Józef, 3, 45
Pinsk, 24–25, 39, 42, 60–63, 85
play, x, 78, 91–93, 149–153, 164, 170, 179, 185, 182, 188, 190, 191–197
Polish, language and culture, 144, 163, 176, 182, 209
Polit, Monika, xiv–xv
politics, role of, 24–25, 25–26, 27–29, 34–35
Pomoc (Help), 12

INDEX

Poznański, Izrael Kalmanowicz, 94
press, 9
Prużany, 86, 156
Przegląd Społeczny, viii, xii, xvii, xix, 9, 11, 37, 39, 55, 56, 64, 86, 88, 102, 154, 166, 172, 198, 202
Purim, 107
Puszcza Mariańska, 198

R

Rechman, 211
Reichensteinowa, Ada, 17
religion, 15–16
Riger, Sh., 140
Ringelblum, Emanuel, 208, 210
Rosen, Borukh, 132–133
Rosenberg, J. B., 34, 35
Rosenberg, James N., 21, 22
Rosenblum, Zofia, *see* Szymańska, Zofia
Rosental, I., 139
Rossolimo, Grigory Ivanovich, 143, 173
Rozenboym, Tereza, 51–52, 55
Rożyszcze, 156
Równo, 39, 53–54, 79–80
Rumkowski, Khayim Mordkhe, xi, 94–141, 103; charges of abuse, 132–133; charges of sexual abuse, xiii–xvi, 96, 133–136; and Nahum Sokolow, 125–126
Rundstein, D., 32, 33, 34
Rusak, 117
Ryfka, child in Otwock, 158–159, 162–164
Rzeszów, 78

S

Sarner, Yakov, xi, xii, 91–93
Schaff, Maks, xii, xviii–xix, 1, 11–12, 44, 51, 64–71, 210
Schmelkes, Dawid, 210
schools, 26–27, 29, 36 47–48, 72–74, 91–93, 181–182; publications, 88–90; in Otwock, 147
Shapiro, Robert Moses, xiii–xiv
Shedlets, 139
Sherman, Miriam, 30–33, 41
Sherman, Max, 33
Shoykhet,
slöjd, 177
Słonim, 24
Sochaczew, 22

social work, xx, 1, 5, 6, 8, 17, 37, 43, 50; August 1923 legislation, 36–37
Soloveichik, Hayim, 85
Sokolow, Nahum, 125–126, 137
Soviet Union, 30–31
special education (special needs education), xi, xvi, 4, 13, 29–35, 98, 112–113, 142–205
Spektorowa, P., 199
sports, 191–197
St. John of God, 200
Stanisławów, 25, 86
Studzieniec, 99, 198
Stryj, 17–18, 38
summer colonies, 49
Sura, 157–158, 161
Szkoła Specjalna, 149
Sznejerson, Mendel, 142
Szczepaniak-Wiecha, Izabela, 7, 36
Szymańska, Zofia (Rosenblum), xi, xvi, xvii, xviii, 1, 158, 201, 202, 206–207, 209, 210, 211; descriptions of her work in CENTOS in Otwock, 142–148, 166–197; name, explanation of, xx

T

Tarlovski, Tsvi, xi, xii, 72–74
Tarnopol, 86
Tarnów, 77
Taubenfeld, Anna, 210
teachers, 91–93, 96, 113–115, 136–139, 144, 169
Temkin-Bermanowa, Barbara, 207–208
Terman, Lewis, 144–145, 173, 189
therapeutic methods, 187–190
Towbin, D., 27
TOZ (Towarzystwo Ochrony Zdrowia Ludności Żydowskiej, Society for the Protection of the Health of the Jewish People), x, 82, 208
Twerski, I., 199
Tworki, 200

U

Unger, Michal, xv
Unzer kind, 9, 75, 100, 150
Uściług, 81

V

Vaynrib, Sore, 116, 137, 138
Vilna (Wilno), xvi, 37, 39, 81, 82, 83, 99, 199

Vincenz, xviii–xix
Vogelówna, Dr., 69
Vulf, Sh. Z., 99

W

Walasek, Stefania, 7, 8, 16, 36
Wańkowicz, Melchior, 206
Warburg, Felix M., 21
Warsaw, ix, xiv, 8, 12, 31, 37, 39, 76, 79, 83, 87, 96, 137, 138, 139, 143, 145, 154, 164, 165, 167, 173,186, 189, 190, 194, 196, 200, 201, 203, 204; Association for the Care of Deaf Jews, 199; Assocation of Friends of Children School Clinic, 189; Committee for the Care of Orphans, 30–31, 34; Dom Opieki dla Opuszczonych Dzieci Żydowskich (Care Home for Abandoned Jewish Orphans, located at Płock 26), 203–204; ghetto, vii, xvi, 207, 208, 209, 210; Home for Orphans, 168, 184; Institute for the Deaf and Blind, 198; JDC in, 20, 32, 33, 34, 53, 75; Kalman Lis in, 149, 208; orphanages in, 12, 39, 42, 182, 199; Zofia Rosenblum in, 143, 206, 209
Wasserman tests, 189
wedding customs, 156
Week of the Orphan, 17, 208
Welfle, Mrs., 33

Wieliczka, 79
Wilczyńska, Stefania, ix, 12–13, 52, 208, 210; and institutionalization, attitudes toward, 54–58
Wilno, *see* Vilna
Włodawa, 211
Włodzimierz (Vladimir-Volynski), 80, 81, 86
Wołyń, xvi, 23–24, 25, 42, 47–48, 79, 81
World War I, 11, 18; postwar relief, 11–17

Y

YEKOPO, 15, 82
Yiddish, language and culture, 48, 70, 88–90, 144, 176, 182

Z

Zaromb, 27
Zaydler, R., 137
Zdołbunów, 156
Zelikhowska, Andzhe, 131
Zionism, xv, xviii, xix, 2, 18, 31, 55, 61, 126, 127
Złoczów, 44
Złoczew, 87
Zofiówka, 142, 188, 208
Zshak, Aharon, 117
Zwiahel, 23–24
Żółkiewka, 86

www.ingramcontent.com/pod-product-compliance
Lightning Source LLC
Chambersburg PA
CBHW051115230426
43667CB00014B/2590